BY THE SAME AUTHOR

Mine Enemy Grows Older

MAY
THIS HOUSE
BE SAFE
FROM
TIGERS

by Alexander King

1960

SIMON AND SCHUSTER
NEW YORK

LIBRARY OF CONGRESS CATALOG CARD NUMBER: 59–13151
MANUFACTURED IN THE UNITED STATES OF AMERICA
BY KINGSPORT PRESS, INC., KINGSPORT, TENN.

To Al and Dolly and Nina Hirschfeld,
for all sorts of wonderful reasons

My friend *Norman Prelick happens to be a Zen Buddhist at the moment. He used to be a Communist once.*

It figures.

But suddenly, a couple of years ago, he saw the true light and since then he's been thoroughly illuminated.

At any rate, every time this character comes to visit me and finally gets ready to leave, he stops in the doorway, folds his hands Hindu fashion, lowers his fourth-dimensional eyelids and says:

"May this house be safe from tigers."

He does this every time.

The other day, when his senseless little orison had fallen on me again, I said to him, "What is the meaning of this idiot prayer you're always uttering over me every time you leave here? What the hell does it mean, anyway?"

Norman looked surprised and even a little hurt, and finally he gave off the familiar long-suffering sigh of the frequently misunderstood.

"What's wrong with my prayer?" he said. "How long have I been saying it to you?"

"Oh, about three years, on and off."

"Three years," he said. "Well—been bothered by any tigers lately?"

Perfectly correct.

So, since it is surely one of the most effective benedictions I have ever encountered, I've decided to share this powerful and potent spell with the rest of the world.

CHAPTER ONE

WHEN I WAS BORN I weighed a little less than
three pounds. If you look at a broiler that size, you can see
that it's barely enough to make a decent meal for two ordinary
people. Since there weren't many incubators around in those
days, they just wrapped me from head to foot in some ab-
sorbent cotton, put me in a frying pan and placed me in a
moderate oven for the next three months.

(I'm dead serious about all this, and, what's more, an Austrian scientific publication of the year 1900 called *Medizin-
ischer Beobachter* devoted two and a half columns to my peculiarly rancid condition at that period.)

They basted me with olive oil every twenty minutes and
they also turned me over each time, so that I didn't get too
well done on any one side. After a while my poor parents,
who were terrible cooks, both of them, delegated this whole

dreary chore to a little deaf peasant woman who had been something of a pensioner of theirs from 'way back.

And then, about my third week in that frying pan, I suddenly developed a fierce rash all over my belly, and this time it certainly looked like I was headed for the garbage pail for sure. One morning Dr. Tschurtschentaler, the gifted medico who divided his time between giving me last aid and administering comfort to my shattered begetters, observed that the deaf troll who took care of me had the habit of imbibing considerable quantities of raw snuff. Luckily for me, this competent pediatrician was also something of a sleuth, and he noticed that she often dropped great gobs of her high explosive onto my infant navel, and so he sensibly deduced that this must inevitably be the cause of my flagrant inflammation.

Just think how fortunate I am that all this happened nearly sixty years ago. Nowadays they would instantly remove my navel and replace it with a plastic button that I could whistle "Mother Machree" through for the rest of my life.

The other day my dear wife, Margie, asked me, "And how did it all begin? I mean, for instance, your realization that you were going to be an artist. And when did you first discover you had such a gift of gab?"

I explained it to her in detail. When I was six years old my father took me to the great art museum in Vienna, and there in one room I saw all four walls covered with paintings by Pieter Breughel. It rocked me. I didn't realize that any man could ever acquire so much skill and learn to render his visions so magnificently for the whole world to see. From that moment on, that Breughel room became a sort of shrine to me. I went back to it again and again, and I even made several copies of "The Tower of Babel" with some water colors that my people had bought me for my birthday.

2

I realized at once that whoever had made these pictures was certainly one of the world's outstanding magicians. There were other magicians too, but somehow this one had done something more enduring, something that had left a permanent mark on the walls of the earth. I had already seen a sword swallower, and he was nothing to sneeze at either, but Breughel's pictures had, after all, outlasted Breughel. I would be *another* Breughel.

As time passed, I wavered somewhat, particularly when the next circus came around and I saw a flock of trained cormorants. Let me tell you about this act. The arena was flooded with water and a tall, lean Chinese sailed out on this artificial pond in a skimpy little bamboo boat. There were a dozen cormorants sitting on the edge of this frail craft, and when a few circus attendants emptied some buckets of live fish into the water those birds instantly dived overboard and retrieved all the fish. That is to say, they brought them back to the Chinese man, who took the fish out of their beaks and dropped them into a red-lacquered container. When I asked my father how the man had managed to train the cormorants to do this, my father pointed out to me that each of these birds had a tight ring encircling its neck and that this ring very definitely prevented him from swallowing the fish.

My father said, "The Chinese man later on removes the rings and lets them eat their fill. You see, cormorants are naturally fabulous fishermen and they have learned that unless they retrieve their prey out of the water there will be no supper for them afterward."

I was absolutely enchanted. Breughel instantly took second place in my heart, and I began to look around our neighborhood for a flock of suitable cormorants.

So you see, I was still very fickle at that age. But whatever profession I became interested in, or enthusiastic about, it always had one basic element in common with each of the oth-

3

ers: They were all different aspects of one central theme, which was—magic!

I was going to be a magician of some kind, that was settled in my mind when I was six, and I can truthfully say that, in the pursuance of this goal, I have not wavered even once during the following fifty-three years.

When I was even less than six years old, I had a rather curious experience I'd like to tell you about.

You see, in the entrance hallway of our apartment there stood a large mahogany grandfather clock. Well, late one afternoon it happened quite by accident that I discovered the little side door to this timepiece, and before I knew what I was doing I had opened it and stepped inside. It was a somewhat close fit, but in a way it was quite an ideal hiding place for a smallish child. It was pretty dusty in there too, and after a while, when a couple of cobwebs settled ticklishly across my ears and nose, I tell you I was damned uncomfortable in there. But, for some reason or another, I remained inside that clock for more than half an hour.

And then quite a natural thing happened—my mother began to miss me. Suddenly she was loudly calling my name and clattering all over that house in search of me. I heard her opening all sorts of room and closet doors, and, as the minutes passed, her voice became really quite frantic. My father, who had been taking a nap in his study, was now noisily aroused, and in a very little while, when the maid too came in, from the market, that whole apartment was in an absolutely bloody uproar.

Finally, as I looked out from the tight and stuffy clock case, I could see my distraught mother standing in the middle of the living room, with both her hands to her face, completely shaken by sobs of maternal anxiety. I, in my upright sarcophagus, began to cry too, and my tears, mingling with the dust and dirt all around me, ran in thick, brackish rivulets straight into my mouth. I realized, of course, that all I had to do was to step out of that goddamned clock and all that wailing and grieving would be over in a minute, but for some mysterious reason I heroically suppressed my blubberings and wept silently and heartbrokenly along with my dear mother for the bitter, irreplaceable loss of her darling son.

At last one of the heavy, brass-covered weights which furnished the clock's motive power came to rest solidly on top of my head, and the clock stopped.

My father, who noticed it, stepped over to the door, opened it and found me standing inside.

Mad, isn't it?

Well, there was a tremendous reunion among the four of us, big holiday treats and everything. And, do you know, this day became a landmark in our lives. We held an anniversary of it every year, until I was finally too tall to get into the clock.

This date was henceforth known in our small circle as The Day That

> *Hickory, dickory, dock,*
> *Poor Alex was lost in the clock.*

As for the gift of gab—I discovered the great power of it when I was eight. At that age I attended a tough but very wonderful Jesuit academy, and my favorite teacher in that school was a priest called Father Francis. He liked me very much too, and although he never showed any open partiality toward me I was well aware of the fact that he had a kind, fatherly eye on me.

At any rate, once during some hectic weeks at the academy when Father Francis had to attend a good many executive meetings, he asked me to read aloud to the rest of the children from a history textbook during his frequent absences from the classroom. I did this with great eagerness and joy, of course, but I soon discovered that it was very difficult, really almost impossible, to hold the attention of my fellow students with the dry, unrewarding text in that book. So I slowly began to improvise certain elucidative asides of my own, which, I must say, went over much better with my fellow students, and after a little while I hardly bothered to refer to the book at all and just talked on about whatever I myself had been reading in my spare time at home.

The results were phenomenal. Our class was the best-behaved class on the floor, and Father Francis earned a great many compliments for the exemplary behavior of his pupils. It stands to reason that, in due time, I was found out. Somebody snitched on me, and I was at once automatically demoted from my role as official reader.

But the die was cast—and that wasn't all that was cast. I myself was cast adrift on an ocean of careless verbiage that has carried me, as you can see, to an impenitent and verbose old age.

As a matter of fact, when I was nine years old I went off to spend a summer in Hungary with a school friend of mine, and there one night, just before bedtime, I remember, I started to tell him and his four brothers and sister some kind of story. In the midst of this telling, the lights were suddenly put out and we all had to turn in for the night. However, the minute the grownups were gone the children all crowded around my bed and pleaded with me to finish my little tale for them.

And now comes, as Joyce would say, the "hazelhatchery" part of it.

I had seen, earlier that day, that each of those kids owned some rather beautiful sea shells. Now remember, Austria was a completely landlocked country and sea shells were at all times of the very greatest rarity indeed. I don't recall where or how those children had managed to get hold of their rich swag, but it suddenly came to me, there in that dark dormitory, that if I played my cards right I just might manage to make myself a very profitable deal with all those eager little listeners. In short, I offered to tell them the end of that story of mine, provided each of my auditors agreed to give me one choice item out of his sea-shell collection.

There was no haggling. They all agreed.

But at that moment so long ago, 'way back in Hungary, an ominous precedent was set, a precedent that jeopardized for all future time the wholesomeness and the immutability of my tender little soul.

Before that summer was over I had told them a whole slew of interesting stories, but—by the use of prolonged intermissions, sudden pretenses of deadly fatigue, and other cunning and judicious devices—I had, by the time I was ready to go back to Vienna, bilked those five innocents out of every last one of their precious sea shells. In the end, I even carried away in my simple childish luggage my school friend's most cherished treasure, a tiny starfish.

Indeed, that little starfish remained a talisman of mine throughout the years, and you will be pleased to know that at this very moment it is prettily reflected in the top of my Margie's mirrored dressing table. Margie loves that starfish just as much as I did. You see, she comes from Nebraska and is an inland girl too.

Also, it must be obvious that there is nothing wrong with *her* gift of gab either, since she managed to talk *me* out of it.

CHAPTER TWO

IT HAPPENED within comparatively recent years that on Sixth Avenue, and along some of the other rather shoddily commercial streets of New York, certain Japanese magicians set up shops where the more obvious American house pets were put on sale. Very soon after these businesses became established I decided that the minutely accomplished people who operated them must have access to some extraordinarily potent enchantments indeed, since everything alive that was sold in their stores, from the quiet insect-consuming orchid to the most frenetically agitated Siamese cat, prospered and flourished while still in Japanese hands but seemed to go into almost instant decline the moment it arrived at my home.

These days I no longer keep any animals around the house, but once, quite a while ago, I was for some reason or another pretty deeply involved in raising hundreds and hundreds of tropical fish, and I must say I derived a great deal of fun and even satisfaction out of this expensive pastime.

But I finally had to give it all up, because early one morning, while I was watching the stupendous accouchement of an overgravid *fundulus gularis*, a shattering flash of illumination came upon me. To tell you the truth, the effects of that bitter moment of enlightenment have never completely faded from my mind. Even now I sometimes still find myself under the unhappy spell of it, although it all happened more than thirty years ago. Yes, to this very day I always manage to pass the façades of the various pet shops in town in something close to a double trot, just out of fear that I might get an accidental glimpse of their suffocatingly overcrowded aquaria.

You must understand that it's not that I'm afraid of being tempted back into my costly hobby again. No, no! Not a bit of it. Quite the contrary. It's only that I can no longer bear to look at all those dopey fish opening and closing their god-damned mouths a million times a day. It just gets me down. It gets me down because I know that those poor bastards aren't simply breathing or gasping for air. I know for a fact that they're all really *screaming—screaming*—like crazy. Yes, screaming and giving off heartbreaking, soul-shattering sub-marine howls. And, do you know what it is that they're all shouting?

They're shouting, *"Look at Me! Please Look at Me!* I'm so *Original!* I'm so *Irreplaceable!* I'm so *Darling!* I'm so *Cute!* Just *Look* at *Me!* and see how *Unique* I am! Look at me and *Love* me! *Love* me! *Love* me! Why don't you *Love* me? Please! Please! Love* me! *Love* me! *Love* me!"

That's what those poor suckers are all saying. It's awful!

And what makes it so terrible for me is that I know only too goddamned well that that's exactly what everybody else all around me is constantly saying too. I just don't care to have a swampful of pop-eyed, screaming fish go on reminding me of it all the time.

Yes, I guess the pride in one's own uniqueness is what keeps everybody going in this erratically operated sausage machine. I suppose that's why a lot of people go off their rockers nowadays, because pride in one's work, for instance, is certainly disappearing out of our world. It's impossible to be proud of the crappy things that most people have to do to earn their living—and, believe me, I don't mean that any sort of real labor is ever debasing in itself. Just look at all our millionaires happily pfooshing around in their hobby shops, getting sawdust on their eyelashes and covering themselves with all sorts of decorative calluses which they can proudly show off at their clubs later on.

But what *can* be utterly debasing to the human spirit is if you have to earn your keep by performing some monotonous, mechanical gesture of such minute insignificance that even the smallest sense of achievement is totally absent from your endeavors.

Remember, in my time I have known whimsical hod carriers, dignified sewer inspectors and even poetic chimney sweeps.

Hey! I knew chimney sweeps. . . .

You see, I'm writing about the days when automation seemed only a passing, seasonal rash on the body of our existence, and when it was still possible for a man on any occupational level whatever to find at least some sort of *excuse* for accomplishment in the work that had somehow blindly fallen to his lot. In fact, I will now give you an example that has just come to my mind which, I think, will adequately demonstrate this very healthful condition in human affairs.

When I was still quite a young man—so young, in fact, that I hadn't even been married for the first time—I was, of course, living down in the depths of Greenwich Village.

Where else?

10

I had a measly ground-floor apartment in a place called Minetta Alley, a dead-end street that is no longer in existence. Back in those distant, wonderfully livable years this property had not yet been improved to accommodate the higher-income brackets. My neighbors all around me were mostly writers, painters, sculptors and all sorts of other colorful riffraff, and I daresay these excessively original people, in company with their various wives and mistresses, created at that time, in that particular place, the only true Bohemia this country has ever known.

The best proof of this is that the cunning real-estate boys in the Village are garnering fabulous dividends to this very day on the mere memory of it all. Yes, those heartless liars have somehow managed to fix it in the public mind that the Muses and their Dionysian devotees are still living in riotous concubinage—right below Fourteenth Street—at eighty dollars a room.

Well, as I've been telling you, once upon a time when I was still a very young man and occupying a ground-floor apartment in Minetta Alley, around eleven o'clock one spring morning, just as I was getting shaved near an open window, I happened to see three garbage men who were about to tackle the tons of refuse that had accumulated over the weekend. Not a particularly significant or memorable vision, you might think, and under ordinary circumstances you would be quite right. What made this a special occasion worthy of commemoration here is the fact that one of those three men was obviously quite new to his job.

Now, just think about him for a moment.

He was a raw beginner in the sanitation game—and "raw" was the word for him, because the whole back of his neck was chafed and rubbed open by the stiff, unyielding collar of his brand-new uniform. Everything he had on was either too wide or too long for his pathetic, post-adolescent torso, and although he had rolled up his sleeves until the cuffs looked

like two oversized cloth doughnuts, they still managed somehow to cover the larger part of his poor abraded knuckles.

The other two S.D. operatives who were with him were,
just as evidently, a couple of well-seasoned, thoroughly blasé
veterans of the debris world. One of them, who was sure-
footedly riding the treacherous seas of garbage on top of the
truck, had a huge Slovak mustache that came down almost as
far as his chin. His partner, a skinny, long-armed, Ichabod
Crane sort of person, even had *two* mustaches, each of which
bristled irritatedly over a bloodshot eyeball.

Well, then, the couple of characters on the ground began
to tackle the mountain of garbage in front of our doorway,
and I noticed with considerable uneasiness that the young apprentice, in the manner of novices the world over, had un-
erringly selected the most ambitious job of the morning for
himself. He had picked up the largest and most ostentatiously
overloaded crap can in the whole goddamned alley, and he
proceeded to stagger crazily in the direction of the garbage
truck with it.

The very moment that he did this, his benign elders automatically stopped their own vacant meandering and gave their
complete attention to these megalomanic doings.

It stands to reason that even by his greatest efforts the young
understudy was unable to raise his burden any farther up than
the hub cap of the nearest wheel. When he got as far as that,
he just stood there panting for a moment, and I could see that
during his stupendous exertions a black banana peel had tumbled playfully across his minute nose, and this, plus a broken
ostrich feather which had fallen up against his left ear, gave
him the look of a soiled Pierrot who was just about to arise
coquettishly out of the city garbage dumps.

And so there he stood, irresolute, for about thirty seconds,
until he noticed with sudden horror that both of his elderly
confreres were quietly but sternly watching him.

Naturally, he got quite panicky. I understood him perfectly.

12

I knew that that was exactly how the students of Giotto or Cimabue must have felt when their master's eye had fallen critically upon their early efforts. That's what it means to be an apprentice anywhere. I suppose at Princeton and at Sing Sing the old-timers are sure to make life miserable for you, simply because they themselves were made to suffer when they were only young aspirants. Now that they in their turn have finally matured into old stinkers, they're certainly going to make you pay for the raps *they* once took.

That's human nature for you!

Do you notice that whenever a particularly nasty or swinish piece of business happens to be pulled off on you, the knowing ones in your midst are always ready to tell you that there is really nothing to be surprised at, that you've simply been exposed to a rather common phenomenon, something called "Human Nature"? Well, may heaven preserve me from "Human Nature," whatever the hell it is.

At any rate, as I've been telling you, this young garbage juggler stood there for about half a minute, harassed and wild-eyed, and through all that time the poor punk realized only too well that pretty soon he'd have to bestir himself toward some kind of action. It must also have been quite clear to him, as it certainly was to me, that those two dear colleagues of his had not the slightest intention of giving him any kind of a hand. Not yet. Not until he'd exposed his incompetence a little more dramatically or had managed to inflict a solid hunk of damage to his own person, or to the surrounding premises at least.

And then the poor bastard, shaken by a sudden spasm of mad resolution, tried to heave that monstrous can straight up to the brink of the truck and, by this witless and desperate maneuver, gave himself such a stupendous blow under the chin that I could plainly hear his teeth cracking in his jaws, forty feet away from me. Great streams of perspiration rolled out from under his cast-iron cap and his eyes began to waggle around hysterically, like the eyes of a demented chameleon.

Twice more he tried to get that preposterous load straight up, past the jutting promontory of his chin, and each time I expected to see him literally decapitate himself, and to see his goddamned head roll right across the alley up to my window. After the third brutal blow, he turned as pale as death and slowly closed his eyes, and for a moment I was sure the miserable wretch was going to keel over in a faint.

And then, and *only* then, destiny, in the form of Ichabod Crane, stepped forward and relieved him of that oversized cornucopia of crap. With the silent simplicity of an animal, he elbowed the youngster aside and quietly took charge. But even so, he did it with the facile assurance which is the immemorial attribute of great achievement in a familiar but recondite undertaking. For a few heartbeats all three figures remained quietly immobile. Then, with truly reptile grace, old Ichabod swung that enormous load a little to one side, gave his body an astonishing spiral whorl, shifted his neck and head horizontally, like a Balinese dancer—and, in less time than it takes me to tell you, that can was fabulously propelled to the high outer rim of the truck, where it remained, tremulously poised, for just one breathtaking, wonderful moment.

It was absolutely beautiful!

The rest was equally expert, and just as marvelous a thing to observe. You see, when that can finally came level with the Poseidon of garbage who was stationed on the top, he gave it just the least bit of a kick with the side of his boot, and then, slowly and ever so gently, it tipped forward and, after giving off an absolutely stupendous sigh, fell over with a grand swoosh and disemboweled itself in one vast hemorrhage of schmutz.

After the can had been emptied it was bounced neatly down onto the sidewalk again, and before it ever had a chance to come to rest Ichabod gave it one deft effortless twist with a little English on it, and it rolled clear down to the end of the alley, maintaining its dangerous equilibrium intact until it finally bounced safely off the rear wall and came to rest underneath my window.

All this was done casually and fluently, with a minimum of effort and a maximum of noise. Toscanini himself couldn't have done it any better.

And what did the young apprentice do, while these masterful evolutions were unfolding before him? Well, at first he bounced epileptically around the garbage truck pretending to be of great help to everybody, and later on he did a sliding gavotte alongside that dangerously tilted can as it rolled inevitably to its predestined goal. In short, he did a whole ballet of flagrant ineptitude up and down that alley, while his two sober seniors completely disdained him. After they'd gotten their little task out of the way, those two boys just stood there and solemnly stared at each other.

They stared at each other as Hannibal must have stared at Hasdrubal when the new recruits from Gaul had first made their appearance in the Carthaginian ranks. They stared at each other as if to say, "Just look at the sort of riffraff that's managing to get into the Department nowadays. Yes, yes, yes . . . and there is the whole goddamned younger generation for you, too!"

But that wasn't all of it. Not by a damn sight. I tell you, I was haunted by that crazy tableau long after that truck had left our alley, and even long after the sound of the tumbling cans had stopped echoing in that entire neighborhood. I've thought of it endless numbers of times during the intervening years, and I suppose I'll go on recalling that little episode till the very end of my life. It was, in its own way, a rather significant parable.

You see, I couldn't help going on thinking about those three characters and their probable subsequent behavior, and I couldn't stop speculating about what must have happened to them after they all finally got home that evening.

You can easily imagine it yourself.

Papa, at the head of the table, his mustache dripping with pea soup, the buxom, amiably perspiring mother serving the large family, and the whole family just brimful of shining admiration for the old man. Remember, he's a street cleaner in a rich and wasteful city like New York. That means that he's bound to find something pretty interesting to bring home to his dear ones almost every evening.

That's just common sense.

I'm sure that those kids have at least three hundred Christmases a year. And don't you think for one moment that all he ever rescues out of those thousands of brimming garbage cans is just some useless junk, or a lot of cast-off broken toys. No, sir! I myself have seen whole workable radio sets and fitted vanity cases, and even ping-pong tables in good repair, thrown out of doors by my property-weary neighbors. Yes, it is surely a good and opulent thing to be even just a street cleaner in a town like New York. So much for that.

Well, then, after supper, when the table is cleared and the new gifts have all been properly inspected and gurgled over, and just before Papa is finally about to relax with half a dozen morning newspapers, he takes time out to tell Mom and the family something about the outstanding events of his day. And what does he tell them? He tells them that a new and inexperienced man has, most unfortunately, been detailed to his Division.

"Just a grass-green punk that can't lift his weight in paper napkins," he says. "All thumbs and sweat and gristle, that's him. God only knows who they're gonna send up to us next. I'm telling you, things are getting worse every day. When Andy and me finally quit, all I can say is, *God help the Department!*"

Although this is a melancholy and almost somber thought, it is somehow comforting too, because it is surely a sweet thing to be worthy and irreplaceable in some manly function of high responsibility.

That's how I imagine the older man, or men, felt about the events of that particular day.

And the younger man?

Well, I'm pretty sure that on the strength of his solid civil-service status he'd gotten himself married a little while before. In fact, I'm willing to bet one of my calcified kidneys that his little wife is already four months gone in her pregnancy. I can see them cozily settled in some tiny flat up in the Bronx or out in Brooklyn somewhere, and, what's more, I can imagine that there is hardly any room for the two of them in the apartment at all, because it is so suffocatingly crammed with a lot of overstuffed, antihuman furniture. I also have the feeling that this gruesome setting is illuminated by a lot of modern lamps that throw the cold spotlight of criminal investigation onto all those places in the apartment where nobody could ever possibly want to have them. One of these fiendish beams, a wedding present from his in-laws, shines mercilessly down on the brand-new Sanitation Department coat that has been carefully draped across the back of the best family armchair. It is plain that this ritualistic, almost sacred, garment has already lost a good deal of its official effrontery. Its shoulders slope down in a spirit of unmistakable dejection and the stained and wrinkled sleeves seem to embrace the chair like a deeply wounded aspiration.

Here, too, supper has nearly been finished, and our young hero is thoughtfully bent over the last remnants of his rice pudding. His neck is aglow with the reflections of some soothing ointments and a deep sigh suddenly rises from his manly bosom. His bride, standing in the doorway to the kitchenette, is absent-mindedly resting a salad bowl atop her already visible protuberance. She even pretends to be wiping this innocent dish, when, in fact, she is keeping her troubled, humid eyes

17

anxiously fixed on the face of her dispirited Lancelot.

Our hero gives another tremendous sigh, pushes away the five raisins still afloat in his saucer and slowly lifts his bewildered gaze toward his worshipful helpmeet.

"Millie," he says, "you know, Millie, there sure are a lot more angles to this game than most people imagine."

"I know," says Millie, dropping her pose of preoccupied housewifery and coming purposefully back to the dinner table. "I could tell something was bothering you the minute you stepped through that door," she says. "I just made up my mind not to ask you about it until after you'd finished your supper, but now that you've brought the whole thing up yourself, I'm just gonna tell you something. Remember when you bought the Harley Davidson motorcycle three years ago, and you put a match near the gas tank that first day, and you singed off both my eyebrows and all my bangs? Remember? And remember how three weeks later we drove up to Scaroon Lake with that same bike and we hardly had any trouble with it, all through that whole rainy weekend? Right?

"Well, then, five months ago when we moved into this apartment and you decided to paint the place yourself, remember when you started scraping the walls the whole ceiling fell down, and the landlord threatened to have you locked up, remember? Well, what happened then? You plastered that ceiling for nearly a month and a half, didn't you? And just look at this lovely place now!

"And so I've only got this one thing to say to you: You may be discouraged, and things may look very black to you *right this minute*, but whatever it is that's got you down at this moment, you're gonna come through topside up, just like you've always done. Whatever it is that you've got your mind made up about, no matter how hard and impossible it seems, I just *know* that you—you—*you*—*Clarence Boylan*—are going to *MAKE IT!!!*"

18

CHAPTER THREE

There be three things which are too wonderful
*   for me,*
Yea, four which I know not:
The way of an eagle in the air;
The way of a serpent upon a rock;
The way of a ship in the midst of the sea;
And the way of a man with a maid.

A<small>ND</small>, just as puzzling, of course, is the way of
a *maid* with a *man*. This came home to me when I tried to do
a good deed once and went to a whorehouse in the Village to
find an amiable night's companion for a demoralized friend of
mine.

"Friend" is a pretty euphemistic expression to use in connection with this particular wretch, because what actually kept our relationship going over the years was just that we were both tuned in on a familiar wave length of basic loathing for each other. It was a bond, nevertheless, and we were fully aware of its origins, and its obligations too.

Human relationships are sometimes really quite unexplainable. Remember the original Siamese twins, the ones who actually came from Siam and were exhibited in Barnum's famous museum? Although they were solidly joined at the hips and had only one bloodstream between them, they had some kind of silly quarrel toward the end of their lives, and as a result of it they never again addressed a single word to each other. They ignored each other for seven solid years. That's a fact.

At any rate, my own story happened quite a long while ago too, and this character that I'm telling you about, whose name was Phil, had at that time a most annoying girl friend, who for reasons unknown chose to call herself Corinny. Corinny wore long, Mary Pickford-style ringlets quite a while after everybody else had already given up wearing them, even Mary Pickford. She had some other strange affectations that were equally dated and out of key. For instance, she always rigged herself out in velvet Salvation Army-style bonnets, and I don't recall ever seeing her with a pair of gloves whose finger tips weren't missing. I mean that she carefully trimmed them off, to give the effect of little Eva on her way to Sunday school. Henry James would probably have said about her that "her eyes were perhaps just too round, and too inveterately surprised." What he would have said about her tendency toward hysterical giggling and her undeniable inclination to go on drunken binges is more than I can possibly imagine.

Well, that was the setup. I might also mention that Phil, who was really quite gone about this tramp, was himself almost a teetotaler. He used to take some weak iced tea once in a while, but I don't think he quite approved of Cokes. Too much caffeine.

It stands to reason that their love affair was destined to travel along some pretty rocky detours, and so it came as no terribly great surprise to me that it finally busted up completely. Of course, it hadn't helped any that friend Phil, in addition to his other virtues, was also pathologically stingy. This feature of his character played a decisive role in the bust-up, because it seems that one day Corinny titteringly announced to him that she had decided to take riding lessons—sidesaddle of course, to go with her hats and her gloves. Horses cost about six bucks an hour in those days, and that did it.

Phil used to make his living keeping an antique shop down in Greenwich Village. When I dropped in on him one afternoon, I found him absolutely slaughtered by grief. He was never, under the best of circumstances, any too cheerful, but this time he really hit bottom. It even shook me. He bawled real, wet tears right in front of me, and I was suddenly determined to stand by my measly emotional investment in this beetle and to do something for him.

Unfortunately, there isn't a hell of a lot you can do for a guy whose doll has just put him on ice, but luckily I knew that Phil was terribly horny all the time, and so I thought I'd find him some kind of bed rabbit that would help to tide him over his worst spell. This was a hell of a lot harder than it sounds, too, because Phil was not only terribly tight about money, he was also physically somewhat on the repulsive side. A great little combination, as you can see.

And then I remembered that a friend of mine, an artist called Norton Burger, had told me only a few days before that a new whorehouse-and-gin-mill combination had opened up for business somewhere on Christopher Street, and it naturally occurred to me to recruit some reasonable-looking hooker out of this seraglio without ever letting Phil know where the hell she really came from.

Makes sense, doesn't it?

Excepting, of course, that I'd never before in all my life

been to a professional whorehouse, and I hadn't the vaguest idea how to set my little scheme into motion. I was in my mid-twenties at the time and I must have gotten over the worst of my timidities, because I went, right that same afternoon, down to this *maison de joie* to see if I couldn't score for a friend.

Just to show you how green I was, I went there at about two o'clock in the afternoon. Anybody in his right mind would have realized that nobody, but *nobody*, goes to get himself a prefabricated lay at such a crazy hour as that.

So I knocked at the door of this brothel early in the afternoon, and after a while a baleful Italian eye appeared at a rusty peephole and gave me a bloodshot once-over.

"Yeah?" it said.

"I'd like to talk to one of the girls," I said. "Norton sent me."

"Norton? Norton who?"

"Norton Burger, the artist, who makes sketches of people. Charges fifty cents for a portrait. *You* know!"

"Never hoid o' him," said the guardian of the treasures. "Who you, anyway?"

"My name is Sylvester," I said. "Sylvester Bonino. I live over on Third Street."

The "Bonino" did it, of course. He lowered a reptile lid and mused over it for a moment.

"It's kinda oily," he said. "Dem goils ain't up yet. Wanna walk around de block a coupla times and come back in half an hour?"

"Fine," I said. "I'll be back."

Half an hour later I *was*. The sinister little pimp seemed to have washed and shaved in the interim, which had simply turned his jowls blue-gray, like the skin of a killer shark, and I hadn't the slightest doubt that his map was at least as rough. He wore a tight snap-brim hat and a tight pin-striped suit, and,

22

just as he stood there, he looked as if he'd been freshly clipped out of a film about the underworld.

He opened the iron gate for me wide enough to squeeze through, and I stepped down into the gloom of a typical Village basement—except that there were about a dozen booths fixed against three of the walls. The moment I entered the room an insane mechanical piano began to heave asthmatically, and after three or four preliminary sound hemorrhages an unbelievable, nerve-shattering racket smashed up against my eardrums. It was, of all things, the William Tell Overture. Because the mechanism had certainly been turned up to its loudest pitch, that bloody noise blasted my senses like the sudden explosion of an oversized land mine. I was so stunned by the impact that I fell defensively into the booth that was located nearest the entrance. Then, as if this mad rumpus were not enough to unsettle me, there appeared through the large center doorway about twenty youngish-looking girls, and the moment they crossed the threshold they automatically paired off and started to dance with each other.

To the William Tell Overture, remember?

You can't possibly imagine the spooky effect that this demented saraband had on me. The place had hardly any lights at all, because people who run booze parlors and hookshops know perfectly well that the special illusions that people like to nurture in such places thrive infinitely better if the atmosphere is kept rather consistently murky. There were also imitation vine leaves all over the walls, and over the ceiling too, and hunks of white latticework had been artistically distributed about the premises to give the impression of a romantically secluded grape arbor.

Hideous beyond belief!

Surprisingly enough, the girls all seemed rather good-looking, but what still further demoralized me in this joint was the fact that all of them were dressed up as if they were just ready to go out for a stroll. That's exactly what it looked like. They wore hats and gloves and fur pieces, and it seemed as if somebody, by some powerful act of enchantment, had at the very last moment altered their plans and they had all suddenly been compelled to dance around this dimly lit basement that was absolutely reeking with the smell of carbolic acid.

It sure was weird.

I hardly dared to look up, but luckily the undersized hood who had let me in didn't seem to take the slightest notice of my stupefaction. He just leaned against the side of my booth and watched the dames whirling about for a couple of minutes, before he finally turned his stony glare back on me.

"Which one o' dem goils'd you like to talk to?" he said.

Without really raising my eyes, I pointed silently at the tail of a white fox fur piece that just happened to be sailing past my table, and the moment I made that very slight gesture all twenty girls stopped dancing and nineteen of them quietly trooped out of the room. I also noted with growing uneasiness that the owner of the fox fur was slowly lowering her rump onto the narrow bench that was nailed down opposite to mine. Meanwhile, the tough-looking little blue-jowl had taken himself a powder too. In short, my dream girl and I were alone at last.

Then I just had to look up.

She was wearing a turquoise-blue tailored suit, a pink, gold-embroidered toque and, of course, the dead white animal that had first caught my attention.

"My name is June," she said. "What's yours?"

"Sylvester," I said. "I'm glad to know you, June."

She was a fine-looking broad, pink and white, with blue eyes—of German or Irish stock, very probably. She certainly was one of the healthiest and most cheerful-looking young women I had ever laid eyes on. None of the ravages of sin

24

was visible about her person, and the only thing you might have held against her was that she seemed just a little bit over-weight. Too plump for *my* taste, anyway, but I was going through a Botticelli, pre-Raphaelite stage at the time, and I may have been just a shade too critical of her endowments.

Unfortunately, like so many American girls she looked rather anonymous in her eye-soothing prettiness. If you had lost her in a crowd somewhere, you might have had a tough time finding her again unless she was wearing some kind of class pin or a locket that you had just recently given her.

But that sort of confusion can happen easily enough on any social level in this country, especially in college mobs and such-like gatherings. It has happened to me any number of times, particularly when everybody was wearing beanies and rac-coon coats. I can remember at least three occasions when I had a hell of a time locating my own pet raccoon. You had to have the instinct of a Seeing Eye dog to find your way back to your own cherished ideal on some of these festive occasions.

Well, anyway, June just sat there and beamed at me. Then suddenly another Italian, a giant in a white apron, material-ized at our table and gave my hands a solid, wet slop with a dirty dishcloth.

"What'll ya have?" he said.

I looked questioningly at June. "What will *you* have?" I asked her.

"I'll have Scotch and water," she said.

"I'll have the same," I said.

The dishcloth disappeared. June leaned forward and smiled encouragingly into my dopey deadpan expression.

"You from New York?" she said.

"Yes, I'm from New York," I said. "I guess I got here a little early in the day, didn't I?"

"Well . . . you did . . ." she said. "We don't expect peo-ple mostly until around six or six-thirty—except weekends,

25

when the hours is less regular. But it don't matter, does it? You're here now, so you just have yourself a good time."

The man arrived with the drinks, and I remembered reading or hearing somewhere that bartenders in such places generally served the girls only cold tea. When I lifted my glass to my lips, I heartily wished the bastard had done the same for me, for I suddenly realized why the joint had such an infernal stink of carbolic—those sons of bitches were probably mixing it in their drinks.

But, after all, I hadn't come there to get plastered. I had other things on my mind. So I decided to quickly clear my little problem with the amiable June.

"You see, I'm here on account of a friend of mine," I said to her. And no sooner were these few words out of my mouth than I could see a veil of weary skepticism definitely falling across the face of my bright vis-à-vis.

"A *friend?*" she said, as she took a minute, speculative sip out of her tea.

"Yes," I said. "He's an old pal of mine and his girl friend just died a couple of weeks ago, see? He's in pretty bad shape right now, and so I thought maybe I'd ask one of the girls from here to go out with us some evening this week, and not let on that it's all just a frame-up. I just want her to act like she was the friend of a girl friend of mine, and like she just happened to come along on a blind date, get it?"

As I went on talking, I noticed that June had quietly decided to change her mind about me and my story. When I had finally finished laying my little plot before her, she looked at me thoughtfully and even with a certain amount of warm concern, like a hep elder sister when her kid brother has just confessed to her that he thinks he's about to come down with a dose of clap.

"You're a very nice guy, Sylvester," she said. "There ain't many friends these days that would do as much for anybody.

26

Believe me, *I* know. There's only one trouble about this scheme of yours. You see, if the girls ever leave this place, for a night, I mean, it's bound to run into quite a lot of money. That's only natural."

She noticed that I was disappointed, so she quickly put her hand on top of mine and said, "There's a couple of ways out of it, though, and maybe we can work out something that'll suit you, and suit your friend too, and wouldn't cost you such a lot of money, neither."

"What about weekends?" I asked.

"Weekends!!! Why, that's the biggest business the house does all week. Saturday is ace night for everybody, and even on Sundays we get the leftovers and the returnees, don't you see?"

"Returnees???!!!"

"Sure, they're the ones who were already on their way home after their Saturday night binge, but somehow or other they never quite made it across the bridges and across the ferries—back home, I mean—and before you know it, they're right back here for another refill. I guess some of them just hate the idea of going home, don't you see? No, weekends are definitely out. And Monday the hairdresser comes and washes and does our hair, and the girls like to have Monday quiet anyway, after all that razzle-dazzle—you know, they like to do their own washing, and stuff. Tuesday . . . well, Tuesday . . ."

She had cocked her curly pink-and-white head 'way over to one side and was counting the days of the week off on her plump, dimpled fingers. She was exactly like a busy little housewife whose many duties hardly ever give her any time off to do even some harmless window-shopping. Also she looked like a kindly saleswoman in a department store who is judiciously advising an undecided and inexperienced customer about the advantages and the drawbacks of certain dress

27

materials. She was wonderfully housewifely about my problem and altogether adorably feminine in balancing the pros and cons of her practical speculations. And then I could see by a sudden decisive gesture that she had finally come to a satisfactory decision in my ticklish affair.

"I've got a suggestion to make," she said. "See how it strikes you."

"Go on," I said. "I'm sure it's something good."

"Well, here's my idea, Sylvester, and I really think it's the best way out for everybody. You see, I've got Thursdays off. I like it that way, so I can get a little breather before the weekend. But from the way you talk, I'm sure your friend must be a nice guy, too, and won't give me too much of a hard time of it. So why don't I meet you on Thursday, around suppertime, and we can have your friend meet me then. How about that? How does that strike you? On my own time, I mean?"

"Just fine!" I said. "Just fine! Where do I pick you up—here?"

"No," she said. "My day off is my own and has nothing to do with the house. You come up to eight-seventy-four-B Eighth Avenue. Write it down, so you won't forget it. It's the rear house—you just walk through the hall, and you'll find me right on the parlor floor in the back. Don't forget. Make it around seven-thirty, that'll give me plenty of time to get my rest."

I wrote it all down, of course.

"You gonna bring along your own girl friend?" she asked.

"You bet," I said. "She's very nice, you'll like her."

"I'm sure I will," she said.

"And what do I leave them for these drinks?" I asked.

"If you can afford it, leave three dollars, 'cause they'll be hung up about your not coming upstairs with me. But if that's too much for you, a couple of dollars will be enough, too."

"That's all right," I said. "I'll leave three."

28

We shook hands. I threw the bills on the table, and, as we got up, the gatekeeper automatically reappeared.

"I made a date for next Saturday with June," I told him. "Goodbye, June, see you then."

"Goodbye and good luck, Sylvester," she said.

"You better come oily on Saddy," said the pimp, as he preceded me to the exit. "June is damn popular around here, and she mightn't have too much time for you. Bedder come around six."

"I'll be here early," I said. "You got a lot of good music going on here," I said. "It's just a little too loud."

"Huh?" He looked puzzled. "Dat music is high class, grand opera," he said. "Baldo don't like jazz and he won't have nothin' but opera around here. Nothin' *but* opera! The *best!*"

Aren't Italians wonderful?

So a couple of days later I waltzed into Phil's antique shop to tell him that my wife had found a nice friend for him who was willing to go out with all of us the following Thursday evening. When I stepped into the dinginess of his store, there was Corinny sitting on Phil's lap, and she was dipping some fresh raspberries into a saucer of sugar before judiciously inserting them between her big, yellow horse teeth.

What had happened?

Nothing mysterious, really, when you consider the monsters involved. Those two horrible freaks had simply double-crossed me and made it up again.

I was furious.

I was particularly sore because it meant hanging up a fine girl like June Dorgan (that was her full name), and certainly my little June was worth forty-seven different kinds of Corinny any day, not to mention the *nights*.

I said nothing to those two bastards, of course, but I left

29

Phil's shop absolutely determined to keep my date with June on the following Thursday. I explained the whole goddamned problem to my young wife, and, to my complete astonishment, she turned out very sympathetic about it.

"You can't let her down now," she said. "You take her out somewhere. I'll just meet you later on."

"You mean it?" I said.

"Of course! You were silly to get mixed up in this mess in the first place, but now that you're in it you might as well finish it off the best you can. Remember, this girl may have given up some other plans she had for this night. I think it would be absolutely dirty for you to let her down."

Well, I *didn't* let her down.

At seven-thirty sharp I was over on Eighth Avenue, at the address she had given me, and I headed smack into a real disaster right off the bat.

It was a very warm spring evening and it seemed that most of the tenants in that miserable ruin had decided to catch themselves a little dusty air right in front of their stoop. They were squatting all over the place on broken benches and on three-legged chairs, while their screaming brats were going through deadly calisthenics on the rusty fire escapes and the scarred banisters. But the moment I arrived in front of their door a pall of frozen silence suddenly descended on the cast of that rackety beggar's opera. They stopped sucking at their straws, lowered their bottles and their paper fans, and a few of the slatternly younger women even pulled their kids protectively into the folds of their skirts. It was a real reception, no mistake about *that*, with elaborately muted drums too, because they all knew, with the unfailing wisdom of the gutter, exactly whom I'd come to visit in that mildewed little retreat of theirs. To clinch the matter still further, I had even equipped myself with an idiotic nosegay of some sort, and they'd all spotted it, because I wasn't able to shove it out of sight until I was right on top of them.

30

I literally clenched my teeth as I passed that grim phalanx of staring mutes, and, badly shaken but undaunted, I landed at last in the stone funnel that was their back yard. There I found another, even dingier stoop, but luckily no people, just a garbage can into which I hastily flung my floral offering. My collar was wilted and I was trembling as only a young man trembles who has somehow gotten himself involved in an extremely strange adventure indeed.

I knocked, and an old woman opened the door. She was fattish and slovenly and she was halfheartedly drying her hands on a wet apron as she peered out into the semidarkness.

"You're Sylvester," she said, and, as she smiled at me, she became instantly and unmistakably June's mother.

"Yes," I said. "Am I too early?"

"No," she said. "Come in. June will be out in a minute. I just had my own supper and fed the baby, and I was washing up the dishes."

I stepped into the derelict kitchen and she motioned me toward a low wooden stool whose legs had been reinforced with galvanized wire. I sat down, and only then I got my first look at the baby. He was a solid-looking little boy about a year old, quite naked, and he was sitting contentedly in a small washbasin under the kitchen table. What's more, I could have sworn that the liquid that the kid was sitting in was *coffee*. There must even have been some *sugar* in this puddle too, because a whole cordon of buzzing flies seemed to be guzzling the stuff on the inner rim of that pan.

Before I realized what I was doing, I heard myself asking her about it. "Is that coffee the kid is sitting in?" I said.

She gave a croupy chuckle. "Just a little," she said. "He's crazy about it and I can't get him to get into the pan unless I pour some of it into the water for him. I rinse him off clean later on, but he's sure gonna be a fiend for coffee when *he* grows up."

"How did he get into the habit?" I asked her.

31

"By accident. I once spilt half a cup on top of him when he was bathing and he ain't ever been the same since. He's good as gold otherwise, and I never have any real trouble with him, thank God."

"*Your* baby?" I asked.

"Naw, he's June's. Had him a year ago last Easter. His name is George Patrick."

I would have liked to find out just a little more about these fascinating matters, but June came into the kitchen just then.

She looked simply great. No more sky-blue suits, no more pink-and-gold toques, no fox furs, white or otherwise. In fact, she had decked herself out in remarkable good taste. She was wearing a black crepe-de-Chine dress with Irish lace at the cuffs and the neck, and her hat, her purse and her gloves were positively chic. What's more, unlike me she wasn't a bit flustered. It was also obvious that she wasn't planning for us to hang around for a session of social chitchat. Not her. She just took one more quick look at herself in a little mirror above the sink, threw a kiss to the baby and opened the door.

"I'll see you in the morning, Mom," she said. "Tell the man to leave us a little heavy cream, and take care of yourself."

And that was that.

No false daughterly or motherly gestures, no pecks on the cheek for Mater, no sloppy goodbyes to the infant. Nothing. She was a real, twenty-one-carat jewel.

Of course, after we got out of the yard we had to pass that death watch again, but June firmly held on to my arm and led me past those adenoidal baboons with her head held high, like the Duchess de Montrouge on her way to the guillotine. She was not only magnificent in her disdain but she automatically endowed me with guts too. That was the best part of it.

"Where are we going to meet them?" she said.

Well, there it was—the bitter, unpalatable moment that I had been dreading all along. We had just reached the corner

32

when she asked me, and I slowly disengaged my arm and squarely confronted her.

"June," I said, "my friend's girl never died at all, she just threw him in the bag like a dirty old dish towel, that's what really happened. And he was so down about it that I decided I just had to do something for him. Well, they made it up again a couple of days ago, and so *I* decided to take you out for the evening, myself. We'll have dinner somewhere, if you like, and I've got a couple of tickets for a show later on. And everything else . . . about our arrangements stands just as we planned it. I mean, you're not just going to waste your evening . . . I mean . . . it'll be all just as if everything had gone through the way we planned it . . . see?"

Her face was so candid that during my clumsy discouse her features clearly reflected her fluctuating reactions to my story. I could see that she was a little stunned at first, but as I went on talking her eyes brightened, and in the end she took my hand and gave it a wonderfully reassuring squeeze.

"Now, Sylvester," she said, "don't you bother your head about this even for another minute. This is my night off, ain't it, and I had nothing in mind that I'd sooner do than having dinner with you and going to a show later on. I think you're a real nice guy, and I'm glad you didn't just stand me up, like *some* guys might have done. So let's waste no more time talking about a lot of other people, who aren't here, anyway. The evening is young, ain't it?"

What a girl!

Anyway, we went and had a quiet dinner over at Joel's, on West Forty-first Street. This was a hangout for newspapermen and cartoonists during those years, and the food and beer were of the best. Simple grub, you understand, but certainly infinitely superior to anything served up by the famous Broadway places a little farther uptown. June loved it.

"You know I'm married, don't you?" she said. "Well, when

Fred and me were first going out together he used to take me over to Hoboken to some sea-food places that were really great. Steamed clams, big baskets full of 'em, wonderful fish and lobsters and stuff—really scrumptious."

"Where is Fred now?" I asked.

"Oh, he's been out of a job a long time. More than a year. Sixteen months, almost. He's a nickel-plater and makes good money when he works at it. You know, most nickel-platers are terrible lushes. *All* of them, in fact. It's on account of them poisonous fumes they inhale all the time. Well, anyway, everybody always liked Fred, he's very likable, but he's just too unreliable even for a·nickel-plater. So he got laid off . . . and then we had the kid . . . and instead of its straightening him out it just made him worse. Some men are like that. Well, what with one thing and another, he just drifted off. But . . . I'm managing. We're still married, though, and he comes to see me once in a while and makes all kinds of promises, but, you know how it is with a lush. They can't just drink the stuff, they gotta go swimming in it. But let's just forget about it. Tell me about your girl, why don't you?

"Well, as a matter of fact, we're already married."

"Oh boy," she said, "you're certainly a fast worker."

"I'm going to be an artist," I said. "I already sold some drawings to the New York *World*, and some other places too. Maybe in a year or so I'll get something a little more steady and then we'll be on Easy Street."

"You better be," she said. "You can't just make it on love alone, that's for sure. You better be able to take care of a home before you do anything foolish, because suddenly you find yourself out in the street when it's raining cats and dogs. If you really care for the girl, you'd better watch out."

"I will," I said.

And that's about a fair sample of the tone and the general texture of our confidences during the meal. The rest of the evening she was just a carefree, cheerful companion who certainly seemed to have no misgivings about the ominous rumblings of her own uneasy tomorrows.

We went to see a fine movie which was playing two-a-day over at the old Criterion. It was called *Grass* and was an extraordinary documentary about some tribes of shepherds who traditionally grazed their flocks somewhere in the lowlands of Persia. The film showed one of their biannual treks across high, snowy mountain passes in search of fresh pastures for their animals. This picture still exists, in the files of the Museum of Modern Art film library, and if you consult their schedules you might even see this masterpiece yourself someday. It is well worth your while to watch out for it. The making of that picture was a real achievement for the movie business.

June was absolutely slain by it. When, in the course of their mountain crossing, the tribes had to struggle barefooted through knee-deep snow, and when, later, hundreds of their sheep and goats perished in the icy torrents that had to be forded, she impulsively clutched my hand in wild sympathy for their travail. And when finally the lights came on, her lovely forget-me-not eyes, were filled with tears.

"Well," she said, "some people sure have a hard time of it, don't they? God help everybody!"

We had another small snack in some cookie-nookie on Broadway, and then, since it was already getting on to twelve o'clock, I suggested that I'd better take her home. So we got into a taxi and I told the driver to take us to Eighth Avenue. As I rode along beside her, it suddenly came to me that despite the lateness of the hour some of June's neighbors might still be draped out on the sidewalk in front of their tenement, and I must say the mere thought of it completely soured my evening.

"Let's get off on the corner," I said to her, "and we'll just walk up to the door. All right?"

"If you don't mind, I'd rather not," she said. "You musn't mind what people think, or how they look at you. They're really not any better than you are, no matter what they pretend to themselves. Let's pull right up to the door, and to hell with them, if you'll excuse the expression. Believe me, they've got nothing on *me*. I don't bother anybody and I don't owe *any* of them *anything!* They're a poor lot, just like myself, and some of them are even a lot worse off than I am. So don't you pay them no mind."

And that's the way we did it. We pulled up in front of the house with our cab, and there, sure enough, was the full quorum still in attendance, children and all, and when we passed between them they were again frozen into blind-eyed silence as if we were a couple of spooks that had suddenly come to haunt their festering dung pile.

When we hit the back yard June gave a soft, girlish laugh.

"They'll sit out there all night," she said, "waiting for you to come out again. So you must come inside now and I'll make you a cup of real homemade coffee."

"Isn't it too late?" I asked.

"Not for me," she said. "Mom and the baby are sleeping and we won't bother them any. Don't you worry."

And now, as you've probably been anticipating, another hideous problem, maybe the worst of the whole evening, was still waiting to be tactfully liquidated by me. I had to manage somehow to pay the poor girl for her evening, didn't I? It was her way in life, after all, to sell her services, her society and her tangible assets for cold cash, wasn't it? Well, how in hell was I ever going to hand over the ten bucks that I had reserved for just that purpose?

I mean, after the dinner, and after our confidences, and particularly after the soul-stirring, superb movie we'd seen together . . .

It would have been a real poser for anybody; for me it had grown into a bat-infested sleeping bag.

Meanwhile she took off her hat and her gloves and proceeded to make us some coffee.

"We're moving out of here soon," she said. "I found a nice place over in Brooklyn the other day, where there still are some trees around, and where the kid can play on a sandpile out in the back yard. I've already put down a deposit on it and we'll be getting out of here next month."

"Great," I said. "It won't be too far for you to travel, will it?"

"Only fifteen minutes more," she said, "and it'll be worth it. Mom is a great cook, but here there's nothing for her to work with. She has arthritis but she still has more go about her than somebody thirty years younger. I want her to get a breath of fresh air once in a while, too."

"Don't you have any brothers or sisters?" I said.

"Two brothers and a sister, but they live out in Michigan and around Chicago somewhere, and they never did nothing for us anyway. They got their own troubles, I guess. Who hasn't?"

In these and suchlike conversational gambits we drank our coffee and passed the next half hour. And all during those bitter thirty minutes I was really only half attentive to what she was saying, because—well, because through all that time I was desperately clutching that goddamned ten-dollar bill in my pocket.

How was I ever going to hand it to her?

And when?

It was really too much for me.

At last I had to leave. I picked up my hat and went to the door. The money was in my fist, and I had decided that I would slip it to her *dexterously* at the final handshake. I was sure Cardini * could have done it, and therefore it *was* humanly possible! It goes without saying that I muffed it. The wet, minutely folded bill fell ignominiously to the floor between us.

"I'm sorry," I said, stooping down to retrieve it. "It's just

* The greatest sleight-of-hand magician in the world.

37

a little something for you, June, something to buy something with . . ."

I tried to hand it to her quite openly.

And then she smiled at me, a warm, unforgettable, womanly smile. The Mona Lisa never had anything like it, never. Believe me; I've seen the original.

"That's all right," she said. "I don't want to take it, Sylvester, because it would just spoil the evening for me. I'm sure you understand. If you really feel you'd like to do something, why don't you buy some little thing for the kid tomorrow. I owe *you* thanks." She took my hand, bent forward and kissed me ever so softly on the cheek.

I'm ass-deep in a great little cliché, I thought as I stumbled out into the darkness. I'm mixed up with a whore with a heart of gold—and not even by De Maupassant. Oi!

The next afternoon I was back with a fire truck, with a whole hook and ladder company, in fact, for the benefit of the coffee fiend. Mom was so delighted by the unexpected gift that she completely forgot that I was there. Just as I was leaving she finally remembered me.

"June is gone downtown," she said, "and she left you a letter. I'm so mixed up I nearly didn't give it to you. Here it is."

June's handwriting was clear and blatantly legible, like a conscientious schoolgirl's, and here is what she had to say:

DEAR SYLVESTER,

Thanks again for a wonderful evening. I will remember it a long time. The picture was a real treat and the company was up to it. I am enclosing a little token that somebody once forgot down at the place and never came back for. It is not of any use to me so please keep it and use it and maybe it will bring you luck. It might at that. You will notice that one of the initials is the same as yours.

My best good wishes to you and to your wife.

Sincerely,

JUNE DORGAN

Inside the envelope, wrapped in some tissue paper, was a gold billfold which was formed out of three initials, and one of them was actually a large, very fancy letter *S*.

Some years later when I was in a bad jam I hocked it and got twelve dollars for it, in a pawnshop that was only two blocks away from the house where June had once cooked a hospitable cup of midnight coffee for me.

I finally had to sell the ticket too, for another two dollars. Well, easy come, easy go, *I* always say.

CHAPTER FOUR

M<small>INE</small> (like everybody else's) is a very peculiar and special dilemma. It seems that for the past half century I was so busy with the business of living that I never gave much thought to the idea that my cacophonous carousel was ever going to come to any kind of permanent stop.

Of course, I'd sometimes been quite sick, a hell of a lot sicker than most of the other people I knew, but it had never entered my head that any of these illnesses was anything but a minor interruption in the all-absorbing razzle-dazzle that I was involved in. Even time taken out by obstreperous ulcers and acute renal spasms seemed like just so many temporary intermissions, and it didn't ever seriously occur to me that these occasionally rather alarming and sometimes even bloody

40

breakdowns might, at any moment, come to signalize the final turn of the wheel.

And so, as I'm telling you, I was riding along in my not particularly restful way, when I suddenly looked up and found a doctor shoving a twenty-three-inch flashlight up into my goddamned bladder.

I nearly passed out.

You know how a *man* is built, don't you? Well, then, just imagine that crazy character galloping in *there*, with all that furniture on his back. It certainly took a lot of painful finagling to get that bloody apparatus all the way up into my vitals, believe me.

And what the hell was he spying in there for, anyway? What did he expect to find?

Are you ready?

You'd better sit down.

He found death!

Surprised? You think I'm just kidding? Not a bit of it. I've got the documents to prove it. X rays and crap—the whole kit and kaboodle of it. Yes, I have.

Well, it certainly startled me.

You surely can understand that, can't you? You know how it is about death . . .

Everybody has to die. Of course!

Everybody except *You!*

And there, in the midst of all the exhilarating racket of my life, with most of my fun and even a lot of my very important heartbreaks still quite incompleted, bang! I stopped being my unique, imperishable self and in less time than it takes a light beam to flutter around the earth I had suddenly become— *Everybody!*

Wait till it hits *you*. It'll take your breath away too.

Also, it'll make you think as you never thought before. At first I found it very hard going. Particularly at night.

41

You see, I have a very beautiful young wife; and she's a musician, and very sensitive too, you understand, and I wanted to spare her as much as possible, of course.

Probably the toughest thing of all, for me, was to think of having to leave her. Not that she really needed me. Not a bit of it. She's a beautiful American girl, don't you see? I myself was born in Vienna, and so I'm not the kind of vain ass who thinks there ain't gonna be no more serenades just because his own little harmonica happens to be blighted by mildew. No, not me!

I'd like to call your attention to the fact that being born an Austrian is something pretty special. Not better. Not worse. Just *special*.

For instance, an Austrian school child learns even in his earliest history classes that Austria too has won some important victories on the field of battle. But I remember very clearly that during those history lessons, back in Vienna, our teachers would always gently point out to us that after each of these heroic achievements the Austrians had to pick up the vanquished enemy by his armpits and to hold him up for quite a while, before he was able to function like his old normal self again. It seems we had, first of all, to feed the son of a bitch, him and his starving family too, and then we had to bind up their goddamned sores and go on looking after the lot of them for years and years, or else the whole stinking, putrescent mess was liable to fall right down on us and put everybody out of business.

It certainly made us ponder.

Yes, I discovered when I was only a snotty little kid, 'way back in Austria, that the brunt of victory is not necessarily borne by the conquered.

Believe me, it makes you damned suspicious of all future victories, and it certainly prevents you from becoming any kind of convincing or passionate go-getter. You always have the funny feeling that in the long run, who knows, your triumphs might come to cost you a lot more than they are worth. Dig?

You may perhaps think that I'm exaggerating the Austrian ambivalence of feeling toward success. Well, perhaps I am. But I'm about to go even further and tell you something equally astonishing about the way my ex-countrymen react to disaster.

When I say my ex-countrymen, I don't mean only Mozart or Schnitzler or Freud, although I include them too, of course; I'm referring to everybody. I include all the people who in other countries would be counted strictly among the *squares* —just a lot of egos on the half shell, flying through space backward.

First of all, let me solemnly assure you that I have never in all my life met a single really *naïve* Austrian. In a truly certified Austrian, even naïveté is just a highly sophisticated form of protective coloration. And let me add to this, that no matter what the hell they may be doing or saying or even preaching, they are, the lot of them, ever so secretly and quietly smiling to themselves inside. In church, in school, in jail, in Parliament and, yes, even on their deathbeds, they can't ever seem to stop being sort of vaguely amused.

There is a National Characteristic for you, Professor Jung.

Now, remember, I don't wish to imply that they are chronically flippant or cynical about things; nothing could be further from the truth. What's more, I don't care to go on record that this particular trait of theirs is either a failing or an attribute of any kind. I only claim that, whatever the hell it is, it gives the secret smiler a certain undeniable advantage in facing the varying fraudulent manipulations and setbacks provided in endless abundance by an unpredictable fate.

And so, despite the fact that I'd already lived in the United States for over forty-five years, when I was informed by excellent medical authority that my life was in imminent danger the little old boy from old Vienna who lives inside me began— automatically, protectively and ever so gently—to smile.

It was a great surprise—and a great help.

So that's it, I thought. Finished! Well, it was a damned good show while it lasted, and I'm sorry it has to be curtains now. But, as the French say, even the most beautiful woman cannot give more than she *has*.

After all, it had happened to other nice Austrians too, to Schubert, to Haydn, to Grillparzer and to Peter Altenberg, and they'd all certainly been damned good kids when *they'd* had it. Obviously there was no effective way of avoiding it.

Of course, I still had a lot of unfinished business on hand. Who hasn't?

But, even so, you must admit that not every poor man in his late fifties who is about to die has a beautiful and loving young wife at his side.

I recalled that David Garrick, the famous actor, had, after his many theatrical triumphs, finally managed to fill a huge mansion with valuable furnishings and art treasures, and how one day he had persuaded Samuel Johnson to come and inspect all this valuable loot.

After stomping up and down the many halls and corridors on his poor gouty legs, old Samuel had finally fallen exhausted into an armchair and given off a great puff of exhaustion.

"Well, sir," said the proud actor, "what do you really think of it all?"

Johnson pondered the question for a moment, squinted speculatively at Garrick and said, "Ah, Davie, Davie, I think that all this is going to make *dying* very, very hard for you!"

Maybe that's not exactly the way it all happened, but that's the way I remembered it and that's how I certainly felt about it. Yes, to leave all my rich and undeserved treasures was certainly going to be *very*, *very* hard for me too.

You can guess that I went through a hell of a bitchy time there for a spell, but, as I've already indicated, the national characteristics eventually came through for me, and that, in the end, probably saved the remnants of my sanity.

44

And it was then that I decided to use whatever little time I still had left to write down a few elucidative facts about my life. In the half century that I had already lived, quite a few people, some of them well-meaning and quite a lot of them poisonously envious, had, over the years, evolved a whole mythology of crap about my supposed activities. Samplings of these tidbits could easily be savored wherever my name happened to come up in conversation, and some of this stuff that floated in my direction was not only largely misleading but was also unforgivably dull.

Now, then, I really don't know why anybody ever bothered to *invent* things about me, when the factual circumstances were always so much more scandalous and infinitely more entertaining than the lies ever were.

Another thing, I decided to put down in this book a few facts about myself that nobody could possibly have known about me, because nobody has ever been that intimate with me. *Nobody!* Not even my four beautiful and lovable wives. That also happens to be part of the peculiarly human condition—that nobody can ever really get to know you *ultimately*.

You see, when I first arrived in the United States of America, I was already almost fourteen years old. A finished disaster, in short.

Don't worry, I have no intention of boring you with golden reminiscences of my dear dead childhood. I only want to indicate that before I ever saw the Flatiron Building and the Horn and Hardart restaurants, a hell of a lot of pretty significant stuff must already have happened to me.

For instance, the Volksgarten in Vienna had happened to me, and I shall certainly be filled with disturbing memories of it as long as any sort of rational or irrational thought is left tumbling around inside my noggin.

The Volksgarten is quite unlike anything in America. It doesn't resemble Central Park at all. I really don't quite know how to give you the authentic feel of it. It's more like the parks in France, I suppose. If you've ever been to Paris, then you can guess what I mean. You'll probably recall that the foliage is sometimes very cunningly draped into quite fantastic patterns of formality. On the other hand, wherever that kind of architectural finesse has been avoided, the trees and bushes are nevertheless so ingeniously placed and arranged that their special charms and qualities are always displayed to the greatest possible advantage. Also, the occasional statues that one happens to come across in the midst of all this fabulous greenery are, invariably, excellent examples of the sculptor's art and not just a lot of ossified pastry cakes.

You may think that I'm only hitting the pipe of the past, and that nothing on God's earth was ever as cute as all that. Well, for once you'd be quite wrong, because I've been back and seen it a couple of times since and it's still all there—the velvety moss, the shaded, sun-speckled walks, the stupefying rows of tulips, and even the boozy smell of the little white jasmine stars. I found it all intact.

Only the people have most certainly gone to pot. That's true enough. But the Volksgarten still stands unaltered and exquisite in all its heartbreaking perfection.

And don't blame me too much for falling back into time for a moment, because when a man is as sick as I am almost everything he looks at, or thinks about, becomes a touchstone that seems automatically to evoke the past.

I think Proust has demonstrated pretty plainly that nostalgia can build a most effective bridge for itself out of the moist crumbs of a stale vanilla cooky. So you can just imagine what sort of morass of memory I must get mired in whenever I happen to get a look at Seurat's "Grande Jatte," for instance, which I did just a week ago last Sunday.

Well, anyway, I generally used to play in the Volksgarten near the Theseus Temple, a chaste many-pillared Greek-style

46

structure especially erected to set off the beauty of the surrounding foliage. The children I played with were also a lot different from the kids I later got to know in New York. The boys always tipped their caps to everybody, even to each other, and hardly anybody ever showed up in the park without chaperonage of some sort. I most frequently came alone, because I had my poor parents completely bulldozed and I had somehow managed to wangle it around that way. I was an only child and my folks really didn't quite know what the hell to make of me. It's not that they were such permissive parents, it's simply that they had never had any experience with any other kids and, luckily for me, they never managed to churn up any sort of real faith in their own parental authority.

I liked particularly to go to the Volksgarten on Tuesday afternoons, when most of the children would come to do some guileful swapping of the duplicates from their stamp collections. I also collected prints of famous paintings, which I frenziedly cut out of art books and various pseudocultural family magazines. I used to bring these clippings along for swapping too. It stands to reason that most of these pictures were reproductions of nudes, and I think I can safely say that I had the largest collection of such masterpieces of any twelve-year-old in Vienna at that time. I didn't have a particularly dirty mind, I just liked naked women. I liked them dressed, too. In fact, I had quite a crush on a long-legged, tousle-haired little girl called Hortense who used to come to the park with her French governess, who, despite my unchaperoned condition, had fortunately taken quite a liking to me. Her name was Mlle. Viret, and she was always dressed in black taffeta with a thin line of Val lace around her wrinkled throat.

At any rate, I used to listen avidly to Mlle. Viret as she talked to us about her own childhood in Burgundy and about the great wine festivals that she had witnessed in her native province, and you can believe me, I often became quite drunk with the borrowed ecstasies of the old girl's past. Actually, I was just a little afraid of Mlle. Viret, which was just as well, because occasionally in the early spring, when the air was simply loaded with the heady smell of white lilacs, I found it extremely difficult to manage any sort of rational behavior at all.

It was a wonderfully magical time. And, as if there were still not enough of all that lavish beauty, there was a quiet pond in the background where every form of breathtaking wonder was offered up in shimmering, rippling duplicate. There were swans too, of course, and like cloyingly familiar metaphors they added their suave banality to the somnolence of the enchanted afternoons. Luckily I was still too young to take exception to their facile picturesqueness.

I finally did get around to that too just a couple of years later, up in Central Park in New York City.

As you see, I finally did come to America, and I managed to smuggle all of my sloppy memories ever so cunningly past the unsuspecting customs inspectors, and, what's more, I've carried all that dangerous contraband everywhere around with me ever since. Believe me, I don't overhaul it too often.

I can't afford it.

Still, like most Europeans I am inordinately fond of parks, and since I happen to live in Greenwich Village I generally mosey over to Washington Square, where in the summer months some eruption of scrofulous greenery makes a desperate attempt to remind you of nature. Most of these poor arboreal cripples never really get to bear anything besides crumpled paper bags, torn kite strings and a few rusty tin cans, and each spring dreadful new ruptures and prolapses appear even in the cement trusses that have been prophylactically applied only the year before.

But it is much better than sitting in a crowded parking lot, and so there are always a few hundred passionate nature lovers who go on congregating there, to smoke, to tell lies and to spit on each other's shoes. It's particularly tough on the girls with open-toed slippers.

Now, then, since I've lived in the Village for quite a long time, it seems that I must have spent at least a couple of decades, even just recreationally, within general sight and smell of Washington Arch. During most of that time I seem to have met and talked to nearly the identical group of people, and quite by accident a little while ago I fell into the habit of making myself a few brief notes on some of their more amusing conversations. Nobody in the park knows anything about this, or it would only make them sickeningly self-conscious; after all, the chief virtue of these palavers lies exactly in their shameless, unedited effrontery.

The same people come to occupy the same benches almost every day. It's like the Austrian *Stammtische*, the tables in the coffeehouses of Vienna where the same gossipy mob sits down every afternoon and evening of the year. The only difference is that in the Village you imbibe Popsicles, Gymgicles, and Fudgicles, instead of coffee with whipped cream.

At any rate, I was down in the park last Tuesday, and when I finally came home that evening I made myself some rather elaborate memoranda on what I'd happened to overhear there. It seems that I'd accidentally stumbled in on one of the season's truly momentous caucuses, and if you'll be patient with me for a moment, I'd like to give you just a little taste of what went on down there that afternoon.

You see, the blithe spirits who congregate on or around my own favorite benches are always looking for some well-lit highway that will lead them inevitably to a wide plaza where they'll be able to make a fast and easy buck for themselves. The trouble is that they're attempting to achieve this dizzily solvent condition by simply trying to capitalize on the fact that they have for quite a few years been more or less idle residents of Greenwich Village. Naturally that doesn't make their problem exactly an easy one, for, after all, they really have nothing additional to sell besides their already highly unmarketable talents.

But every once in a while somebody pops up with an idea. It's always the same idea, and nothing ever comes of it. The idea is to produce some kind of show, preferably a musical of some sort, since all their wives and mistresses either sing or dance or something, but certainly it must be a show that will liberally employ all their special devious gifts, such as they are.

Well, that's exactly what they were going on about last Tuesday when I was fortunate enough to drop by. It was an executive session, and when I arrived the meeting had already been under way for about half an hour—which means that general rancor was already knee-high and I didn't garner even a single sign of recognition when I sat down.

They did make room for me on the bench, though, because they knew that I had just recently had six blood transfusions. In fact, only a few weeks ago a few of the people sitting right near me had ill-naturedly and rancorously gone up to the hospital where I was entombed at the time and had had their veins tapped in my behalf. But I'm an old-timer down here, and I realized that this was not necessarily a signal of special regard for me; indeed, as one of them assured me afterward, they would have done just as much for a dog. An Afghan, preferably. Style counts for a lot in the Village.

Well, anyway, sitting alongside and standing in front of me were Boshko Pfenning, Mort Kurtz, Troy Bunthorne, Sandra Plevin, Jack Guilford and Professor Haupt. Besides these there were present about a dozen or so shamuses, kibitzers and dorbitzers of various assorted and frightening genders, and most of these extras were just squatting on the ground, leaning against some consumptive elms or directing their adenoidal breathing down the backs of our necks.

I understood at once that another one of their shows was

50

again under way. In fact, "The Arch Follies" was going to be its working name, and there obviously had already been quite a hassle about this rancid little title of theirs. But before I dish you up any more of this witch's brew, let me tell you something about Professor Haupt. He is an honest-to-God professor at N.Y.U., who comes here quite often because, as a refugee from Central Europe, he too is probably hopelessly addicted to parks—and also I suspect that all these Village characters do sort of vaguely remind him of his own youth in Schwabing and he can't quite seem to resist browsing nostalgically among the mangy local fauna.

Well, I soon discovered that one act of the prospective show had already been completed, in outline at least, and even the professor had agreed to submit a few lyrics for a specialty number of some sort. I also noticed that Boshko Pfenning, who seemed to have missed most of the preliminary meetings, was, therefore, compensationally opinionated and objectionable about everything. By the way, this Boshko person fancies himself something of a nature boy. He eats only in health-food stores, wears, even for the Village, outrageously ill-assorted garments, and is, all in all, just a swarthy bundle of fat, loudmouthed cantankerousness. Also, he is a poet.

Now, then, for reasons which completely eluded me Boshko pretended that this whole theatrical project was really under the special aegis of Professor Haupt, and so he insisted on hurling all of his raucous questions and complaints exclusively at that lean, defenseless refugee.

I'll try and reconstruct some of the spirit of that little get-together for you. Just after I'd sat down, Sandra Plevin, officially a model and also famous as a very sexy little bed rabbit (from Winnetka, of all places), was starting to beef to the assembled group about the complete hopelessness of their windblown aspirations.

"You're never gonna get your ass off the ground," she said.

"This is the fourth year I've heard about a Village show, and all I ever get out of these executive meetings is a corrugated rump from these goddamned benches."

Sandra has fine blue eyes and they simply shimmered with disgust and indignation.

"You fellers are all out cold on your hoofs," she continued. "The lot of you are just boozed up on nothing but hope-dope, and nobody ever even bothers to give you a hot foot. 'The Arch Follies'! Now, there's a name for you. Why don't you guys give yourselves up, and maybe some sucker will turn you out to graze in some abandoned subway station, for crissake!"

Before anyone could make an appropriately lurid reply, Professor Haupt, who never made a pass at Sandra and whom she therefore deeply respects, gave a mild and extenuating defense of the circumstances. He pointed out that there was really no particular harm in all these plans. He indicated that even if nothing ever came of them they were nevertheless aimed in the right direction.

"You are all still so young," he said, "and now is surely the time for a lot of ambitious projects and even hopelessly high-flown ideas. I'm sure that all of you must look at the dawn of each new day as a wonderful unopened surprise."

"Oh my God!" said Sandra. "I get up every morning and hardly dare get out of bed, for fear of stepping into all the hideous crap that is left over from the night before. Every day seems just like an unopened shit bomb to me!"

"Never mind all that personal stuff," said Boshko severely. "Look here, Perfessor, I'd like you to hear something I've just written, something that might be the making of this whole show. Give it its character, so to speak. Put it over, in fact."

"I'm sorry, Boshko," said the professor, "but I have a class in just about fifteen minutes."

"This will only take three," said Boshko, "and remember, it concerns the welfare of the whole country."

"Well," said the professor, "the welfare of the country comes first."

"I'm glad to hear you say that," said Boshko. "I know you're a learned man and that you kneel at the shrine of world liddature. That's why I persume to trouble you. Aldough, with your classical prejudices, you would probly not care so much for some of the more really modrun udderances."

"Frankly, Boshko," said the professor, "I have nothing whatever to say about the show. It's these boys and girls here that are active in the whole matter, and I only promised to help them all I could."

"Exactly!" said Boshko. "But dese boys and girls are already infected with the virus of uptown snobbery—by the virus of phony liddature that has lost all contact with the gudder. Now, François Villon, he was a poet of the gudder, wasn't he, and he was never published in his own lifetime either. He was hanged by the neck until dead—am I right?"

"Such is the legend," said the professor.

"Oh, so you think it's just a *legend*, eh?" said Boshko. "Hedging, as usual. Well, Perfessor, I'm just a plain man. I don't say 'intestinal fortitude' when I mean 'guts'—and I belong to the Guts school of wriding, the wriding that is the hope of America, the raw, low-down speech that serves our evvyday purposes, see? And you, who pertend to care about liddature, ought to be concerned about that kind of wriding."

"The professor has already promised us fifty bucks cash when we're ready to put on our show," said Morton Kurtz. "What the hell did you ever contribute to anybody?"

"I'll tell you what I'm ready to contribute," said Boshko. "I'm ready to contribute a piece of work, a playful little rhyme, a diddy, that the people might some day take to their hearts like 'Sweet Adeline' or 'Silver Threads among the Gold,' which intellectuals scorn but which even little children sing at their games."

"What kind of children is he talking about?" said Sandra, "and what kind of games can those little bastards be playing?"

"Simple harmless games," said Boshko, "because they're just the simple children of simple, common people, you snob!"

"Please!" said the professor.

"All right," said Boshko, "here's my contribution. Take it or leave it—I scorn to press my case."

"You also scorn to press your pants," said Guilford.

"Shut up!" said Boshko. He took a dirty piece of paper out of his pocket, put on his girl friend's green harlequin eyeglasses and started to read:

> *"Her name was Jennie Fechtel*
> *She had a Techtel Mechtel . . ."*

"Just a minute!" said Guilford. "What in hell is a Techtel Mechtel?"

"Techtel Mechtel means affair," said Boshko. "It means a romance."

"In what language is that?" said Sandra.

"It was originally Yiddish," said Boshko, "but the people have adopted it. It has become hallowed by common usage and it is now part of the American language. T. S. Eliot and his pansified British friends wouldn't understand it, but they're not supposed to. Please let me go on.

> *"Her name was Jennie Fechtel,*
> *She had a Techtel Mechtel;*
> *Her lover was a modest Undertaker.*
> *He sent her calla lilies,*
> *His fingers had the chillies,*
> *Through strategy he finally did make her.*

> *"To charm her, and to calm her,*
> *He offered to embalm her;*
> *He made her up just like a youthful orphan.*

She loved the shroud and make-up
And hoped she'd never wake up;
Their love nest was a double-decker coffin."

Boshko cleared his throat and put the paper back into his pocket, and I could see that he was deeply moved. "Well, Perfessor," he said, "that's it! How does it rank?"

"Ranks right along with 'Silver Threads among the Gold,'" said Sandra. "It's a natural."

"I'll take care of you later, tootsie," said Boshko. "What do *you* say, Perfessor?"

"Well," said the professor, "I'm not competent to tell you whether it would fit the show. You must admit it isn't exactly wholesome, but it is certainly a very, very vigorous effort. Very, very vigorous indeed."

Boshko gave a loud snort of contempt, turned away from us and opened his arms in a wide and direct appeal to the mute and simple millions for whom he had spoken.

"And that's all he's got to say," he moaned. "He says it isn't *wholesome!* Well, that just goes to show you what American art is up against today!"

But Boshko was rather nice to me later on, when I asked him to let me make a copy of his little opus. "They're all jealous," he said, "particularly our learned friend from N.Y.U. He just wants to do a fresh version of *Iolanthe*, or some of that other Gilbert and Sullivan fairy crap."

"If you think the prof is a fairy," I said, "you just happen to be 'way off base. He's got plenty of balls, believe me. He spent two years in a concentration camp, and he came out of it alive and good-natured, and, what's more, I understand he's a damned fine teacher still."

"Granted!" said Boshko. "But the essential fiber is gone, because it was never there. The world ends, for these academic characters, on the funeral pyre of Keats."

"You mean Shelley," I said.

"What's the diff?" said Boshko. "It's a dead world, ain't it? The prof hasn't come up for air in forty years. If he did, he'd just keel over from fresh-air poisoning."

Boshko, was, of course, quite wrong.

About a week later I ran into Professor Haupt up at the Forty-second Street library, and we both went out front for a while to have a smoke.

"Did you ever get around to writing anything for the Arch Follies?" I asked him.

"I've made a try," he said. "It isn't exactly easy for me. You see, they need lyrics for songs, and lyrics, in the modern American sense, are quite distinct from traditional poetry. There has to be a certain allowance for—well, for the musical liberties that the composer may want to take. You can't write too tightly or else he'll find himself hopelessly bound by the words. It is very tricky and requires a special type of skill which, I'm afraid I don't possess. I'm trying, just the same."

"May I see anything you've done?" I said.

"Well, it isn't quite completed yet. The beginning and the end are still in mid-air. But you're welcome to look at what I've got so far. It's just rough draft, of course. I got the idea for it from a fellow refugee who is confined in a sanitarium at the moment. In fact, he's been there for quite a while. He came over on the same boat with me, and shortly afterward he obtained a position out West somewhere. And then something went wrong, and he was suddenly asked to resign. He is an altogether charming and learned man, and his dilemma forms the basis of my projected lyric. It is perhaps a little special as a subject, but then again I myself know of four or five other immigrants who had pretty similar experiences. And yet, on the other hand, perhaps the American public may really be more familiar with these mute and dim calamities than I imagine. Well, at any rate, here it is."

56

This is what he gave me.

Lyrics still to be written about the hero's arrival in this country. He states his qualifications: forty years old and a Ph.D., and of nine living languages master. Has composed Greek and Latin poetry, but seems haunted by relentless disaster.

Some friends who took pity on my damaged fate
And wanted to help in my need
Secured me a post in a Midwestern state,
Where they felt I was bound to succeed.
My students seemed fond of my history course,
But one day the D.A.R. landed in force,
For they claimed I endangered the nation.
It was vainly I pleaded and tried to make clear
That their rebel forefathers were hallowed and dear.
I suppose it got lost in translation.
Oh, it loses so much in translation.

I know that my clothes never fit me quite right.
I seem overanxious to please.
I bow far too low when I'm saying good night—
It's an old European disease.
The Danube and Rhine roll in three-quarter time
In a tempo so dated it's really a crime,
And I find all my thoughts a vexation.
I eat standing up while the jukeboxes blare,
And I season with ketchup my hamburgers rare.
Those hamburgers lose in translation.
Oh, they lose such a lot in translation.

I spent quite some time out on terrace cafés,
I loved to see life rolling by.
I drank only wine, or some café au laits,

57

But I fancied myself quite a guy.
I've sat at the Dôme in the spring of the year,
On the Ring in Vienna I drank Pilsner beer,
But I've found myself quite a new station.
I sit in the park with a frankie and Coke,
And I'm ever alert for the point of a joke,
That seems to lose much in translation.
Yes, the laugh's sometimes lost in translation.

The last stanza is still unresolved.

"It's fine, Professor," I said, "just fine. You must finish it."

"I'll try to," he said. "I wish I could really help them to get a show on. Not to show off my silly little lyric, but for the sake of the adventure."

"Tell me, Professor," I said, "are you happy in your job?"

"Yes, because I love talking about the things that interest me. I'm sometimes disturbed and even a little depressed by the chronic pessimism of my young students. They seem so anxious to play it safe from the very start. They behave like a bunch of small tradesmen who are all facing an inevitable bankruptcy together. I want to laugh at them and say, 'Behold this ancient failure who only *means* well and is still quite, quite unafraid.'"

"You're a good kid, Professor," I said. "You're certainly a very good kid, but, whether you know it or not, you belong to a dying species. How about a cup of coffee?"

"Solid!" he said.

CHAPTER FIVE

THERE ARE quite a few people in this country who
actually believe that artists are somehow exempt from the
common concerns of everyday life.

I've even known some *artists* who sustained such an ass-hole
view of their own condition. They like to pretend that they
are so many Prince Charmings, or, better still, that they are
just so many Ariels sitting on a lot of enchanted islands, sending out Living Color Bar Mitzvah greetings to a world that
never wrote to them.

The truth is that nowadays the world writes to *everybody*,
and, what's more, it writes mostly about unpaid bills and tells
you to fork over by return mail—or else!!!!!

Luckily, I knew the real facts from the very start. I was
never anybody's Little Jack Horner. Even at fourteen, when

I first came to this country, I knew it would be a very tough go to make any kind of living as a painter. Still, I also realized that nothing much could be done about it, since I certainly wasn't going to do anything else.

Of course, things were a hell of a lot better in those years, because there still wasn't such a mad mass participation in the arts, and not every idiot who had shamelessly smeared a lot of colored excrement onto an old dustpan dared to exhibit his nauseating mess in public. You still were expected to undergo certain rational, basic disciplines, such as learning how to draw and to paint properly. "Self-expression" used to have certain meaningful connotations back in those days, because it was assumed that you had to put something *into* yourself before anything could be expected to come *out* of you.

We took it for granted that if you gave a starving man a laxative all you were going to get back was the laxative.

I suppose I sound a hell of a lot like a disillusioned old fogy, but I'm afraid you can't possibly discuss the dirty business of modern aesthetics at all unless you are prepared to talk of it in terms that accurately describe its generally fetid condition. You must realize that so many critical maggots manage to make a fat living out of modern art that hardly anybody with a rational approach to this revolting subject can hope to emerge unsoiled into daylight again, once he has permitted himself to be involved even temporarily with this all-encompassing swarm of rapacious vermin.

Never before in the whole long history of painting has so vast and brazen a fraud been put over with complete impunity. The critics, in free association with hundreds of thieving dealers, are involved in such a large-scale hoax on the public that I'm afraid it will take many, many years before any sort of sane and sanitary condition can be restored.

All I can tell you for your own comfort is that the cool little wallpaper sample or the nonobjective paint regurgitation that some smart cooky has managed to unload on *you* will eventually wind up in exactly that mephitic garbage can where it should have landed in the first place.

Well, to hell with it!

I only mentioned it at all because for almost a quarter of a century I threw over my so-called career as an artist and went into equally sordid but at least financially more rewarding enterprises. Also, nobody around me ever pretended that he was after anything more exalted than money. No pus-mouthed, petulant pansies dinned great aesthetic truths into my ears, and when payday came I got my dough without any bonus of highfalutin horse crap. I sometimes had a lot of fun doing my work, too, and I only started to paint again very recently, when I was immured for six and a half months in a government hospital down in Lexington, Kentucky, where I couldn't possibly do very much else.

Maybe it wasn't exactly like that. Sometimes I had wanted to paint in the intervening years too, but I thought I'd had enough of the goddamned hassle and heartbreak for one lifetime.

Evidently not!

I hope I'm not giving you the impression that the world of art, that is to say of painting, is quite alone and unique in its putrescent coma. Not at all. The American theater, of which I've also had quite a bit of experience, is in just as nauseating a condition, and the fakes and phonies who breed on it talk even louder and longer about High Dedication than the lemurian monsters in the art racket.

Of course, the theater is, by its very nature and condition, the most facile playground for every sort of exhibitionistic freak who happens to be on the loose. And, boy, are they active!

Believe me, the fairy directors, the actors, the stage managers and the nameless, unidentifiable ninnies who are eternally milling around backstage are surely enough to give you the authentic and eternal whim-wham-willies.

Sometime in 1942 or thereabouts, I decided to put on a play that I myself had written. I produced it at the Malin Studios in the West Forties and it ran there for about a dozen very surprising performances.

The play was called *Night Watch in Syria* and had to do with some activities that might presumably have occurred on the afternoon and evening of the day when Jesus was crucified. Let me tell you at once that it was a very reverent play indeed, and that I certainly allowed no flat-footed, ranting actor equipped with a wig and false eyelashes to mimic the sacred personality of the Saviour. I left that sort of revolting hocus-pocus to the professional and quasi-professional religious groups. In fact, Jesus didn't appear on the stage at all, and only the shadows of three crosses fell diagonally onto the backdrop, just a few seconds before the curtain came down on the first act.

Incidentally, because I was afraid that—for reasons which I'll explain later—the spectators might perhaps miss the significance of this highly subtle piece of symbolism, I myself stepped before the footlights and explained it all to them.

At any rate, the play has twenty scenes and covers the time from right after the Crucifixion until about three hours after sundown. The action concerns itself with Mary Magdalene's quest for some person, or persons, who would help her to recover the body of Jesus from the cross. The corpses of executed malefactors are generally assigned to a mass pit, and it is Mary's desperate desire to give her Lord a proper and becoming entombment.

Now, then, during this search of hers the Magdalene eventually visits nearly every stratum of society extant in Jerusalem at that time. First of all she goes to the home of an ex-admirer, a rather witty sybaritic millionaire, who is quite shocked that Mary should ever have gotten herself involved with such a penurious and frowzy outfit. It happens that this rich and erudite bibliophile has considerable respect (mostly aesthetic) for some of the reputed utterances of Jesus, but he bitterly deplores the rabble of professional idlers which has certainly accrued to His doctrine.

Also, he thinks that Mary's almost frenzied preoccupation with His mortal remains would deeply shock and disappoint Jesus Himself. He points out to her that the Saviour had at all times maintained that only the spirit of man was truly deserving of serious regard and had repeatedly disparaged all of the other perishable earthly trappings. "You are like a tidy little Jewish housewife who is just deeply concerned with achieving a respectable funeral service, and not at all like the worthy disciple of the true Son of God."

Now, despite her considerable intelligence and her high state of exaltation, Mary has quite a bit of trouble refuting this very reasonable and pertinent argument. But she is beyond reason and pertinence. She feels that in this man's mouth everything is likely to turn into an accommodating piece of sophistry. She has spent foolish years listening to him and to his kind, and yet she has never been able to find in anything they said a truly conclusive answer to the great, unappeased questions in her heart.

She tells him so. "I have tasted of the bread of life," she says, "and I will never again be content with less. I'm sorry, I must go on."

She refuses his offer of sanctuary and decides to seek help somewhere else.

She next goes to see the Roman captain who was present at the Crucifixion and whose men eventually come to throw dice for the cloak and sandals of Jesus.

Of course the captain is equally horrified to find that a girl of Mary's upbringing and exclusive tastes should be mixed up with the casuistries and cabals of the most sordid riffraff in Jerusalem. He, too, respects the personality of the dead man, chiefly because He was very brave in His dying. Nevertheless, he feels that He was hopelessly compromised by the cowardly behavior of His followers, who openly deserted Him in the hour of His greatest need.

And, believe me, this is also something very, very tough for a fine and high-spirited girl to account for, at least in terms that the captain is likely to understand.

At any rate, he will do nothing for her, except, perhaps, secure her safe passage out of the town until the high tide of bitter feeling against the Nazarenes has somewhat subsided.

The next step down in the social scale brings Mary to a tavern where certain salesmen of bathroom tiles, only recently arrived from Rome, are noisily discussing the afternoon's events with mine host. The obliging innkeeper sheds as much light as he can on the situation, but he, also, is quite unable to account for some of the undoubtedly wealthy and well-connected people who have somehow gotten involved in all these cranky, antisocial activities.

One of these salesmen, a man who will someday certainly own his own business, finally asks the innkeeper some leading questions. How many followers did the man have? Two hundred? Two thousand? How many? He thinks it is worth looking into. One of the rumors he has heard, earlier in the afternoon, concerned a stranger happening that was supposed to have occurred shortly before the Crucifixion.

"They tell me that somebody lent him a kerchief to wipe his face on while he was carrying the cross up the hill," he says. "Well, the person that told me this story claims that after he'd wiped off his sweat and returned the kerchief to the woman who gave it to him, his face was printed right on that scarf, in full colors!"

The other salesmen loudly and appropriately deride this crazy yarn. They claim that such a story goes quite naturally with the infernal climate and certainly doesn't merit even a moment's serious consideration.

"I'm not so sure," says the first salesman, who is obviously a man of vision. "I'm not so sure. You see, if he's got at least a couple of thousand followers, I can see a chance where somebody can make himself a neat little pile of shekels out of this same yarn."

He now turns purposefully to the innkeeper. "Listen," he says, "I've got a job lot of some damaged linens back in Rome, and for a few drachmas I could get some crummy art students to paint me some kind of faces all over that material. I could send them out here to you, and if you wanna be the distributor for this territory, I'm willing to cut you in for a decent share. What do you say? People at county fairs might gobble them up for keepsakes—get it? Are you in? What do you say?"

The innkeeper is not only delighted with this live proposition, his own spirit is almost immediately fired into rich, creative exuberance by it.

"You know what else we can do?" he says. "We might get ahold of the cross that they nailed him onto, and cut it up into a lot of little crosses, and we could sell them for lucky charms to all the suckers around here."

"Man, you got a real head on your shoulders," says the salesman. "I'll tell you what. Let's make it a real legal partnership and rent out booths where this stuff can be sold only by specially licensed concessionaires. How does *that* hit you?"

The innkeeper is positively ecstatic.

They solemnly shake hands.

"We oughta have some kind of a name for this new little firm, too," concludes the salesman. "Let's have something simple and clean—something that gives it a local flavor too. I think I've got it! Yes, I've got it! Let's call it *The Nazarene Novelty Company!!!*"

As you see, I make clear in the very first act of the play that when poor Jesus was not yet cold on His cross somebody already had some lively angles on how to make a buck out of His agony.

The scene now shifts to the less exclusive side of that same tavern, where two Roman sailors are having a drink with a local boss carpenter. The carpenter is obviously standing treat, and he also tries to give the two seamen some inside dope on the day's happenings.

"You see, it's real tough for the likes of us to make a living in Jerusalem these days," he tells them. "The building trade is all shot to hell, and all we carpenters ever get to make is crosses for executions. I guess that's what must have given *him* the crazy twist that started him downhill in the first place. It even makes *me* think, sometimes. Besides, he got in pretty bad with the priests recently, on account of he chased a lot of influential merchants out of the Temple just a while ago."

"Why did he wanna do a thing like that?" asks the first sailor.

"Some people are always looking for trouble," says the second sailor. "It's in their nature, they can't help it. Had a man like that on board, last trip out of Naples. I bet *he* was one of them Jonahs too."

"Well, that depends how you look at it," says the carpenter. "You see, the Jews sometimes come here from a long ways off to bring their offerings of livestock to be sacrificed in the Temple, and all this truck of theirs has to be in perfect shape, too, or else the priests won't use any of it. Understand? For instance, some poor farmer's walked maybe thirty miles into town, started out 'way before sunup, to bring a couple of his pigeons as a thanks offering for his son's recovery from sickness. And then, when he hands them up for sacrifice, the priest tells him that the pigeons ain't healthy enough to be accepted,

66

that they got a clot on their tongues or a rupture on their eyelids or something. So what can the poor guy do? He's come all that distance already anyway, and he don't wanna go back to his wife and tell her he didn't get around to making a sacrifice after all, so he buys a fresh pair of birds or lambs or chickens or whatever the hell it is, right here in the Temple, where a lot of dealers have set up their stands and, as everybody knows, are right in cahoots with all the priests. They get a kickback, see?"

"Sure sounds like an awful raw deal to me," says the first sailor.

"It is!" agrees the carpenter. "And it got *him* so sore, when he saw it happen again one day, that he just got himself a rawhide whip and drove all those leeches right out of the temple. Drove the lot of them right into the gutter, that's what he did!"

"I wish I'da known him," says the first sailor. "He sounds plenty okay to me."

"He *was* okay, in lots of ways," says the carpenter. "Trouble is, you can't just make enemies. You gotta have friends too."

"How come he didn't never manage to have himself any buddies in this town?" asks the second sailor.

"Oh, he *had* some, all right," says the carpenter. "But the people who were supposed to be his friends all let him down cold when the real trouble started. They all scrammed and let him take the rap."

"I think I get the whole idea now," says the first sailor. "Seems to me like he got in wrong with a lot of powerful poultry dealers, and in the end this kosher-chicken mob finally nailed him. Am I right?"

"I think maybe that's just part of it," says the second sailor. "All I can say is, I'd sure like to take a good poke at one of them louse-bellied followers of his. Man, would I like to lay a hand on *them*."

The sailor who has spoken last does not suspect that in the

darkest corner of the tavern sit the very disciples he has just execrated.

In fact, Mary has come to this place specifically to see if she could perhaps get some help from them. However, after even just a look at these worthies she realizes only too sadly that she couldn't possibly expect anything but tears and self-reproaches from all those pathetic whimperers. She gives them whatever words of comfort she can spare and proceeds on her own self-imposed mission.

And so, as the day slowly turns into evening, she continues on and on in her drooping quest, until, just a little before ten o'clock, she finally lands in the cellars of the Thieves' Guild of Jerusalem.

Here she meets a really tough hombre called Joel Ben Sasra, the chief union organizer. This lad is enormously amused by Mary's seemingly great concern for a poor executed carpenter, and the only way he can understand it at all is to assume that she is indulging in some new form of particularly decadent slumming.

But then, when Mary tells him that Jesus had, that very afternoon, blessed a thief who died beside Him on the cross, Ben Sasra finds himself stirred into sudden, unfamiliar wonder.

Because, if thieves are blessed on the cross, then the time for miracles may indeed be at hand.

(Remember, this is *Jerusalem* in the year zero, and not the Bronx or Bucks County.)

At any rate, in the light of this extraordinary information, he impulsively agrees to abduct the desired body from the custody of the established authorities. At a price, of course. In fact, he finds himself so completely moved out of his chronic cynicism that he decides to steal the corpses of the other two malefactors as well, and to give them decent burial too, out of the union funds.

A couple of scouts are quickly sent off to case the lay of the land, and in a very short while these emissaries return with some rather disappointing news. It seems that Pilate has already granted permission to Joseph of Arimathea to remove the sacred remains for the purpose of proper burial.

Well, even so, Ben Sasra, who is obviously Mary's first convert, sticks to his original decision. He will remove the bodies of the two thieves at least and see that they are duly and decently laid alongside their more naturally deceased fellow outcasts.

This is, in its way, a truly stupendous gesture of well-doing on Ben Sasra's part, since one of the thieves, the unblest one, is completely unknown in Jerusalem and has never paid either an initiation or a membership fee into the local union treasury.

At the news that Jesus is to be taken from the cross and reverently interred, Mary falls quietly onto her knees and begins to recite the Lord's prayer—

as the curtain slowly descends.

So much for the play.

Now, then, 'way back in those dim years before America had yet perfected the vitamin-enriched atomic fallout, a boychik called Leo Shull, who currently publishes a very successful actors' trade paper called *Show Business*, used to get out that same sheet by means of a penurious, but somehow more sincere, mimeograph machine.

Leo had at that time quite a few other speculative raisins rampant in the show-business pudding, and outstanding among these was a kind of actors' club which he had dubbed "Genius Incorporated."

Here, amidst a good deal of hideous professional gabble and some truly stupefying tobacco smoke, every imaginable form of stage-struck lummox could, over a strange but cheap cup of coffee, revel and expand without limit in the company of his revolting peers.

So naturally I took my modest assault on reality, my play *Night Watch in Syria*, down to "Genius Incorporated." I must say, Leo Shull was not only quite excited by my little creation, he was instantly ready to be of help to me with it, too. To tell you the truth, I suspect that due to some peculiar but certainly very helpful gland condition, Leo was, in those distant days, not only at ease but even rather exuberant at the mere mention of any impending turmoil.

So he at once set about to apprise his large floating congregation of theatrical vagrants that pleasant mischief was afoot, and, in less than three days he managed to siphon off for my inspection about fifty aspirants, who were all prepared to take part in my impending opus—without immediate financial nexus, of course.

But at the first meeting with my prospective players I suffered a rather demoralizing shock. A good many of the candidates who offered themselves to be cast for the roles of the twelve apostles in my play were quite unmistakably flagrant pansies.

I couldn't understand it. Leo was an extremely hep character, and he surely must have noticed that some of these boys were pretty swishy. Still, I didn't feel like discussing it with him, first of all because I was very grateful for the trouble he had taken, and also because I didn't want to appear less worldly in these matters than he. I finally browsed around his diocese myself for about a week or so in the hope of finding some possible replacements, but in the end I had to give it all up. Leo had certainly selected the best material available, and most of the creatures that he had discreetly edited out of his chosen roster turned out to be such revolting monsters that there could be no question of employing them in anything except maybe a Broadway musical.

In the end, I concluded that my dilemma was probably quite a common occupational hazard in show business and so I soberly decided to make my peace with it.

70

Still, it was certainly an eye-opener.

You can just about imagine what sort of time I must have had with some of those leaping gazelles in the following three weeks. Luckily they weren't *all* fairies, and I hoped that by grouping the worst of them in some stylized, obliterative way I would somehow cunningly manage to mask from the audience the nancified contortions of my early Christian fathers.

I'm not going to torment you with any of the detailed horrors of my daily rehearsals. I'm just going to mention that because the whole production was inevitably carried on everybody's cuff, my little group just never seemed to get around to properly memorizing its roles.

I know perfectly well that things are quite different nowadays. There must be a lot more stage-struck people around or something, because I myself presently know dozens of actors, dancers and even singers who will do any goddamned thing you ask of them, and do it most conscientiously too, on the mere promise that they'll appear before a live audience in some mildewed cellar down on Second Avenue somewhere.

I didn't have it so good. No, seventeen years ago I had to give so-called individual coaching lessons to each of those thirty-two wretches, which simply meant that they were learning their goddamned parts with me in public.

But finally it was done.

The hall was hired, the tickets and the programs were printed, the unions had already assigned three contemptuous loafers, at thirty-nine dollars a day, in my direction, and then —and only then—I sent out a couple of desperate calls for help to Boris Aronson and Abe Feder.

Boris is, and was, my all-time favorite stage designer, and Abe Feder was in those days a highly esteemed, highly paid and highly unpredictable theatrical-lighting expert.

Abe looked over the premises, shnoofled some really ruinous predictions into my ear, voiced a few staggering conjectures and, after shrugging his shoulders with devastating Hebraic misgivings, departed at last in a cloud of profound depression.

But Boris, who always has been an angel, and also luckily has a very low threshold of tolerance, at once gave me some really excellent advice.

"It is a sad play," he said. "You have no money for good costumes, so try to light only their heads."

"Costumes?" I said. "I'm not having any kind of costumes at all! If those fairies of mine get themselves draped up in some of those Biblical drags, they'll swish up such a goddamned dust storm the audience will simply cough itself to death."

"Well," he said, "then don't let them have any kind of make-up, either."

"Don't worry, I won't," I said. "But tell me, Boris, what am I going to do with that dirty back wall?"

"Get some long, narrow flats of some kind," he said. "Let them go 'way up beyond the proscenium and try to put them at different levels. And if you can afford it, get a simple, wide staircase that can easily be moved around. It's corny, of course, but I don't see that you have any other choice right now. Treat it like a modern dance recital. After all, the important thing is the play."

He gave me his sweet, commiserative smile, raised his hand in a gesture of blessing, and left me.

I followed all his instructions to the letter, of course—all but the business about the make-up. You see, I couldn't quite control that. I'd told everybody that make-up was out, but, when the evening of the performance finally rolled around, a few of those exhibitionistic schlemiels had smeared themselves from their hairlines to their navels with every imaginable sort of theatrical crap.

When I got sight of these pixies in that condition I suddenly got a terrible feeling that, despite all of my frenzied coachings

72

and rehearsings, they were still, somehow, unpredictably going to manage to bitch up my play. It was then that I decided to step before the curtain after each of my many scenes and to give some sort of elucidative commentary on what had gone before. I know this must sound insane, but I was far too desperate to bank on mere reason.

And that's how it was done.

The critics who came to review my play, and I must say most of them came, were very good-natured and generous about the little presentation. Naturally they all thought that my daffy footlight monologues were strictly part of the script, and a couple of them liked that feature of the show best of all. Burton Rascoe, who worked for the *World Telegram* at the time, was really wildly enthusiastic about the play. It was, in the end, something more than just a *succès d'estime*.

So there I'd had my second baptism of theatrical Seltzer with a Biblical play, and, quite properly, it was no laugh.

I'll tell you about my first one just a little later on.

At any rate, right after the curtain had come down on the last scene, Alan Collins, the head of Curtis Brown, a distinguished literary agency, came backstage and introduced himself to me.

"I was quite delighted with your little play," he said. "How long is it scheduled to run, anyway?"

"Just one more day," I said. "I hope we'll take in enough dough to give the actors a couple of meals out of it."

"I'll tell you why I'm asking," said Mr. Collins. "You see, I get a five-hundred-dollar bonus check each year from a source that doesn't exactly enchant me. Well, I've got that check in my pocket right now, and if you'd like the use of it to keep the show running a little while longer, I'll be glad to sign it over to you."

"Mr. Collins," I said, "you give me sudden intimations of Florence in its most princely days. With that kind of generous

73

endowment we can surely keep the show going for at least another week. Just wait until some of the pansies in my cast hear about this, they're liable to come up to your office with an embossed Maypole and do a ribbon dance right in your waiting room."

"Well, then please let's be sure to keep it all very, very quiet," said Mr. Collins. "Curtis Brown is, after all, a most sedate and altogether undemonstrative firm. Here's the check, and good luck to you!"

And, so saying, Mr. Collins, that undemonstrative man, walked straight out of the theater and also straight out of my life.

In these last few pages I seem to have said quite a few peevish things about actors, haven't I? Well, I'm afraid I'll just have to let them stand. If I considered this matter more maturely, heaven only knows what else I might say.

I know that this world is infested with creatures of truly overbearing vanity, but I certainly don't have to be enthusiastic about the fact that quite a number of them have taken this up as a career and are trying to make their living at it.

On the other hand, I have nothing but the tenderest thoughts and the greatest sympathy for *actresses*. I think it is most becoming to them to be what they are. I don't quite know how it is, but they don't offend me at all. To tell you the truth, I find most of them really quite appealing.

Perhaps the explanation lies in my knowledge that the word "womb" in Greek is *hystera*. "Hysteria" and "histrionics" are obviously derived from this significant source. And, fellers, that's all I'm gonna say about it now, because—well, because I do not choose to run at this particular time.

CHAPTER SIX

I'M QUITE OFTEN DISGUSTED by how much of man's precious existence is passed in anxious preparation, in boring harness and in hopeful readiness for things that are destined never to take place at all. I'm sure that large and infinitely depressing tomes could be written about the long, boring periods of waiting that everyone is compelled to undergo in this ridiculously short life span of ours—and how completely wasteful and debasing most of these lingering states of pointless expectation really are.

I don't mean that it is necessarily unprofitable for people to sit still. I certainly don't endorse a lot of senseless running around. We've got too damned much of that too. I seem to live in a world of almost relentless activity that never leads to anything but physical and mental exhaustion. Even the ones who just are waiting for opportunity to knock the panels out

75

of their doors are absolutely seething and frothing with wild inner fermentations. I'm dead set against all that hope-orama stuff.

As somebody very wisely once said, "Approach death at a walk; take in the beauty of a china doorknob."

In short, keep your eyes and your heart wide open, and all the wonders of the world will constantly come home to you. I don't think you can possibly conceive of all the miraculous and surprising things that have fallen into my life merely because I've always been so avidly alive to the rich potentials of my daily existence.

It may well be that I was sometimes even a little too avid. And, surely, more times than I care to think about I have been just a little too imaginative. I can tell you that my overly active imagination has frequently bollixed up a lot of quite ordinary doings that anybody else could easily have managed to keep within rational bounds. Indeed, this fatal gift of mine has occasionally led me into some curiously labyrinthine involvements from which no exit seemed feasible at all.

There were times when my life suffered vibrations of such wild, fictional wave lengths that I've often been compelled to tone down the fantastic and improbable things that have actually occurred to me, merely to make them reasonably acceptable to people whose lives were more wholesomely humdrum.

For instance, sometime in 1947 I read a humorous story whose pivotal point, farfetched and yet very cleverly conceived, duplicated to an astonishing degree something that once happened to me some twenty or twenty-five years ago. The basic events of this tale had no great bearing on my own case, but the critical climax that promulgated the disastrous payoff was almost completely identical with a certain crazy denouement in my own life.

Suppose I tell you about it.

76

First of all, let me tell you that I've never cared much for dogs.

My indifference toward them stems from the same source that makes most people so desperately fond of them. I always think of dogs as vulgar love proletarians who are forever working overtime at the business of affection and loyalty. Any scoundrel or fool who happens to dispense them food with reasonable regularity can be sure of their blind devotion. Nauseating!

But I *do* like cats.

No cat ever flatters you for more than maybe half a minute. You can feed a cat on capon liver for twenty-seven years and she'll walk into your living room, tail high, eyes coldly appraising, as if she were seeing you or your dreary belongings for the very first time. Called to a hundred times, a cat may ignore you—and then, without rhyme or reason, she will jump into your lap, rub her head affectionately under your chin and purr like a simmering percolator. You get affection as a free gift, not as a payment or a bribe.

So much for my attitude.

The particular cat I am here concerned with was called Lulu. I had guarded her virtue for two solid years—and I must say she co-operated handsomely. It was a great surprise, therefore, when on an evening in late June she suddenly gave birth to a couple of measly kittens. Lulu seemed to be just as much at a loss as I to account for this fantastic disgorgement, and she acted exactly like a puzzled spinster on whose innocent doorstep destiny had decided to play some embarrassing tricks.

At any rate, she refused to feed the beggarly little runts, and I had to step in with the usual baby-bottle routine. The net result of our mutual efforts was disastrous. The kittens died. They died without ever having opened their eyes on a world full of trouble and wonder, and I was very sorry for it.

77

Now, then, two dead kittens would cause no difficulty in any small town or village in the U. S. A., but in a city like New York they became a major problem. Indeed, situated as I was at the time, they became something of a calamity.

It happened like this. I put the little corpses into an empty shoe box, tied some string around it and left the house with the intention of depositing my bundle in the garbage can in front of my door.

Simple enough.

Unfortunately I had, at that time, an extremely nosy neighbor who enjoyed worrying and gossiping about me. His name was Hubert Toplitz, and for his own reasons he liked to think of me as a flagrantly eccentric character. On the morning when I emerged into the street with the funerary package under my arm, Mr. Toplitz was standing in the sunlight next to our garbage can, and, turning toward me with a smirk of hypocritical greeting, he raised his eyebrows expectantly at once, as if he anticipated something pretty unusual from me for that time of day.

Of course I was stumped. I couldn't throw my tidy package into the garbage can and just walk away. Mr. Toplitz was sure to open it the minute my back was turned, and then all hell would break loose. Just imagine him finding two dead kittens wrapped in cellophane inside that miniature sarcophagus. What a flood of sinister conjectures would be released by that morbid discovery! Mr. Toplitz would certainly assume that I practiced some secret Satanic rituals, in which innocent kittens had to be sacrificed on altars too fearful for the human imagination.

All right, call me a coward and a fool—but I just couldn't risk it. The point is, I *didn't* risk it. I said good morning to Mr. Toplitz and proceeded down the block with the dead kittens under my arm.

You might guess the rest, if you know how a big city gathers you into the stride of its momentum and refuses to let you fall out.

I went into a drugstore to phone and left my bundle behind, on purpose. A moment later a soda jerker came panting after me.

"Mr. King!" he screamed. "You forgot your package!" And he restored my gruesome property to me. I had to tip him, of course.

That and similar happenings throughout the morning finally decided me. I had a dinner date out in Staten Island, and I was reconciled to carrying around the two dead cats for the rest of the day, until five o'clock. To get to Staten Island involves a longish ferry ride out into New York Bay, and it was my plan to dump my morbid cargo into the waters of the all-obliterating tides of the Hudson.

Good enough.

At five o'clock I boarded the ferry, along with five hundred eager homeward-bound commuters. I stood at the front end of the lowest deck, ready to heave at the first opportunity. To make my bundle somewhat less conspicuous I had meanwhile managed to insert it into a large brown paper bag.

Unfortunately, a couple of hundred curious eyes eagerly followed each of my movements as I stood at the prow, getting ready to drop my loathsome ballast.

And then it happened again. I saw myself flinging the package. . . . I could just imagine the first moment of surprise among the spectators . . . an outcry from some overimaginative commuter . . . The boat would be stopped, the harbor police would drag the bay for my mysterious parcel, and only heaven knows what they might manage to dredge up before the night set in. After all, the papers were constantly printing lurid stories about parts of human bodies that were fished out of the waters around New York. You couldn't really blame anyone for being suspicious of my strange behavior.

I'm sure that in a tightly packed city like New York where people finally get to loathe each other so that they just have to carve each other up, it must happen every half an hour or so that somebody's dismembered body and giblets get thrown into New York Bay.

I bet that some middle-aged matron who is reading these very lines and taking a coffee break after having carved up her annoying husband is just waiting for the floor to dry before she takes time out to hurl his revolting remains out into the Narrows.

Result? I sneaked back to the benches in the rear of the ferry —disgusted, and resigned to carrying my unhappy freight out to Staten Island.

At last we arrived, and I tottered ashore into the arms of my welcoming friend. He had decided to pick me up in his car to save me the slow bus ride to his home. At sight of my bundle my friend expostulated and began to reproach me as an incorrigible purveyor of needless gifts.

"You shouldn't have bothered," he said. "Really, we've *got* everything. We've even got your favorite dessert—you *shouldn't* have troubled to bring anything."

"Don't be such a fool," I said. "I *didn't* bring anything. I've just got a couple of dead cats in there, that's all!"

My friend laughed, slapped me on the back and waggled his silly head, as if I'd just told him the greatest joke, and I finally realized that no man can hope to stand up against destiny once that old girl has determined to make mock of his intentions.

To hell with it, I thought. He'll find out all about it in due time. And so I didn't stop him when he carefully deposited my bundle in the back of his car, alongside some freshly purchased groceries.

When we arrived at his home he handed my package to his wife, but by that time I was much too far gone to protest. I sat down on the porch with him while the hostess went about busying herself with her housewifely chores. I must say that for a while there I did wait with some anxiety for her scream of shocked surprise when she finally came around to opening my bundle, but I was so busy watching my friend shaking up and dishing out some cocktails that after a few minutes I forgot all about my sordid little time bomb.

But, curiously enough, there was no hubbub of any kind, and when dinner was served, about an hour later, my mischievous package had completely gone from my mind.

But peace wasn't meant to be mine for long.

The ultimate debacle came upon me a little later on like a gentle bomb of delayed poison gas.

In fact, it was when my hostess had just started to cackle approvingly about the unusual quality of the food we had brought that the first alarming smear of uneasiness ominously crossed the quiet horizon of my composure.

"Where in *heaven's* name did you get these delicious steaks?" she squealed. "I don't remember *when* I last had such a juicy piece of beef between my teeth!"

"*I* didn't get any steaks," said her husband. "You know we can't afford such luxuries in the middle of the month." He pointed to me. "*There's* the man who brought the steaks. You can thank *him* if you're eating like a plutocrat! Well, it's certainly convenient to have rich friends. Let's not argue about it now, let's just eat them with humble gratitude and pray to be really deserving of such heavenly bounty."

It goes without saying that I was paralyzed with astonishment. Those two fools were obviously sincere in their thanks to me . . . *and* the woman was actually dishing out what certainly looked like honest-to-God—*steaks!*

What had happened to my kittens?

And then I realized with sudden, sickening awareness that no matter what I could possibly say to them, they certainly weren't going to believe me.

But what came home to me even more shatteringly was the

knowledge that some unfortunate creature who had been sitting alongside me on the ferry bench had certainly that afternoon, to his eternal undoing, accidentally swapped bundles with me on that goddamned boat. He had walked off with *my two cold cadavers* while I had appropriated his juicy supper. Oh God, oh Shenandoah!

But, that wasn't *all* that bothered me. What has caused me nightmares ever since is the thought of the poor man's arrival at his home, where steaks were expected—and *dead cats* were delivered instead.

Just imagine what must have happened to this poor schlemiel if he should have stopped at some friendly saloon for a quick snifter on the way home, and just try to conceive what his wife must have said to him after she found the two ossified kittens in the bag and insisted on smelling his breath.

Am I responsible for a broken home out in Staten Island? If so, I do hope the injured lady will read this and forgive her innocent husband in the name of all the dead little kittens that her spouse had nothing to do with. I tell you, madam, your man is *innocent!!! Take him back!!!*

As for myself, I didn't eat any steak that evening. Anything resembling meat would, for obvious reasons, have stuck in my throat. I had heard about cats having nine lives, but this was the first time that a couple of kittens had finally turned up as medium-rare beef on anybody's dinner table.

Well, I don't suppose such a mad series of experiences has ever occurred to anybody but me, and so you can understand that the funny fictional story I referred to a littler earlier seemed like a mere whimsical echo of the cumulative irritating events that finally led to the bewildering manifestation of steaks instead of kittens at that bewitched meal out in Staten Island.

By the way, if you are still in doubt that *fact* very frequently surpasses *fiction* in the scope of its improbability, I have another small example for you.

Listen to this.

Billy Rose has a friend whose little girl isn't doing any too well in the private school she's attending somewhere up in Riverdale.

"The kid is really quite a bright youngster," Billy told me the other day. "You know how it is, sometimes a kid starts off on the wrong foot and the dopey teachers are down on her from then on. Well, whatever the hell it is, I went up with her old man about a week ago, because he'd been asked to call on the dean or something. He's an old friend of mine, and I just went along for the ride. Anyway, while he was in conference with the head I looked around the joint, and I must say it looked pretty crummy to me. I mean *real* crummy. So when we were driving back into town again, I gave him an excellent idea. 'Listen,' I said to him, 'I looked over the premises and the whole layout of that school, and I tell you, I'd bet my neck that if you made up your mind and decided to put twelve or fourteen gees on the line, you could buy up the whole place, lock, stock and mortgage, this very afternoon. Fourteen gees or fifteen, at the most—I'm sure of it. So why don't you do it? Give your little daughter a decent break,' I said. 'Run the goddamned place to suit yourself, and fire all the bums that don't like it. Yessir, for fifteen gees you can take the whole shebang over—and you can be your own boss.' "

That's what Billy Rose told me. I don't know if the friend ever acted on this excellent piece of advice, but I remember very well that almost the identical situation was the critical fulcrum in a play called *Edward, My Son*, in which Robert Morley starred as the father just a few years ago. In fact, I recall that Mr. Morley actually made a somewhat similar though less outrageous offer to the dean of an English boys' school (where his son was having a rather rough time of it), and that the poor chief of that debt-haunted academy was, in the end, compelled to accept his continued livelihood on just such bitter terms.

I know that Billy never saw or read that play and so he didn't suspect until this moment that he was wildly awash in the spindrift of an established theatrical cliché.

Let me hasten to inform you that I am inordinately fond of Billy Rose, because he is almost the only one among the seven millionaires I've met in my life who is constantly having a real ball for his dough. Billy acts exactly as if he carried all of his loot permanently about his person and were prepared to put every penny of it on the line, if any pleasurable whim came along and moved him to do it.

You can see that he too belongs to a dying species, the American millionaire who is getting his own real ride for his money. *He* doesn't hire any tubercular, bowlegged jockeys to do it for him. No, not Billy. He mounts his own strangely dappled hobby horses and rides them wherever his sweet fancy happens to guide him.

Most of the other millionaires I know are busy figuring out tax dodges that eventually wind up in astringent philanthropical devices or poisonously pious endowment foundations. They establish dropsical bureaucracies whose business it is to dole out scholarships to such mendicant eggheads as have safely passed investigation by their private G.P.U.s.

These characters eat badly and sleep badly, and they generally carry their own skimpy luggage in railroad and plane terminals, and if they ever do have occasion to give anybody a tip for any sort of service they are to the last degree miserly about it. And if you think I'm exaggerating, all you have to do is ask some waiters or porters who have had the doubtful privilege of running into these turtles.

Ugh!

CHAPTER SEVEN

S INCE I WAS SEVENTEEN YEARS OLD, I've suffered untellable agonies from blinding migraine headaches—the classic kind that simply tears you apart. I noticed throughout the years, however, that most of the other migraine people who happened to swap information with me on our favorite subject were, by their own evidence of symptoms, merely afflicted with some acute form of the vapors. But you can be perfectly sure that *I*, as usual, had the absolutely genuine article, in all its disastrous ramifications.

And then, around 1936, my wife's aunt, Miss Leslie, came up here to visit us from Alabama, and it was she who suggested that to relieve these murderous attacks I ought to try a new drug just recently imported from Switzerland which was called Gynergen. Auntie Leslie worked for a vast corporate medical institution of some kind down South at the time, and she told me that they'd had excellent results with this product.

Anyway, after she'd gone back to Alabama she sent me about a dozen Gynergen ampules and a hypodermic syringe with which to inject the stuff. Naturally I tried it at once, and Gynergen worked on me like magic!

And that's how it happened that, for the first time in twenty years, I was able to deal successfully with those infernal migraine attacks. Unfortunately, at the very same time I also fell into a rather dangerous habit pattern: I learned how to casually employ a possibly lethal hypodermic needle! When I think about it now, this surely seems like a most boneheaded procedure for a sane man to get mixed up in, because nobody just offhand makes a goddamned pincushion out of his own carcass. That's just common sense, isn't it?

So, as I'm telling you, there I was, finally rid of my headaches, but from time to time I also used to get some pretty bad renal spasms, which were, of course, the result of a long-neglected case of kidney stones. You can plainly see that along my disaster-ridden production line there was never a shortage of blown fuses, but I did somehow manage to live with my multiple calamities by just carefully doctoring myself, without allowing too much outside medical interference. My general opinion of medicine was really not too high in those days. I used to think of it as just about two inches removed from voodoo.

Nevertheless, I had at various critical times consulted sundry medical practitioners, and let me say to their credit that nearly all of them had advised immediate surgery for the relief of my afflicted kidneys. But, in the meanwhile, they had also very obligingly tided me over my worst seizures with quite a lot of soothing little morphine tablets.

Now, then, when I started to inject this Gynergen stuff into myself with a hypodermic syringe, one of these learned medics, who knew all about my assortment of physical disasters, suggested that I'd get a lot quicker analgesic results from my morphine if I just dissolved the tablets in some sterile water and shot them directly into my bloodstream too.

I suppose you'll have no trouble in realizing that there, at one jolt, I was suddenly involved in some alchemy of a truly shattering potential indeed.

Well, anyway, I started to shoot morphine into myself at a great rate to kill my pains as they occurred, and very often even *before* they occurred. You see, I very soon discovered a few side effects to morphine that were absolute revelations to me. I discovered, for instance, that morphine greatly improved my general attitude and my resistance to the many complex exigencies of my common daily life.

It was absolutely astounding!

I grew calm, as the sages and the saints had been calm. What's more, I achieved this personal nirvana through no long and arduous apprenticeship to some finicky and petulant guru, nor by passing my days in virtuous acts of thorny self-denial. Not a bit of it. Just a quick shot and I was all set.

It was suddenly quite within my own power to become the Dalai Lama, and this by the mere injection of a divinely soothing, never failing and altogether enchanting distillate of pure euphoria.

In short, I was hooked on junk.

I just loved it. I had no hangovers, I felt no ill effects of any kind. I was the puissant master of my colorful destiny, and I understood and forgave all human shortcomings, trespasses and imbecilities, particularly my own.

As you can see, I had found the *real* thing. Believe me, liquor just wasn't anywhere near it. For crissake, liquor couldn't even stop a toothache. Well, morphine *could!* That's how in the next few years most of my teeth happened to fall out. They just never hurt me. I'd find teeth in my food or on my plate or even in my lap, like loose rice, and I never suffered even a single moment's pain.

Well, maybe that wasn't altogether an advantage. In fact, there were a couple of other drawbacks too. Isn't it disgusting? Nothing on this goddamned earth ever works so that you can really sit back and enjoy it. Not even morphine. It's enough to make you give up. But, as I've already indicated, I *didn't* give up. Not right away. Not for ten years or thereabouts, and during that somewhat opaque decade I got to know a hell of a lot about life that I certainly never knew before. First of all, I became thoroughly familiar with scores of crooked doctors and druggists who all knew perfectly well that I was hooked but who, for a good stiff fee, were all prepared to overlook my whimsical little failing. I'm sure they excused themselves with the thought that if *they* didn't fork their expensive poison over to me, some other son of a bitch in the city was sure to do it.

Once I did strike a snag, though, over on the East Side, where a couple of hundred physicians have set up their roosts in a so-called medical building. I had already visited three of the croakers who festered there and, after showing them my X rays and paying my fee, had managed to get three fine prescriptions out of them. Now, the fourth one turned out to be a little Jewish doctor called Ernest Reinzheimer, and he, all of a sudden, didn't seem to care so much for my little story.

"If you don't believe me," I said, "you can call the X-ray man who took these pictures, and he'll be glad to identify me."

"Oh, I believe they're your X rays, all right," he said. "I just don't prescribe morphine to anybody like you."

"Like *me?*" I said. "What's wrong with *me?*"

"You're the type that no rational medical man will ever prescribe narcotics for," said the doctor. "Anybody with any sense of awareness would realize at once that you're extremely addictable. Just listen to the way you talk. You're higher than a kite right this minute, and I'm not so sure that you've even had a shot for the last couple of hours. I'd say you've got the temperament of a born junkie, and any man that gives you dope is—well, he's certainly damned careless."

Of course I took an instant shine to this character, and so I copped out to him.

"That's what I figured," he said. "Well, my advice is, get yourself cured as fast as possible. In heaven's name, go down to Fort Worth, or to Lexington, and let them give you the works. If you don't go, you'll just land in jail sooner or later. Why don't you go down to the Subtreasury Building and apply for admittance to Lexington? Bring back the signed permit for admittance and I'll give you a prescription, so you can last until you get down there."

"I'll go next Monday," I said. "Thanks, Doc, I'll take your advice on Monday. I've got some business to take care of right now, but I'll see you next week without fail."

I was really touched by his friendly, disinterested spiel, but —well, I still had those three prescriptions in my poke, don't you see? You can't just throw away a sure thing, can you? Who does?

Nevertheless, I did take his advice seriously. The following Monday morning I was down at the Subtreasury Building and asked one of the guards for information about Lexington. He pointed to a desk where an old lady was seated at a typewriter and said, "Ask Mrs. McDermott. She's in charge of applications, I think."

Let me give you an idea of Mrs. McDermott. She was positively the most ancient, the most collapsed old doll I'd ever seen outside a coffin. She had little white frankfurter-shaped ringlets, she had octagonal glasses and a tremor in both her hands that made her look as if she were doing a sit-down hula with invisible castanets.

I'm telling you, she was so old she made Whistler's mother look like an airline hostess.

Hell, I thought, how am I ever going to tell this prehistoric valentine about the lousy jam I'm in? She looks like a requiem for a lost cause, and the cause must have been the Civil War.

You know, I was actually embarrassed when I finally got up to her. "I'd like to apply for a cure in Lexington, Kentucky," I said demurely.

She motioned me to sit down, inserted a piece of paper in the typewriter, got her pinky caught in the works, extricated herself and finally gave me a mild, grandmotherly stare.

"Well," she said, "what do you shoot? Deemerol? Heeroin? Or Horse?" ("Horse" is vernacular for heroin.)

"I use morphine," I said.

"A square, eh?" She gave a graveyard chuckle and started to type. That is to say she got half a dozen keys tangled into each other like a multiple crash landing, and I realized that she was certainly going to take quite a big bite out of my morning.

"Is there a men's room around here?" I asked her.

"Yeah, over past that man," she said. "You gotta see him too. He's like a psychologist or something, see?"

Anyway, before I got to the can, where I was planning to give myself a couple of shots, the psychologist grabbed me.

"Sit down, young man," he said. "Sit right down here and tell me what's on your mind."

"The toilet," I said.

"Lexington is the place for you," he said. "Sit down."

I sat down and took a good look at him. He had a terrifying twitch in one side of his face and he blinked his crazy eyes at least twice every second. Those eyes of his, by the way, seemed to have been poured at the Corning Glass works and would have gone perfectly fine on a stuffed hooty owl. I also noticed that most of the fingers on his right hand were so deeply nicotine-stained they looked as if he had just dipped them into a saucerful of iodine.

90

"Greatest place in the world, Lexington!" he said. "Yessir, you'll come out a new man. Straighten out your body *and* your mind. The *mind* is just as important, you know."

"Yes," I said. "I've got to remember to look after it. Now I'd like to go to the can, if you don't mind. Also, I'm not yet finished with Mother Hubbard over there. I'll be seeing you in a little while."

What this poor guy really needed was a good-sized shot of dope; that would have settled his shaky nerves, that was for sure. I didn't bother to tip him off, though, 'cause you never can tell how such an unstable character might react to a well-meant suggestion. I just kept my trap shut.

After I'd taken on my own load of embalming fluid, I calmed down wonderfully. As the Little Flower would have said, Patience and Fortitude descended upon me. So I went back to the old lady. She took a couple or three hours out of my life, but I hardly noticed it. Finally she gave me a carbon of my certificate of admittance to Lexington for three days later. I took this valuable document and hot-tailed it right up to Doc Reinzheimer's office.

"I'm glad you're going," that good man said to me. "It's the only way. You've got a life to live, so don't waste it on junk. You'll be a lot better off without all that poison. Remember, you constantly have to increase your dosages all the time, just to feel even normal. In the end you'll find that you can't get enough, even if someone fills up the whole Grand Canyon with morphine pills for you. So here's your prescription for five grains, and good luck to you."

"Thanks, Doc," I said. "I'll always remember you."

I don't suppose I have to tell you that I didn't go near Lexington that Wednesday. I didn't even go near it that year, or even the year after.

No, things had to get a hell of a lot tougher for me before I was finally reduced to that particular desperate gambit. Meanwhile I used that application to Lexington to very good

91

purpose. I kept changing the admittance date on it for nearly eight months—until the paper wore out, in fact—and even a lot of upright, hardheaded doctors couldn't resist giving me one final kiss-off prescription on the strength of my good intentions.

I did make the Public Health Service Hospital four different times, finally, and I spent about fourteen months there altogether, curing myself of my drug addition. I say "curing *myself*" because that's what, in the end, it actually amounted to. The best the croakers and the prison authorities down there can do for you is to stop you from using junk while you're inside the walls of the institution. Once you hit the street you're strictly on your own, and the tide of crap that engulfed you and sent you sprawling before is again waiting for you right there on the doorstep.

That's why, of course, there are hardly any cures. I've been off the stuff now over five years, but the people that were down there with me, the ones I kept in touch with, are all back on junk again. Every last one of them, excepting me. You needn't bother with any of the silly, fraudulent statistics— you're getting it straight from the horse's mouth. And, what's more, there isn't going to be any change for the better until the whole narcotics business is taken out of the hands of the numskull cops who are administering it now. The head of the Narcotics Bureau is a bonehead in my opinion, and so he's hardly the man to suggest any substantial improvements in this bitterly neglected territory. He wants tougher judges and stiffer sentences, and he particularly wants no interference from nosy doctors and psychiatrists. His name is Harry J. Anslinger, and I believe that his name will eventually go down in medical history as one of the major stumbling blocks to an enlightened policy in the field of human rehabilitation.

I do not know a single physician who is familiar with this subject or a really conscientious penologist who thinks any differently than I do about Anslinger. And I've got him down for a lard-brained cop who knows exactly how and when to cash his pay check—and with this concession to his talents I've just about exhausted everything laudatory that I can say about him. Of course, he didn't invent the monstrously benighted policy of the Narcotics Bureau, he just seems to do his goddamndest to perpetuate it. In this he has certainly succeeded. There is no aspect of American life that is more hemmed in with sinister medieval taboos, more burdened with lurid, rancorous prejudices, and more encumbered with morbid, shrivelhearted self-interest than the law-enforcement end of the narcotics business.

I say "business" advisedly. Remember that most of the cops in this game, the wardens, the keepers and the endless guards and shamuses all over the country have a vested interest, by the very nature of their jobs, in keeping the whole slimy narcotics racket going as long as possible.

Just have *that* in mind for a moment and you'll understand the whole bastardly setup a hell of a lot better than you ever did before. It *pays* a lot of people, and pays them damned well, that *somebody, somewhere*, is permanently hooked on dope. And many of the guys that find it so profitable aren't gangsters or drug pushers, either.

Anyway that's the general picture, and so it stands to reason that the narcotics hospitals can't really do a hell of a lot for you. The guide word is, predominantly, Penology and not Reclamation, no matter what you may have heard about this whole messy theme. There are always two or three decent doctors at Lexington who try their best to be of actual use, who sincerely believe that drug addiction requires a medical and not a punitive form of treatment. Indeed, lip service to such a posture is given in all the crappy literature gotten out

by the responsible jobholders in this field, but in actual practice it's just a lot of horseshit. Every louse who makes a living
at it has a staggering moral ascendancy over the drug addict,
and, what's more, he never misses a chance to let him feel it.

And that's how it all stands as of this moment, I'm sorry to
say.

CHAPTER EIGHT

Because of my stomach ulcers, my bum kidneys
and my high blood pressure, I eat only boiled rice and unsalted
vegetables, three times a day. My friends are quite staggered
by the stoical fortitude with which I pursue this flat and
meager diet, but, strangely enough, I don't mind it half as much
as they imagine.

You know, I think that a lot of the boys of my acquaintance
wouldn't really mind eating all that monotonous rice, provided they were sitting under some rustling banana palms
somewhere and if only, from time to time, they were able to
spot some native tootsie bouncing her precocious titties on the
caressing South Sea breezes.

Well, my beautiful wife very obligingly walks around our
apartment half naked most of the day, and you may not believe

this, but that rice of mine has an absolutely gone flavor due to this simple and yet altogether enchanting décor.

I have other compensations too. I'm always busy making a lot of great plans. I plan, for instance, to rescue American literature from the Southern lesbians and fairies who've got a stranglehold on it right now. I have quite a few ideas how to do this, too. Mostly by means of some sensationally clever comics that anybody can absorb at a glance. I know that it's not going to be done by books that have to be *read*. That's all past, or on its way out, I'm pretty sure about that.

Then again, I wonder if I oughtn't to compile a sort of encyclopedia of strange characters I have known. I've certainly been involved with quite a few weirdies in my time. Not just people with multicolored beards and astonishing clothes, you understand, but creatures whose aberrations you'd have trouble duplicating in any accredited loony bin. Most of them weren't violent or dangerous in any way, they just nourished some quaint personal monomania that, for some reason or another, I happened to find rather attractive.

One of my favorite people, for instance, was a man called Beryl Kipnil, a sculptor, who's been dead for quite a while now. He used to live across the way from me down on Gansevoort Street about a quarter of a century ago, and, if I remember correctly, I originally met him at a pretty awful art exhibition of some kind.

He was a fat, completely bald little man who looked a lot like the Dormouse in *Alice in Wonderland*, and I recall that he had the longest eyebrows I'd ever seen on any human being. He always carried a comb especially to groom these fantastic appendages. In fact, he gave them the minute care that some men, at the beginning of this century, used to expend only on their carefully groomed mustaches.

For some reason or another, he introduced himself to me. Oh, yes—he had an item on exhibit at this jumble shop, and because he knew all about my own work and, he said, had always liked it, he now wanted me to pass an appraising eye over his little opus.

So we marched over to the sculpture section, and there, poised on a rusty iron rod, was some kind of large, strangely tinted plaster lump. At first glance it looked to me like an oversized turnip with a rather unhealthy complexion.

"What is it?" I asked.

Kipnil gave a little ecclesiastical cough and said, "I call it 'The Tragic Turnip.'"

Well, he hadn't fooled me, and I liked him for it.

"It *looks* like it," I said. "Why is he crying? It is a *he*, isn't it?"

"Yes," he said. "It is a male turnip who dreamed of being a radish and never achieved his dream. He has no bite or sting in him, he is just a lowly turnip. But, ennobled by his disappointment and grief, he suddenly breaks into surprising scarlet tears. And that's where I've caught him."

I don't have to tell you that I found Mr. Kipnil a man entirely to my liking. So, after a few other accidental meetings, I began deliberately to cultivate his society. Since he lived just across the street from me, this was easy enough. It was, however, a lot less easy for me to have him as a guest at my dinner table, because he was an extremely farfetched and truly astonishing food faddist.

For dinner he always liked to have some kind of fruit soup, which isn't too bad, but in addition to this he was partial to breaded and baked watermelon or cantaloupe, and no matter how you phrase it this is sure to cause a certain amount of contemptuous shoulder-tossing in the kitchen. Baked lettuce stuffed with bran was also among his favorites. All of these culinary delights had to be served quite cold. Kipnil was convinced that hot food was the main cause of cancer, and he repeatedly warned me against this deadly indulgence. For dessert

97

he preferred bananas in good Spanish olive oil, but he would, and did, occasionally eat cucumber slices dipped in honey. That's what *I* generally gave him. That and water cress that had first been breaded, sugared, and fried in deep vegetable shortening.

If you'll examine this lurid menu a little more closely, you'll discover it's the same as the horrible crap that those great gourmets the ancient Romans used to eat all the time. Everything on their tables was always dripping with oil and honey, and Nero's great banquet, the one described by Petronius, was full of items like the dreck that Beryl Kipnil was particularly partial to.

But, aside from his strange dietary habits, he was a mild and really amusing man, who seemed to have endless time to indulge his curious and multifaceted hobbies. He was a kind of amateur investigator in various esoteric fields, and he trusted no mere dictionary or scientific compendium to give him the answers that he was looking for.

For quite a while there he was agitated by the wonder of penguins. Did they have feathers? Or hair? Or what? He laughed at me when I told him to look it up in the encyclopedia.

"I've spent hours down at the Aquarium studying them," he said. "Nothing like firsthand observation. Take no man's word for anything you can observe for yourself."

"And," I said, "have you found out what the hell they do grow?"

"I'll be ready with a definitive answer shortly," he said. "You see, I'm planning a sculpture group to be called 'Penguin Honeymoon.' Two penguins leaning together, creating thereby the form of an arch—or a large horseshoe, really. I have to have complete certainty about them first, don't you see?"

"Of course," I said. "It all makes sense now."

Well, anyway, we had gone along like this for nearly a year or so, when one day he introduced me to his best friend, who was also a sculptor and who lived over on the Jersey side of the Palisades somewhere. This guy's name was Stanley Crale, and he never worked in any medium that wasn't an unyielding organic substance. But that was just part of it. He used to carve his stuff directly with the stones that he carted home from the Palisades cliffs, and believe me, that stuff is pure disaster—it chips like crazy. But no trouble and no mishaps could cure Crale of the notion that he was involved in something called Creative Integrity. He also occasionally chiseled away on some kinds of wood, if it just splintered easily enough or was in some other way rather unmanageable. In fact, he had carved a portrait of Kipnil out of ordinary coal, and he'd been about *this* little job for about two years, with all the failures he'd had and everything.

They were great friends, those two, and I realized that New York City has so damned many varieties of people that no man, if he's just reasonably sociable, needs to be alone for long here. Yes, no matter how strange his tastes and predilections might be, he's always sure to find *somebody* who'll go along with his cuckoo opinions and his nutsy outlook.

I must say I found this tremendously reassuring.

And then one day I had a terrible shock. I read in the paper that Kipnil had been arrested the night before and—due to some strange answers he'd given the cop, and later on the magistrate in Night Court—had been shooed off to the psychopathic ward of Bellevue Hospital.

What could have happened?

Stanley Crale over on the Palisades had no phone, but an obliging neighbor finally got him on the wire for me. He was, of course, equally stunned. "I'll come right over," he said. "No, maybe I'd better go to Bellevue first. Thanks for telling me. I'll see you later."

Well, about two hours afterward he knocked on my door, and he was simply breathless with indignation. "I've been up to the hospital," he said, "and those savages just won't let me see him."

"Why did they grab him?" I asked.

"Absolutely nothing!" he said. "You know, there's an old stable over on West Twenty-third Street that hasn't been used for about twenty years, and they still have a dirty old horseshoe hanging over the door."

"A horseshoe?" I said.

"One of those golden horseshoes made out of wood, excepting this one's all tarnished and dirty and no use to anybody any more. It's about a yard high, and Berlie was trying to get it down last night when suddenly a cop grabbed him."

"So why'd they take him to Bellevue?" I asked.

"They say he talked queer to the cop, and to the magistrate too, and so they just shooed him into the booby hatch. I tell you, it's absolutely disgraceful. You know, I'm getting sorer by the minute and I've got a good mind to go right back there and insist on talking to him. In God's name, just think of what they're *feeding* that poor man."

"Why don't we get a lawyer," I said, "and he'll tell us about the best way to proceed."

"A lawyer!" he screamed. "Heaven help us all if that's what we're reduced to. No! I'm going back to Bellevue this minute. I shouldn't have left there in the first place."

"I'll go with you," I said.

"No, I better handle this myself. You know why they thought he was crazy? He told them he needed that horseshoe for an armature for a Penguin Honeymoon. Isn't that disgraceful? Those morons probably didn't even know what an armature is. Well, I'll let you know what happens. I'm off now."

"Phone me!" I yelled after him.

"Never use a phone if I can help it," he said. "I'll drop back myself later on."

But he didn't come back, and so I got kind of worried and called up an amiable lawyer that I know and told him all about the circumstances of the case. "Look into it for me, please," I said, "and, in heaven's name, let me know the minute you hear something."

About an hour later he called me back. "You and your god-damned pals," he said. "This Stanley Crale character who went up there to get him sprung—well, they've got *him* in a strait jacket in the violent ward right this minute. And, what's more, I absolutely forbid *you* to go anywhere near Bellevue until further notice, you hear? Because, the way you all act, *you'll* just wind up in a padded cell yourself. That's an order!"

"So what are we going to do?" I said. "We just can't let those poor bastards rot in a loony bin, can we?"

"Don't worry," he said. "I've found out quite a lot about Kipnil's family. They're very well heeled—brokers or bankers, or something—and when I talked to his brother he didn't seem particularly upset about the whole thing."

"They're bankers?" I said. "Why, this guy lives in a hole that even rats wouldn't build a nest in, and he cooks his horrible food on a rusty hot plate that he found out in the back yard seventeen years ago."

"He's got an income, my boy," said the lawyer, "and his brother tells me that under his grandmother's will he collects about fifteen thousand dollars a year."

How about that?

Well, the family did get him out, that very day. Got them both out, in fact, and around twelve o'clock at night they both came around to see me.

"You've been very kind," said Kipnil. "You know, we don't as a general thing approve of lawyers, but your friend proved to be unusually decent. I'm much obliged to you for having

101

engaged him in our behalf. Of course, my sudden release did spoil a little thing that I'd just started at the hospital."

"Spoiled something?" I said. "What was it?"

"Well, I has just begun to model a little bust out of some kitchen soap," he said. "A bust of the chief psychiatrist up there, a man with a truly prehistoric face and an absolutely frantic manner. He also had a laugh that sounded like the mating call of a caged hyena. Wonderful man, really. I'm sorry I couldn't finish it. You know what I was going to call that little portrait? *Run for Your Lives, Boys! Sanity's at Large!!!*"

I've told you about my friend Kipnil in such detail because I wanted to show that his only really overt act against society, in all the years that I knew him, consisted in that one childish attempt to get that old horseshoe off that abandoned livery stable.

You see, I'm quite convinced that the really dangerous people in our midst are invariably the respectable bounders who work in advertising agencies or on some of the successful news magazines around town. Now, those characters with their astringent Brooks façade, if *they* ever go off the deep end, and they often *do*, really pull some tricks that could frighten the kinks off a monkey's tail. Boy, during the last thirty years some of the most buttoned-up and constipated among these commuters have flung huge steel filing cabinets out of skyscraper windows. They've attacked elderly charwomen over their wash pails, and on one memorable occasion a certain editor, who shall be nameless, deliberately forced his secretary's hand into the mail chute out in the hall and it took the ambulance men two solid hours to extricate the poor girl so that she could quietly go to the nearest hospital for a six-week nervous breakdown.

So, you see, I'd much rather be surrounded by mild eccentrics who practice some innocent piece of daily aberration and really never harm anyone than by the frozen-assed executives with their socially acceptable fronts and their madly churning subcutaneous rages.

These are the lads who finally run amok on Madison Avenue or go screaming across Rockefeller Plaza and suddenly take a fiendish bite out of some visiting maiden lady's buttock.

Yessir!

Run for Your Lives, Boys! Sanity's at Large!!!

Somehow this brings to my mind someone else I was rather friendly with during those colorful years—namely, the distinguished Russian-born painter Dimitri Pilniak. I recall with particular pleasure his fiftieth birthday, quite a while ago, when he invited Arshile Gorki and myself to his home to help celebrate the occasion.

"Next vick I em exectly heff century," he said, "and, remember, is a grate milestyone in histery. So you must calm, the boat ahv you."

I'm not going to try to give you more of his fabulous accent, because in all fairness the only way to render it properly is by a tape recording. Just remember that Pilniak looked and spoke exactly like the hetman of a Cossack settlement that had taken up temporary quarters on New York's Lower East Side.

"He is really fifty-two or fifty-three," Gorki said to me later on, "and it is not that he is trying to make himself younger —he just likes to say 'half century' because it's a nice round figure, it's a monumental figure, and it has more style than an odd number. Pilniak is all style."

At any rate, we pulled up at the house a week later and found five other guests already assembled when we got there. The spirit of the event seemed to have boiled over even into the hallway, where some paper lanterns had been hung to indicate to the neighbors that things were certainly going to hum at the Pilniak campfires that night.

Actually the party proved very gay but certainly well within the bounds of middle-class decorum. Pilniak gave me the key to this condition before I even sat down.

"We will not upset the neighborhood," he said, "because artists are the only *living* organisms, the yeast, so to speak, in the dough of civilization. We must not upset the inert tissues with too much fermentation. Things are bad enough for them, poor souls."

In the end there were seven guests altogether, and of these I most clearly recall Mr. Christian Stanwood and a Jewish rabbi whose name, I believe, was Dr. Rohrstock. This celebration took place during the prohibition era, remember, and I shrewdly suspected that Dr. Rohrstock, aside from his other virtues, had been invited also because, under the law, he had access to certain quantities of sacramental wine, a few bottles of which very promisingly adorned the festive board. Nameless in my memory, but nonetheless persistent in their prevailing images, are two female models who were also part of the evolving gaieties of the evening, and whose bodily configurations would have brought tears of ecstasy to the eyes of Aristide Maillol. You will guess from this that these ladies had no ankles whatever, but I recall that they did have truly heroic capacities for eating and drinking. They stowed away the potables and the grub like a couple of famished shipwreck victims who had luckily been cast ashore in a flourishing delicatessen emporium.

It was wonderful and awe-inspiring.

I also recall quite clearly that these ladies were handily abetted in their labors by two bearded, surly-mannered sculptors—which, by the way, was par for sculptors as far as my experience went.

Mrs. Pilniak, our gracious hostess, supervised the proceedings with a steady but unofficious hand, while the half-century-birthday baby kept bouncing around the little apartment full of hospitable concern for the welfare of his guests.

And now it is high time that I tell you something about the Pilniak children, two handsome young boys who had obviously been appointed to wait on table, to empty the ash trays, to make themselves generally useful in various ways and to smooth the progress of the joyful occasion. These youngsters performed their duties with such truly selfless devotion and so much mature composure that I made several attempts to compliment them on their efforts, but, to tell you the truth, I was kept back from speaking to them as freely as I would have liked to, because—well, because both these boys had all their clothes on *backward*. Their jackets and their shirts were buttoned right up the rear, and their bright little neckties kept bouncing gaily up and down their backs as they rushed about the premises changing the dishes and fetching heaping platters of fresh food out of the kitchen.

Naturally I was deeply puzzled by this astonishing hunk of costuming, but since nobody else remarked on it I kept my own trap shut about it too. After all, I didn't want to seem less hep about such unusual proceedings than a couple of dopey sculptors.

But, a good deal later on in the evening, when the party had both metaphorically and literally unbuttoned itself to some degree and the host had just smilingly wandered into the little window nook where I happened to be sitting quite alone, I finally upped and point-blank asked him about it.

He raised his eyebrows in evident surprise, and I noticed that in answering me he definitely lowered his voice, as if to prevent others from hearing what was obviously a social *gaffe* on my part. He put his hand on my shoulder, as a wiser, older man naturally would, a man who had already reached the "heff century," and said, "So, you do not understand the symbolism, eh? Strange!"

105

"No," I admitted, "frankly I don't."

"Ah well," he said, "it is really quite simple. You see, when you dine in a restaurant you surely must have noticed that every time you want the waiter's attention his *back* is turned to you. Didn't you ever notice that?"

"You're quite right," I said. "It's happened to me endless numbers of times."

"Aha! Well, then, here in Maison Pilniak, just as fashionable as the finest restaurants, the waiters also permanently have their back *toward* you. But—*here* they can still *see* you!"

I don't have to tell you that I felt like a complete numskull. After all, the thing was obvious.

On another occasion Pilniak especially endeared himself to me by a highly skillful piece of deliberate buffoonery, which took place at a party that I was giving for the painter George Grosz, who had just recently arrived in this country. There was a huge mob of people present at this shindig, and literally outstanding among all the celebrities who had assembled to honor George was the gigantic figure of Hendrik Willem Van Loon. You may recall that Van Loon was at the height of his fame thirty years ago, since his book *The Story of Mankind*, a popularized history of the world, had already sold into untold editions and made his name known among the literate and illiterate the country over. He had illustrated this work with hundreds of clever little black-and-white sketches, so that those who couldn't even read when they *ran* were able to garner the essence of the book by merely riffling the pages.

Now, then, for some reason that I was never able to discover, Van Loon chose to just barely acknowledge the existence of poor Pilniak when they were introduced to each other, and someone told me later on that Van Loon even snubbed my charming Muscovite friend by deliberately ignoring his outstretched hand. What aggravated the matter still further was that about a dozen pretty young women were

106

worshipfully hovering around the Dutch giant when this unprovoked piece of rudeness was taking place. I believe that these dear girls were even shaken by spasms of approving titters when they saw the shocked expression of discomfiture on the face of the physically smaller man.

I myself, as the permanently preoccupied host, had of course only sensed rather than seen this awful contretemps, but I did notice that immediately after the introduction Pilniak had slowly wandered off toward one of the heavily draped ballroom windows, as if to seek silent communion with his thoughts. Even from the distance where I stood, it was obvious that something pretty disturbing must have happened to dampen the high spirits of the usually ebullient painter. I was just about to join him and to ask him the cause of his strange depression, when I saw him suddenly wheel about and wangle his way resolutely back into the Van Loon orbit. He slid dexterously past several conformations of adoring young ladies, until he once more directly confronted the disdainful Vesuvius. I came closer just in time to see Pilniak grab one of Van Loon's large, reluctant hands and proceed to shake it hysterically up and down like a loose pump handle.

"Maestro!" he screamed. "Maestro, I will not go home to my family without telling them that I have shaken this wonderful hand—the hand of genius, the hand of creation!"

Van Loon took the monocle out of his eye, looked wearily down at the exuberant Russian and, finally, directed a mild belch of approval in his direction.

"Maestro!" Pilniak shouted. "Maestro! This is one of the greatest moments of my life, to stand here and to shake the hand of *such* a writer, the favorite writer of my *whole* family —because I tell you, Maestro, that *Main Street* is positively the *greatest* book ever written in this country. Maestro—I thank you!"

107

CHAPTER NINE

I'M SITTING HERE in a small town in Massachusetts at the moment, because summer has come again and my
wife is once more cavorting around, musically, in a local
theatrical tent. This is not a traveling circus or a Chautauqua
enterprise by any means. The management of this divertise-
ment merely revives certain successful Broadway musicals for
the benefit of the surrounding rural communities. Of course, as
you have probably surmised, it is not an entirely altruistic undertaking; the producers hope to make themselves an honest buck by it too.

So, meanwhile, I'm interned here for the duration, and I
spend quite a bit of time listening to the exuberant voices of
children who are exercising their high spirits on the other side
of the small lake which lies before my doorstep. It occurs to

108

me as I sit here how reassuring it is, in a time of mass ama-
teurishness in most fields of creative endeavor, that the seasons,
at least, have remained expert professionals. Spring and summer make their casual appearance, and neither one of them
shouts for attention, or screams, "Looka me!!! No hands!!!"
No, they've got their fine, competent hands in everything, and
they even have a couple of fingers to spare with which to goose
my thoughts playfully back into the lovely past, when their
performances, if memory serves me right, seem to have been
even more astonishing than they are now.

The voices of those sun-drunken children which drift
through my open window all day long bring back the summers
when I myself was just such a young splasher in magical
waters, and they awaken the memory of other young voices
long ago—voices which, mingled with the pleasant coun-
terpoint of clattering dishes and silverware from the nearby
hotel terraces, formed the enchanting sound track for many
of my own early years in the mountain and lake resorts of
Austria.

If I ever told you about the places where I used to spend my
summer vacations as a child (on the Wolfgangsee and the Salz-
kammergut, for instance), if I ever spread myself about it in
detail—I mean, if I told you about the incredible, heartbreaking beauty of some of my native landscapes—why, I'm sure
I'd be responsible for large-scale mass suicides all over the
country, on account of the poor people who would suddenly
realize how defrauded and utterly bankrupt their own childhood surroundings had been.

And don't you bother to tell me about the silken mists that
hover over the bayous of Louisiana, or the pale, stark skies that
spread their translucent moonstone austerity over New Eng-
land. It's all great. I've seen it. I'm seeing it now. It's just all
happening on another planet, that's all.

I particularly don't want you to rave to me about corn pone

and collard greens, because I've had 'em, up to here. In fact, I've even sampled spoon bread sloshing around in sorghum or bacon grease, and all I can tell you is that somehow it never really quite *sent* me. Not like the mellow homemade cheeses and the tiny, fragrant strawberries, and the crackling dark bread crusts that the gods once lavishly dispensed to their favorite children in the highlands of Austria—because, to put it bluntly, I was at home there as a child. Don't you see, even an Eskimo suffers spasms of nostalgia for the igloo where he nibbled his first delicious lump of walrus flipper; his eyes are bound to go dim with unutterable longing when he is reduced to sucking reminiscently on a thin, sooty icicle while he is perhaps hospitably marooned in some benign foreign land.

Here is a dilemma I myself have never finally managed to resolve: What *am* I, anyway? I don't mean in the vast interplanetary scheme of things, nor in the eternal conundrum posed by the elusiveness of the human identity. I mean, what the hell is my *true nationality*, anyway? I'm certainly assimilated into the life that is lived all around me, and yet every so often I catch myself thinking in Austrian, and the mere sound of the lilting, slovenly accents of my native land never fail to give me the authentic goose pimples. I know from experience that I'd absolutely die if I ever had to live permanently in any part of Europe, and still there is a detached hunk of awareness loose somewhere in my organism which tells me that the whole of my adult existence was just lived in a furnished room that some good-natured landlord generously put at my disposal; nothing in it actually belonged to me. Maybe that's why I was always so frantically anxious to acquire a thorough command of the American lingo—because I was ever so damned eager to strike my taproot firmly into the spring of the American consciousness.

Well, I never made it. Not really. I'm a permanently displaced person, and I always have been. I've visited Austria any number of times during the past forty-five years, and after a while it always struck me as a dingy attic in which some muddleheaded go-getter had installed a jukebox and a Coke machine. It wasn't smart, and it wasn't *gemütlich* either. Maybe it *never* was. It well may be that when I talk about my childhood I'm probably just telling you what my heart remembers. And yet the Vienna I once knew, the Vienna of Francis Joseph with the feathery side whiskers, was certainly possessed of all the things you can still hear in the boozy waltzes of Johann Strauss—and if that's too schmaltzy and too low-brow for your taste, just listen to what his namesake, Richard, has provided as a theme song for that Austrian booby Baron Ochs in *Der Rosenkavalier,* and you'll get the hang of what is really wrong with me from 'way back. You'll understand then that I'm just incurably afflicted with homesickness for never-never land, and that this is surely a desperately inappropriate piece of psychological ballast to carry around with you in a frenziedly competitive society. The mystery was, and still is, how I ever managed to make any kind of living at all, because, on the face of it, it must be obvious to anybody who has listened to me so far that I was certainly well equipped from the very start to become a truly sensational failure in life.

I did make it in that direction, too, any number of times, but officially I've been declared bankrupt only once (in the courts, I mean), and otherwise I don't think I've ever in my life been more emotionally solvent than I am right at this moment—mostly due to my happy marriage, and also because I'm at last rid of my ghastly drug addiction.

This took some doing, as you can imagine, because, as I've already indicated, opium sustains one so marvelously during every form of financial or emotional hangup. The only thing that can ever rival it as a crutch for a limping soul is a really successful love affair. Well, the first three times I went down to get cured, my heart was quite unattached and so naturally I bounced right back onto my hill of white pills the minute the first little wriggling crisis came along.

By the way, the third time I landed in Lexington I was accompanied to the doors of the institution by a Federal officer whose name was Lovelace. When the big steel gates clanged shut behind us, I turned to him and said, "You had a very famous namesake once, Mr. Lovelace. He was one of the greatest brawlers, poets and lovers at the court of Charles II. Ever hear of him?"

"Yes, someone else once mentioned him to me a couple of years ago," he said.

"You know, he wrote a fine poem once, which was addressed to his mistress, while he was locked up in jail. Did you ever hear it?"

"No, not that I remember."

"Her name was Althea," I said, "and he wrote to her, 'Stone walls do not a prison make, nor iron bars a cage.' What do you think of that?"

"I certainly admire his spirit," said Mr. Lovelace. "I'm just wondering what kind of jails they had in those days."

He was quite right. Things must have changed a good deal since then, because Lexington held me for four and a half months and I must admit I felt very definitely confined during every minute of that whole miserable time. I had a room all to myself during that third hitch, but I had a very interesting gallery of neighbors living up and down my corridor. It was rather a select group of doctors, chemists, engineers and all sorts of other highly skilled professional men who had somehow fallen into the drug swamp and were now being dry-cleaned for the umpteenth time.

In the corner room, on the right of me, there lived a handsome young eye specialist, Dr. Herbert Craddock, who eventually confided in me that he had once had very serious aspirations to go on the stage. Nothing was easier to believe. He was

112

well over six feet tall, blue of orb, blond of mane and tawny of hide. A typical girl trap no matter where you put him, but certainly the ideal sex foil for the matinee mob. Instead he had become a first-rate eye surgeon, and in the medical library I even found some books he had written on his particular specialty some years before. After I got to know him better, I realized that unfortunately the science he adorned had never quite managed to answer the real basic quest in his wayward heart. Somewhere along the line he had defrauded his true nature, and because he had probably made the wrong choice he had been on junk, on and off, for about eleven years. He'd been back to Lexington six times already and had kicked at least a dozen of his habits in darkened hotel rooms back in Bar Harbor, where he came from.

One day, when he asked me to cue him on his part for a play that I had written especially for the inmates at the hospital, I let him in on my secret deductions about him.

"You know what I think is really wrong with you?" I said. "I think you're hung higher than a kite because you never gave this acting fixation of yours a real break. I think you should have *tried*, at least *failed* at it. That's my honest opinion. How come you never chanced it, Doc?"

"Because my mother was a widow, and I'm her only son, and she made unbelievable sacrifices to send me to medical school, that's why. Don't you see, I couldn't possibly let her down and maybe take some stinky job in a summer theater, or become an extra in a Broadway musical, after she'd practically annihilated herself in working for my education. Later on I somehow turned out rather good at my job, and when I was interning, one of the top men in town even took me on as an assistant. So, you see, I made a very successful career of being a physician, and it was only when I occasionally took part in some of the amateur theatricals in our community that I had myself some pretty bad moments. I purposely stayed away

113

from them a couple of times, but that only made me feel worse. I suppose you're probably right about me. You don't have to be Sigmund Freud to guess that junk is just something I keep on feeding to my roaring frustration so it'll keep quiet long enough for me to go on earning a living. But let me tell you one thing. I've been back here six times already, but never before did I feel so certain of a permanent cure as I do this time. I really feel it deep down inside of me, that this time I'm surely going to make it."

"From *your* mouth into God's ears," I said.

About three weeks later I woke up one morning and found that I had a small but painful swelling on my right eyelid. Naturally I went next door and consulted my neighbor.

"It's just a small cyst," he said. "Put yourself on sick call, and I'll cut it out for you this morning."

"Will it be painful?" I asked.

"Not a bit of it. Don't give it a thought. You're in good hands."

Around eleven o'clock I went down to the eye clinic and he promptly operated on me. He was right; there was no pain at all.

When I was ready to leave, he stopped me in the doorway. "I'm going to ask them to prescribe a goof ball [a barbiturate capsule] for you. The hack will hand it to you tonight at bedtime."

"Fine," I said. "Many thanks."

Sure enough, during the nightly medical ministrations Steve Ransom, the attendant on my floor, came around to my room and handed me a goof ball. He handed me a small glass of water too and waited in the doorway until I had downed it. After he had gone, I turned out the light and went to bed.

About ten minutes later my door was slowly opened, and, because there had been a good deal of cigarette stealing on my floor lately, I quickly turned on my bed light. In the doorway stood my handsome neighbor, obviously quite distressed by the sudden illumination. I couldn't have been more surprised.

"Yes?" I said. "Is there anything wrong?"

"No, not a thing," he said. "Don't talk so loud." He came over to the bed and stretched out his hand, as if he expected me to give him something. I must say he had me quite rattled, because I'd known junkies to act very strange sometimes and of course I hadn't the vaguest idea what was on his mind.

"What is it?" I said. "You want a smoke?"

"No!" he said impatiently. "Stop your kidding and in Christ's name hand over that goof ball."

"What goof ball?"

"The one Ransom handed you just ten minutes ago."

"Oh! I'm afraid I took it. Wasn't I supposed to?"

"You *took* it! Well, that's a nice howdeedoo! You didn't *need* it, did you? You're not having any *pain*, are you?"

"No, I'm not," I said. "I'm sorry, Doc, but I simply didn't realize that you expected me to save it for you. Nobody tipped me off. You didn't say anything to me, did you? I'm awfully sorry, really I am."

His face was such a terrible thing to see that I quickly turned off the light.

"Good God," he said, "how in hell am I ever going to get to sleep tonight?" He fell into a chair near the doorway, and in the dimness I could see he had buried his face in his hands like an Orozco peasant at a Mexican funeral.

"Goddammit," I said, "why didn't you tell me earlier that you wanted the crappy pill? Besides, Ransom stood right there when I took it, and he waited until I'd swallowed it, too."

A deep moan came out of the darkness. "Of course he did. He always waits for you to swallow it. You're not a simpleton, are you? You could have stashed it behind your molars until he was gone, couldn't you? You could have just swallowed the water, the way all my other patients do. That goddamned goof ball is my fee for the operation, don't you see? I've got to have at least one operation a day or I don't close an eye the following night. That's why I always have to hustle like crazy to dig myself up some measly piece of surgery before I quit the clinic at four o'clock. What in God's name am I gonna do now?"

I got out of bed. "I know somebody who's got four aspirins," I said. "Would they be of any help to you?"

He got up and tottered out into the hall. "Never mind," he said. "I've got four hundred of them. No, I'm afraid I'm just in for it now. My patients always manage to save their barbiturates for me, even if they are handed to them in *liquid* form. They just wait till the hack gets out of the room, and they spit it right back into the glass the minute he's gone. That's what *they* do. But never mind. I'm sorry I'm so bitchy about it. I'll see you tomorrow."

He went next door and left me standing there in the middle of my room, terribly sad and utterly bewildered.

As I climbed into bed again, I realized that Dostoievski, whom I'd been reading late that afternoon, was certainly a hep kid, with the real low-down notions. Somewhere in that book of his he had said, "The human heart is a dark, dark forest."

It was during my last stay at Lexington that I had a queer run-in with an occupational therapist, a lady called Verna Fern. I first met Verna a few days after my arrival, when I was still lying in bed with about 103 fever. While my mind was being sucked helplessly down a deep funnel full of morbid, hallucinal images, a bustling middle-aged nurse suddenly bounced into my room and put a funny-looking wooden frame across my diaphragm.

"And how are we *today?*" she shouted. "Shall we raise your bed a little?"

116

Without waiting for an answer she raised my bed and I could see that behind her thick, rimless glasses her crazy eyes were rolling around like a couple of loose marbles. She isn't real, I thought to myself, she's just another one of my ghastly figments and I'll just have to start wrestling with her in a minute or so. But a few seconds later I realized that I was wrong; she was only too damned real. In fact, before I was able to rouse myself to any form of protest she had already opened a vast string reticule, and from somewhere out of its depths she produced two enormous strands of wool, which she put purposefully down on my chest. Let me tell you that I had never before in all my life seen anything as ugly as the colors in that mess of wool. Luckily there were only two strands—a dreary, washed-out lavender and a vomitorious bile yellow. An absolute horror. It must be that the fever made me terribly sluggish or something, because I said nothing at all to her when very quickly, and very dexterously, she started weaving those repulsive strands back and forth across that idiotic frame of hers. At any rate, I finally understood what her mad doings were all about. She was the O.T. nurse, who gave the patients all sorts of interesting little tasks to perform just to take their minds off the fact they were puking out their guts and suffering from a couple of thousand other interesting withdrawal symptoms. Well, I decided to wait until she finally got the hell out of there before I'd throw her playful little apparatus into the garbage pail.

Meanwhile she was weaving away like a busy little spider that was bent on catching every single fly of common sense still loose in that bloody hospital room. Also she talked, of course; and, like most professional do-gooders, she had a special tone and even a special vocabulary that most such dopes invariably use when they start talking to timid children.

"Now, isn't that pretty, the way we've got that started?" she said, giving a cackle of self-approval. "See the little holes in the sides of the frame? Well, the wool goes in *this* way, and it crosses over to *here*, and, if you want to, you can spell out somebody's *name*—if you like, your *wife's*, or your *girl friend's*, if you know what I mean. And when the little rug is all *finished*, you can even send it *home* to her. The hospital packs and ships the whole thing for you, all you have to pay is twenty-six cents in stamps. Now, that isn't too much to pay for a nice present, *is it?* Why don't you try it yourself! *Go ahead!*"

She handed me some wool, and merely to stop her jabbering and just to get her out of the room I made a desperate attempt to focus my attention on her disgusting contrivance. But it was plain to me in a minute that she had no intention of leaving unless I actually started weaving, so with my special sickroom docility I inserted some of her revolting wool into a couple of expectant frame holes. She stood there watching me for a spell, and then at last she slowly gathered up the rest of her trash and, to my infinite relief, she finally took a powder.

And that should have been that. Excepting, of course, that I'm a hopeless schlemiel about certain things, and so, even after that demented creature had gone away, I somehow couldn't quite stop myself from weaving. In fact, it seemed that I was particularly well endowed to perform this dreary piece of imbecility, and in less than half an hour I even had five letters of the alphabet quite clearly defined in pale lavender and sunbleached baby crap. Anyone could plainly see that the word that I was planning to weave was going to be "Alice."

After a while, I suppose, the fever must have gotten the better of my creative spasm, because I seemed to have dozed off. When I suddenly woke up again, the little public-spirited arachnid was back in my room once more. She was the one who had probably awakened me with her wild exclamations of delight, since the echoes of her exuberance were still bouncing off the walls when I opened my eyes.

"Wonderful!" she screamed. "Absolutely wonderful! You've got the name almost done! Now, won't Alice be *glad* when she *sees* this?"

"Yes," I said, "I suppose she *would* be, if I only *knew* anybody by that name."

"You *don't* know anybody called *Alice?*" she said.

There were thirty seconds of complete silence after her question. For the first time since I'd met her, her voice had sounded normal and quite unaffected. It had lost all its silly, patronizing overtones.

"You don't know anybody by that name?" she said, and absent-mindedly she proceeded to lift that frame off my aching gut.

"No!" I said. "I don't know anybody by that name and, what's more, I never did, and I hope I never will, either."

"Well," she said, quite sternly, "then why did you pick *that* particular name for weaving?"

"Why? Because the poor bastard who probably died in this room before me scribbled 'Alice' right on the footboard of this bed, that's why. There it is! You can see it for yourself!"

She didn't even bother to look. I could see that I had managed completely to derail her altruistic chestnut cart. I tried to explain to her why I had done what I had done, but it was perfectly plain that she wasn't paying me much attention.

"Are you married?" she suddenly asked me.

"Yes," I said.

"What *is* your wife's name?"

"Margie," I said. "Don't you see, this wool is really unbelievably repulsive. These colors were obviously picked by some sadistic fiend who's got it in for junkies and is trying his goddamndest to give the sick people in this hospital a hard time."

"This wool is contributed by charitable wholesalers," she said, "and no one ever before has complained about it."

"I'm sorry," I said, "but I'm particularly sensitive to colors, and so with this hideous mixture of washed-out tints I couldn't possibly weave anything for my Margie, could I? Besides, what is this thing supposed to be, anyway? Is it a doily? Or a napkin? Or a pen wiper? Or what? It's a crazy size that I'm sure nobody could possibly have any earthly use for. Who in God's name would want such a thing around the house, anyway? See what I mean?"

"Yes," she said, "I see." She placed the frame back on my stomach and quietly walked out of the room.

I realized, of course, that I had peevishly and frivolously tampered with the equilibrium of a human soul, and I must say I felt quite foolish about the whole thing. I decided to make it up to her. I would apologize. So I got out of bed and in my bare feet I went out into the hall after her.

When I got outside she had already reached the central desk, where the patients' records were kept, and I could see that she was busily scribbling in somebody's dossier. I was dead certain that it was mine, so I waited until she had finished and had copped herself a walk. The minute she was outside the door I rushed up to the desk and quickly started riffling the grim pages of my medical history. I found her entry under "Psychological Notes and Observations." She had written her entry in a strong, almost masculine hand: "Patient is of very unstable temperament. Possibly paranoid."

The bitch! I went back to my room, crawled into bed and at once set about viciously raveling the wool out of my half-completed design. In no time at all that whole horror was crumpled on the floor like a dismantled bird's nest. I somehow felt that I'd gotten even with her and that I'd properly vindicated my integrity by destroying the nauseating evidence of my compulsive piece of craftsmanship.

I don't know how long I was lying there, brooding over my triumph, when I suddenly heard the tripping of an all too

120

familiar footstep along my corridor. In a flash it came to me that the silly oaf was about to pay me still another visit—with a strait jacket, maybe.

Well, she surprised me. She came into my room, her face simply wreathed in good will. She lowered her eyes, she simpered girlishly, and she proceeded to do a whole choreographic evolution on the subject of her belated regrets. Finally she simmered down and even rested one of her shanks in a comradely fashion on the footboard of my bed.

Frankly, I thought she'd gotten to look quite a bit older since the last time I'd seen her, about twenty minutes before. But that often happens with nervous dolls of a certain age; they gotta watch themselves.

"I came back," she said, "because I'm ashamed, the way I walked out on you. You know, lately I lose my temper quite often, and Dr. Zimmermann made me promise just yesterday that I'd be off on my vacation next week. Well, I suppose everybody gets tired after a while. See what I mean? But never mind about that. What I really came back for was to see how Alice is doing."

She positively beamed at me; she even attempted an encouraging wink of common connivance between us. "Well," she said, "let's get a look at Alice again. How is she doing *now?*"

I pointed to the floor.

"*There* is Alice," I said.

She got off my bed and looked stonily at all that raveled disaster. Her eyes hung so far out of her head, you could have hung a couple of coats on them. You see, to her mind, or whatever the hell she had fermenting inside that skull of hers, this deliberate piece of destruction on my part was tantamount to a major crime. As far as she was concerned I had, in fact, coldbloodedly murdered Alice.

She passed a limp hand across her forehead and kept on staring hypnotically at the floor, but after a while she finally pulled herself together and looked straight at me. Those strangely assorted features of hers were puckered into a mask of frozen indignation. I'll grant you it was the indignation of an infuriated snail, but, if anything, that made it somehow even more impressive.

"You know what you are?" she said, barely moving her lips.

"No," I said, "what am I?"

"You are a *monster!*" she said.

And then she turned around and, like an ill-adjusted puppet whose center of gravity isn't too securely pivoted, she staggered out of the room.

She didn't write anything in my dossier this time, but I was by no means finished with her. Not by a damn sight. The rest of it was all my own fault, of course.

You see, a few weeks later when I felt well enough to get out of bed, I talked to some of the people around the institution about this strange creature. To my great surprise they all thought very highly of her and her work—her influence, I should say.

"You bothered her very much," said Dr. Zimmermann, "and I'm not really surprised. As a matter of fact, she's absolutely wonderful with our routine mental cases. She has angelic patience with them, and only a very few really violent ones have ever failed to respond to her. She's been here many years and I really don't know what we're going to do if she ever quits. No, my boy, you've got her quite wrong. She's a real sister of mercy, that's what *she* is."

Well, I must say it bothered me. I thought about it for a while, and then one day I asked Zimmermann to give me a pass to go and visit her over at the building where the loonies were immured, because I'd decided to make my most contrite and elaborate apologies to Miss Fern. Early the following Saturday

I did go over there, and I had reason to feel quite privileged, too, since all the overtly psychopathic patients were very strictly segregated from the rest of the population.

When I finally got there, Miss Fern was unfortunately away, fluttering on some of her endless errands of mercy, no doubt. At any rate, I decided to wait for her. I was sitting in a large, high-ceilinged room—more like a reception hall of some sort, with a desk and some bookcases along one side, but 'way over in one of the far corners an elderly bug was crouching underneath a tall window, busy with what seemed to be a very concentrated piece of knitting.

After waiting around for about ten minutes or so, I got pretty bored and went over to watch this cooky a little closer. He didn't look up when he heard me approaching, and, if anything, he seemed to turn even a little farther away from me. He *was* knitting, all right. What's more, he was in a pretty big hurry about it. He was a guy in his late fifties, with a close-shaven head and a deeply lined, rather Mongoloid face, and he was wearing the mud-green uniform that was the identifying mark of all serious mental patients in the hospital.

I watched him for a while and wondered what in hell he could possibly be making that required him to give it such high-powered, concentrated attention. Also, as I stood there, it came to me that he was for some reason or another employing a rather time-wasting and clumsy system of stitches. You see, just by the merest chance it happened that I *knew* something about knitting—knew quite a bit about it, in fact—and, like most other men with such dubious talents, I was just ass enough to be quite proud of this particular accomplishment of mine.

I had learned how to knit about ten years before, on a very snowy afternoon in December, when I was living with my second wife, Annis, down on East Ninth Street in New York City.

123

It happened like this. I had a bad cold at the time, and so I had decided to stay in bed, when suddenly, late in the afternoon, the goddamned doorbell started to ring. My wife had gone out on an errand of some sort and so I had to go to the door myself. When I opened it I found a crushed little refugee standing out in the hall, smiling like a death mask, and carrying some kind of pathetic cardboard suitcase. I knew he was a refugee the minute I laid eyes on him, because it was plain that his overcoat had certainly been the height of style in Dessau or in Hanover about five years before, with enormous lapels and a belt right under the armpits. A real horror. I was also sure the salesman who had sold it to him had called it an *American* overcoat. He had his silly little hat on ass-backward too, with the bow on the wrong side of his head, and in my experience only bedeviled refugees and thoughtful Chinese ever made such flagrant blunders with their headpieces.

"Yes?" I said.

"Could I please speak to the lady of the house?" he said.

"The lady of the house isn't in. Anything *I* could do?"

He was the saddest little dog-eyed runt I'd seen in ten years, and because a terribly cold blast was blowing under my bathrobe I asked him to come in. Now, that's where I made my great mistake. A man on your doorstep is just a peddler, a nuisance, an outsider against whom you are perfectly free to shut the door, but once he's inside the house with you, once he's taken off his terrible hat, he becomes automatically a man who is there by your special invitation, a guest almost.

So there we were, staring at each other, *I* in deep distaste and he in abject humility.

"What are you selling, anyway?" I said.

"Wool," he answered.

"*Wool?*!?!?! In God's name, who wants wool?"

"Nobody," he said sadly. "I haven't sold a single box in three days."

"Let's see it," I said.

I don't know why I wanted to see that goddamned wool. After all, it couldn't have made the slightest difference, but the born shopper in me somehow just couldn't manage to shut up, I suppose.

He opened his suitcase, a real pressed-paper article with fancy foreign labels on it, the sight of which would have broken your heart, and he displayed his treasures. Wool, sure enough. Blue, red and white were what he had on hand, but he was ready to supply other colors too, on the payment of a small deposit.

"How much is it?" I asked.

"Four dollars a box," he said.

"Four dollars?!?!?! Who in heaven's name wants four dollars' worth of wool? Never mind, don't tell me! Oh God, oh Hiawatha!"

So I bought a box of red wool from him, and I suppose you've guessed by now that he didn't have change of a five-dollar bill. It was really too much.

"I'll go down and get change," he said.

I think I've already mentioned that it was snowing like crazy, but I haven't yet told you that this perambulating disaster didn't have any rubbers on, so when he offered to hurl himself out into that blizzard to get change I just stood there and glared at him while streams of sulphur and smoke were just pouring out of my nostrils. He really had me going.

"I have another suggestion," he said. "I have some knitting needles that cost a dollar a pair. If you like . . . ?"

"Let's see them!"

He produced two good-sized wooden daggers and handed them to me.

"They look more like tent pegs," I said.

"No, they are knitting needles," he insisted. "Maybe you'd like to try them. I show you how."

Well, by the time my gallivanting wife got home, there were the two of us lolling all over my disheveled bed, involved in a frenzy of knitting. At any rate, he had taught me some kind of simple, effective stitch whereby I had managed to use up a hell of a lot of wool in almost no time at all. So just to play it safe I quickly bought two more boxes from him, because, after all, who knew where in hell I'd find the guy again, and by the time he left I already had about fifteen inches of stuff well under way. Later in the evening, I heard my wife in the next room talking to someone on the telephone and telling them not to drop around that evening.

"You better make it some other time," she said. "You see, he's knitting. . . . Yes, knitting. *K*, as in knock-kneed, *N*, as in Neanderthal . . . *Knitting!* That's right. . . . I don't know what it is yet. I don't think *he* knows either."

The poor dear was perfectly right. I had started quite aimlessly, for the sheer joy of exercising my newly discovered skill, but before I knew it the whole thing had gotten a little out of hand. When I first began, the width of my creation had been only about the size of a necktie. By the time the evening was over it had widened out to cover most of the bed, and heaven only knew where it was all going to finally end. It did end, though, about three weeks later, when I ran out of wool, and by that time I had probably completed the largest piece of meaningless knitting south of the Yukon.

For many years afterward, every time we had to move, a great bundle of knitting about the size of an old-fashioned cookstove would fall down on us and have to be stowed away at great expense in a specially constructed fiberboard container. I simply couldn't bear to part with this jewel. It wasn't pretty, and it certainly wasn't useful, but—well, it was all mine, and I was genuinely proud of that piece of imbecility.

Now, then, when I stood in that hospital waiting room down in Lexington and watched the little madman going through that wool like a cyclone, my whole career as a knitter flashed back into my mind and I realized that here at last I'd found a kindred spirit, a soul literally caught in the meshes of its own weaving. But, as I've already mentioned to you, he was certainly using a mighty inefficient stitch, and I was really pained to see him waste all that superfluous motion. And then I noticed something else. Rolled up in the corner, right behind him, was the work he had obviously already finished, and all I can say is that the pile of knitting that *he* had managed to accumulate made *my* effort in that direction look like the merest piece of amateur effrontery. His bundle of fungus reached about halfway up the window frame and it stood out at least five feet from the wall. Man, he *really* was hot. What in heaven's name could he possibly be knitting? And he was so purposeful about it, too, and at the rate he was making it he was obviously planning to weave a net large enough to cover the whole goddamned institution. And not a bad idea, either.

"You're not using a very good stitch," I said to him. "You're rewinding the thread twice, and it only wastes effort and it gets you nowhere."

The little madman turned his head slowly in my direction and gave me a fast sidewise look, like a Muscovite spy in a Hitchcock film. That puss of his really startled me. Who knows, the son of a bitch might just lean over and bite my ear off, or do me some other kind of painful damage. He could get away with it, too. He had a diploma for it. So I kept on talking.

"It's faster if you just loop it over once," I said, "and shove it over directly on the other dagger."

I realized I shouldn't have said "dagger." It might give him ideas.

"It's faster if you just loop it over once," I said, "and shove the thread over on the other chopstick. Let me show you."

Without a word he turned fully toward me and handed me the weapons. Well, so far, so good. He was at least disarmed. I just hoped I hadn't lost the hang of it. I wound some wool around my forearm and three of my fingers and started clattering. Saved! I still had the whole thing under control. It was like roller skating and bicycle riding; it stayed with you till your first cerebral hemorrhage. I knitted on feverishly for about two minutes before he gave any further sign of life.

"You're all right," he said. "That's a very good stitch. Let *me* try it."

I handed him back the dirks, and he positively smiled at me. I knew he was smiling, because his eyes disappeared altogether and two enormous, greenish fangs protruded at each side of his mouth. Also he drooled a little. We were pals, that was obvious.

And now *he* started. He was an expert, you could see that at a glance. In a little while he had amalgamated my system and added to it a little twist of his own that was a palpable improvement on both our methods. I tell you, that wool was disappearing like spaghetti into a suction pump. He finally took time out just to give me another big smile. He even patted me affectionately on the hand.

"Wish I'd met you a lot sooner," he said.

Whatever his dark plans, I had certainly given them a decided impetus.

"Yessir!" he said. "I'd have been nearly done by now, if I'da run into you six months earlier." He gave a sort of zoological cackle 'way in the back of his throat, and his face became suddenly so stylized with additional wrinkles that he looked like a bas-relief road map of the Appalachians.

"You certainly caught on fast," I said. "You're a plenty cool knitter yourself, believe me. That stitch you're doing ain't easy. No sir!"

We beamed at each other like a couple of old knitters in a bughouse.

And just then out of the corner of my eye I suddenly caught

sight of Miss Verna Fern standing beside her desk. Of course I couldn't tell just how long she might possibly have been standing there watching us, but the minute I spotted her I leaped over to make my devoirs.

Poor girl, I could see she was still sore at me but, even so, I was certainly quite unprepared for what happened next.

"Get out of here!" she said, pointing an arthritic index finger commandingly toward the doorway.

"I'm sorry, Miss Fern," I said, "I just came over to see you and to explain . . ."

"Get Out!!!!!"

The indignant snail just wouldn't listen, so, properly crushed and looking mighty foolish, I started toward the exit. But just before I hit the hallway and went out through the iron gate, I turned around once more to take one final look at my old friend, the lonely weaver of Lexington.

That fine man had meanwhile inserted both his thumbs in his ears and was wriggling his fingers ecstatically around his temples. And just as the big steel locks were clanging behind me, I could hear him give out a long, a fierce, a triumphant rooster crow.

A few days later, Dr. Zimmermann, who had given me the pass for that abortive visit, told me what had gone so disastrously wrong with it.

"This friend of yours, the mad knitter," he said, "has been completely un-co-operative and uncommunicative for about fourteen months now. He is my patient, so I know that Miss Fern took unusual pains with him during all that time. She just got nowhere. She was the one who had actually gotten him started with his knitting in the first place, but he's flatly rejected any other overtures on her part since then. Well, anyway, you can see her position, can't you? She steps out of the room for a few minutes, and when she comes back there *you* are, a complete outsider, laughing and fraternizing with this

129

guy as if there wasn't a damned thing wrong with him. All I can tell you is, I've recommended that she'd better take another couple of weeks' vacation right away, because I'm really quite worried that her own mental stability isn't any too great at this moment. I honestly think you've actually broken the poor girl's heart—or her spirit, anyway."

Oh, to hell with them, I thought. After all, I can't tell every sap I run into every silly little thing that's happened to me in the past fifty years, can I?

Still, I hope Verna Fern will read this, so that she can now find out why Rumpelstilzchen and I managed to hit it off so well that day down in Lexington. We grooved it together because we just happened to have a lot in common from 'way, 'way back.

Don't you see, Verna? Come on, Verna! No harm was intended.

I just hope she isn't dead.

CHAPTER TEN

For the duration of the summer I'm living at 44 Evergreen Street in Framingham, Massachusetts. I'm very conveniently located here, too. Across the way is the Union Hospital; down the street are four physicians; on the corner is a nursing home; and, within less than a kidney-stone's throw from my house there are three lively undertakers; so, you see, I'm cushioned against all possible contingencies. However, I'm hoping to fool the lot of them. I work hard all day long, from ten to fourteen hours, in fact, and nothing ever happens here to distract me in any way. My wife is off to rehearsals or to her performances, and the only thing that occasionally breaks in on my solitude is somebody's radio. In the smaller towns of America you don't have to have a radio of your own; everybody is so goddamned public-spirited you get blasted right out of your chair with the slop-over from their noise boxes.

Once a really significant thing happened to me during such a consistent radio barrage by remote control. It was when I was living in an embalmed little community called Wallacauga, down in Georgia, because some hep cooky in Lexington had wised me up that there was an old croaker in Wallacauga who was pretty liberal with his dope prescriptions.

I was lying down in my room one afternoon—at the Beauregard House, to be exact, an enterprise that had obviously been leased from a tribe of supervisory cockroaches—when somebody's radio suddenly started blasting away at me. This broadcast originated in Pittsburgh, or Washington, or someplace quite far up North, and it was nothing less than a heartfelt appeal to my soul, by none other than the Right Reverend Mr. Billy Graham, of all people. Here I was, ass-deep in sin and morphine, and there, a thousand miles away from me, this worthy man was hustling like crazy for my salvation.

Touching, ain't it?

Well, he gave it the well-known works, as usual, and when he had finished in a shower of glory, somebody else came on, a sort of celestial vacuum cleaner to pick up the outlying debris.

"If you are at home now," this voice said, "why don't you reach for your telephone and call us up? Call us up this very minute! There are fifty lines open to receive your calls. Go on, reach for your phone now, this minute, and accept salvation on the telephone! Do that, brother, we are waiting for you! Go on, reach for it, and accept salvation *now!*"

Since I have practically no sales resistance to speak of, I reached for the phone and dialed the long-distance operator. "I want to talk to the Billy Graham Tabernacle," I said to her, "and remember, I want to *reverse the charges.*"

So now there followed the usual long-distance sound effects, but after about half a minute the connection was made and I could hear the operator talking to the party at the other end. She asked this lucky man whether he would accept the charges for a call from Wallacauga, Georgia. The answer wasn't too clear at first, but after the question was repeated four or five times he finally got the hang of it. The moment he understood what was wanted, his voice suddenly sounded quite cranky and he even began to squeal a little, as if somebody had just stepped on his naked tail. I could hear him consulting a couple of other people too, and the decision seemed to be in the negative.

"We can't accept any charges," he said plaintively. "I'm afraid we just can't do that."

"Why *not?*" I screamed into the instrument. "Just chalk it up to my heavenly account, why don't you? I know it's quite a bit overdrawn at the moment, but I'll be all straightened out, and I'll have a clean slate, the minute you guys deliver my salvation. You said so yourself! In no time at all, I'll be all cool and solvent again, that's what you just promised on the radio. Didn't you?"

The good-natured Georgia operator let all this foolishness go on, first of all because it probably broke up the boredom of her day, but also, I suspect, because everybody in this country is greatly in awe of all salesmen for religion; I understand that even among the higher anthropoid apes these gentry enjoy a certain preferential status. So the nonsense proceeded.

Another voice got on the phone. This one was a whole octave lower, like a celestial floorwalker's, and he certainly wasn't going to take any of my silly guff. "You ought to be *ashamed* of yourself," he said. "You ought to be ashamed to trifle this way with the safety of your immortal soul!"

Then he hung up on me with a bang.

"Sorry," said the operator, "but they won't accept the charges."

"I heard him," I said. "Cash on the line, that's them! Just like everybody else. I should have known it. Well, let that be a lesson to *you*, miss!"

Then I hung up too.

Cast your bread upon the waters and it shall come back to you as Fig Newtons. Nuts! I thought.

But my time in Wallacauga wasn't altogether wasted, because I did locate the croaker who wrote scrip for junkies. His name was Cornel Twining, and he roosted right above a cheesy-looking drugstore on the outskirts of the town. After I'd slipped him a sawbuck he handed me my prescription and I went right downstairs to get it filled. Unfortunately the joint was closed. While I stood there peeking into the dark interior I heard footsteps clattering down an outside staircase, and when I looked up, there was my doctor, waving some keys in the air and running toward me with a big, friendly grin on his face.

"It's closed," I said. "You got the keys?"

"I sure have. I'm the druggist too." He pointed meaningfully at his gray alpaca jacket, and then I remembered that when he'd written my prescription upstairs he'd worn a white cotton one. You can see he took his roles seriously—dressed for the parts and everything.

He lifted another five dollars from me for the poison, and when I looked back at him from the road later on I could see him taking off his costume even as he was climbing up again to his mildewed eyrie.

A real Southern lulu!

I hung around two weeks in that horrible bunghole and he slipped me my load of dope every three days. Then, finally, one day he nixed me.

"You come back again in two months from now," he said. "Remember, young feller, I gotta think about my future."

"Your future?" I said. "You look like you're over eighty."

"I'm over ninety," he said. "Ninety-three, to be exact. How would it look if I spent my hundredth birthday in a Federal clink?"

"You'd look great there," I said.

"Now, you just skedaddle along," he said. "You come back again in June and I'll try to fix you up again."

"Okay," I said. "Will you give me fifty grains for a hundred dollars? For the road, I mean."

"Can't do it. Too dangerous. Give you twenty grains for the same price, though."

"I ought to belt you in the eye," I said.

"I wouldn't do that, if I were you," he said. "I'm justice of the peace of McNeill County, and McNeill County dishes up more justice by the square inch than all the rest of the South put together. And *you* know what Southern justice is, don't you, son?"

"Yeah," I said. "I smelled some of it all the way up in New York."

But, of course, I gave him my C note, and he handed over the twenty grains—which left me with just thirty-five dollars in my kick to get along on indefinitely.

Luckily, one of my New York friends, Dave Schoedsag, had given me the address of a cousin of his who lived somewhere around there too, and so I at once proceeded to work on this valuable lead. It took me nearly three days to locate this elusive pus bag, and when I finally found him he turned out to be a retired tobacco auctioneer. His name was Philbert Stewcombe and he was fifty-six years old, a chronic drunkard, a foulmouthed braggart, and a bachelor in a highly aggravated state of acute satyriasis. The booze that generally gurgled inside his fat belly made such a racket you could barely hear what he was saying—not that you missed anything. He lived 'way off the hell and gone in some nettle-covered timber crack to which you first had to take a train, then a bus, and in the end you just had to swing from tree to tree, like Tarzan; and, when you finally found him he'd be asleep with all his clothes on, in an abandoned sawmill around which even the local rats always made a wide detour. I leeched onto this udder for two months and did some typing and correspondence for him, which just gave me enough money to cruise around three states in search of doctors that would write scrip for me. One day I found a lot of dirty women's clothes piled up in his cellar, and when I asked him about it he seemed quite disturbed by my discovery. Later on, when we got more familiar, I found out why. He belonged to a little co-ed correspondence club that swapped its soiled underwear through the mails.

A real daisy, this Philbert.

Believe me, when the next civil war breaks out I've got my Southerners all picked.

I don't know why I don't seem to be able to stop talking about my goddamned drug addiction, but somehow it always keeps coming back into my mind. Only this morning I suddenly remembered how I once landed down in Lexington for a cure just a few days before America was about to go through its annual emotional hemorrhage on Mother's Day.

On the afternoon after my arrival I happened to be well enough to go down to the commissary to do some shopping, and, to my great surprise, there was quite a brawl going on there. I'd never seen anything like it. The inmates were jawing the storekeeper and bawling the crap out of him, and I must say he seemed to be defending himself rather ineffectively.

"What's wrong?" I asked a junk pusher called Randy Murtagh, who was standing right in front of me.

"They run out o' cards, dem sons of bitches," he said. "Dey oughta be hung up by deir balls!"

"What cards?" I said.

"Muddersday cards," he said. "Dey didn' lay in enough o'

136

dem cards, and now dey ain't got enough to go 'round, de bastards!"

I couldn't help laughing.

This was a mistake, because I nearly had my teeth knocked out.

"Funny, eh?" screamed Murtagh, grabbing me by the neck. "Waddaya laughin' about, ya wall-eyed mope? Ya wantcher terbaccer juice smeared all over dem bannistairs? I'll cockalize you, you bastard!"

"Hold on a minute!" I yelled. "In God's name, leggo of me! If they ain't got any goddamned cards left, I'll *make* you one!"

He released his hold on my throat a little, but he still kept his hooks clamped on to my shirt collar. Mayhem and disaster were still hovering over my reckless head, unless I somehow managed to get through to this numskull and succeeded in appeasing his bovine wrath.

Fortunately somebody spoke up for me just then.

"Leggo o' him," said the man standing behind me. "He's an oddist, sure enough, an' ef he wantsa he can make ya a bedder card dan any you could buy down here."

So Murtagh finally let me go, but he followed me up to my room, where I immediately had to sit down to paint him a Mother's Day card.

It was my best.

I did a blond, curly-headed baby putting a pair of horn-rimmed eyeglasses on a fat St. Bernard dog. In the background, hovering over this little pudding, I painted a smiling, bosomy type of woman wearing a plaid shawl and a cameo pin. A real mother, with no nonsense about her—not one of those blue-rinsed horrors that sits around getting plastered in Schrafft's every afternoon of the Christian calendar.

Randy was almost moved to tears. "You're a bastard, all right," he said. "How de hell did you know what she looked like? It's great! *Man*, I owe you a carton of Luckies!"

137

"Never mind," I said. "I can't smoke now, I got an ulcer."

Randy looked hurt. "I can't take dis for nuttin'," he said. "You want me to knuckle somebody dat's bodderin' you, maybe, somebody dat did you doit, or sumtin'?"

"Not at the moment," I said, "but I'll let you know if anything comes up."

I did let him know, that same evening, as a matter of fact. I went to his room and told him that one hundred and twenty-three of our fellow collegians had come to me by twos and threes all afternoon and had demanded that I make them all Mother's Day cards—or else.

"Whatcha want me to do?" Randy asked.

"I want you to tell those dopes to lay off me," I said. "I ain't no goddamned slot machine to puke up cards for them, am I? You go ahead and give it to them plain and strong, Randy. Remember, you promised!"

"You got me in a spot," he said. "It ain't as if dey wuz hi-jackin' ya for butts, or somethin'. After all, everybody is got their feelin's, ain't dey?"

"Oh crap!" I said. "You know who had the gall to come to me for a card just a while ago? Sandy Fenster, the character who smacked his old lady in the snoot right in open court, 'cause she testified that he was trying to pimp on his own sister. He let her have it right in front of the judge, too, and he got an additional year pasted on him just on account of that. Remember? Well, this loving son and all-round family man is pestering me now to make him a goddamned Mother's Day card. How *about* that?"

"Well," said Randy, "if ya bring it down to dat, I ain't been such a big bargain around de house neider. There wuz times when my old lady got me so sore, too, dat I had to quiet her down some myself. I never hit her hard, or anything like dat, but I just had to put de open hand to her once in a while, or she'd of driven me plain nuts. You know how women are."

138

"So you're not gonna keep your promise and stand by me, is that it?"

Randy Murtagh looked positively sheepish. This lout who on the slightest provocation was likely to knock a guy's eye out and eat it for a grape, was maudlin with sympathy for all those frustrated Mother's Day greeters.

"Have a heart," he said. "You gotta mudder yerself, ain't-cha? You know how it feels."

"Don't talk about *me!*" I said. "If my mother ever got a Mother's Day card from *me*, she'd have me locked up in a booby hatch. What the hell kind of a sap do you take *me* for, anyway?"

Randy put his hand, about the size of a twelve-inch gramophone record, a long player, flat on my chest and shoved me out of his room.

"Beat it!" he said. "Beat it, you heartless son of a bitch! You don't *deserve* to do time with decent people!"

You can imagine the rest.

Of course I spent the next eighteen hours painting Mother's Day greetings for one hundred and twenty-three lardheaded forgers, junk pushers and assassins who had all suddenly fallen into the national mood of the most profound filial piety.

What's more, I had to paint two extra ones: one for the warden and one for the chief psychiatrist.

How in hell can you ever really figure people?

All I can say is that I personally would rather deal with the dangerously cunning than with simpletons. A man with a tricky mind is bound sooner or later to disclose his aims, to expose some of the angles that he is playing, and you can take your defensive measures accordingly. The people I can't figure, and the ones who always worry me stiff, are the out-and-out dopes. It is my long and bitter experience that a sincere sap is the most dangerous person in the whole world, because you can't possibly anticipate what he's going to do next. The really unpleasant surprises in my life were never provided by the activities of the sly or the devious; they invariably happened to me because somebody terribly well-meaning and utterly stupid stumbled across my life line.

Which brings me inevitably to talk about a truly monumental dunce called Schlingel Concuss. His real name was Sam Blotsky, but his mother always called him Schlingel, and they lived on the Grand Concourse, which she, of course, pronounced "Concuss," and that's how that moniker permanently stuck to him.

Schlingel practiced what in my circles is generally referred to as Creative Stupidity. You see, some people manage to muddle along in their foolish condition as best they can, but there are others, equally afflicted, who refuse to settle for just simple stupidity—they insist on being *creative* about their morbid predicament. These chosen ones are inclined to lavish pretty fancy embroideries on their mental stultification; they tend to dwell very circumstantially on the painfully obvious; and don't be fooled, sometimes they have even been known to carry substantial works on relativity or existentialism under their sweaty armpits. The best thing to do is to deal with them exactly as if you were a wild-animal trainer. I mean, don't ever take your eyes off them, because they're just liable to decapitate you if you're careless enough to turn your back on them, even for just a moment. Remember!

At any rate, I had known Schlingel for about ten years, on and off, and because he sometimes ran errands for me, or stayed home and answered my phone when I had to go out, I always kept pretending to myself that he had certain tangible functions in my life. Actually, he always screwed up everything under his jurisdiction, and deep down in my heart I certainly had no illusions about his true worth in the world. But, as I've already indicated, some of my oldest relationships have been founded on nothing more substantial than just a series of

140

carefully fostered misunderstandings, and I suppose such go-ings-on also required a special form of inertia on my part, too. Whatever the hell it was, I certainly seemed to have it.

As for Schlingel himself, he was over six feet tall, fleshy, with no eyebrows or eyelashes to speak of, but he was com-pensationally endowed with an enormous mop of greasy, nat-urally ill-groomed hair. Whenever Schlingel had occasion to laugh, which was often, he would lean 'way back, open his alarming mouth and disclose a frankfurterish growth in the back of his gullet that bounced around like a bell clapper in a Disney cartoon. (And please don't bother to tell me that that was just his uvula. *I* know better.)

He was a formidable bundle, in short.

Now, then, I was between wives at the time, and living quite alone on West Fifty-sixth Street, when Schlingel ap-peared at my house one Friday afternoon, dragging an enor-mous dog behind him.

"Out!" I said. "You know how I feel about dogs in New York City. You can't bring that buffalo in here. Get rid of him this very minute, you hear me?"

"Please!" he said. "Please, this is an emergency. I know you don't like dogs, but this a matter of life and death."

"Where is the death warrant?" I said. "I'll sign it at once. That dog should have been exterminated long ago."

"Please, please, don't drive me to despair," he said. "I'm at my wits' end and I beg you to hear me out."

"Okay," I said, "take that monster out into the hall and then you can talk to me about it."

"All right," he said. "I knew you wouldn't fail me."

But it couldn't be done. That miserable cayoodle refused to be separated from Schlingel even for a moment. He knew when he was cheek by jowl with an intellectual equal, and so when he was taken out into the hall he nearly broke down the panels of my door to get back to him. So what could I do?

I had to let him stay in the room while his master "broke his mind to me," as Shakespeare would have put it.

"All right," I said, "the place is already beginning to smell like a neglected dog kennel, so please make it snappy."

"You know my girl friend, Gussie?" Schlingel said.

"You mean *Gertrude*," I said. "Yes, I've met her three or four times. What about her?"

"I'm planning to marry her."

"*Mazeltov*," I said.

"Next year, I mean. You know she's very sensitive and her nerves are not really too good."

"I'm not surprised," I said. "What's Gertrude got to do with this?"

"It's *her* dog," he said. "She absolutely adores this dog, but her father can't stand him."

"I think Gertrude has terrible taste," I said, "which of course I always knew, but I'd like very much to meet her father. He sounds like a right guy to me."

"I'm sorry, but this is really not a matter for joking," he said. "You told me yourself that Gussie, I mean *Gertrude*, was a real surprise to you."

He was quite right. Gertrude was an honest-to-God Jewish beauty of the finest type, a Rachel or a Rebecca straight out of a Doré Bible. How she had ever gotten mixed up with a lummox like Schlingel was the thing that surprised me most about her.

"Gertrude is all right," I said, "but remember, I've had some earlier intimations that she was capable of being foolishly indiscriminate."

"Please, stop joking," he said. "This is a real crisis. You see, Gertrude just dotes on this dog, and finally her father gave her permission to keep it in the house, providing she kept it out of his way."

"I suppose it makes sense," I said, "if you happen to be pathologically fond of your daughter. Luckily *I* had only *sons*, so this particular problem never came up. If my boys were ever reckless enough to bring home a dog, I just chased them all the hell out into the street again. Anyway, what happened after the father gave this monster house room?"

"Gertrude kept *her* in the living room—it's a *she*—and the living room was the best place because the family only used it when company came. See? But then about a week ago a terrible trouble started. You know, Gertrude's father, Mr. Pomerantz, is a cantor in a synagogue. He's a very religious man, and very nearsighted too, and he absolutely refused to get himself new glasses, and so, about a week ago, every time he went out to *shul* he started falling over all kinds of dogs that were congregating all over his stoop. Every time he opened the door, about twenty dogs would start jumping all over him, and a couple of times they nearly knocked him down. You see, they live on the lower floor of a two-family house over in Queens, and when the stairs were always crowded with all those dogs, tearing at his clothes, it made him absolutely furious."

"I would gather from your comprehensive little outline," I said, "that this enchanting pet of Gertrude's was, and probably still is, in heat. Am I right?"

"Right! And the old man was just fit to be tied, of course, but Gertrude kept pleading with him that it would only last a few days, and to please be patient, and that everything would be all right in a little while."

"Aha! But this bitch got out somehow and got herself laid," I said. "Well, that's women for you, you can't keep them out of mischief once they've got their minds really set on it. Is that what happened?"

"No. Something much worse. Their house is located against a hillside, and the hill slopes up past their living-room windows. See what I mean?"

"Oh," I said, "so the male dogs got into the parlor and this little treasure of yours is now pregnant. Right?"

"No, it's nothing as simple as that. The dogs couldn't get into the living room either, because all the windows are barred. Her father had those bars especially put up against burglars. No. You know what those terrible dogs finally did? They urinated into the living room through an open window."

"They *what?!?!?*"

"That's exactly what they did. They must have been doing it for a whole week, too, and, what's more, they absolutely ruined the Pomerantz piano. The top was open and now the whole works are rusty. I saw it myself."

I roared like crazy, of course.

"You mean those frustrated pups got so furious they peed inside the piano? I've never in my life heard anything funnier."

"Neither have I, except that it's heartbreaking too," he said. "Gertrude's father nearly had a stroke when he found out about it."

"How *did* he find out?"

"He was vocalizing in the living room when one of the biggest dogs in the whole neighborhood lifted up his hind leg and let *him* have it."

"Well," I said, "you certainly must build your whole career around this little episode. I'll write you a monologue and you must tell it all just the way you told it to me—deadpan, I mean—and people will come from far and wide and pay good money to hear you tell it. It's the greatest night-club act anybody could possibly imagine. Remember to keep this dopey dog sitting at your feet while you're going through your routine, and Gertrude is sure to have a very rich husband one of these days."

"That's not what I came to see *you* for," he said.

"Oh yes, I forgot about that. What *did* you come to me for?"

"Gertrude is heartbroken, of course. The dog was disbarred

144

from the house, and things are just terrible. But Gertrude has a friend who was a waitress for the summer up in the Catskills, and she is coming back on Monday, and this girl offered to keep Flora, that's the dog's name, until we can find a permanent home for her. Incidentally, Gertrude wrote you a letter."

He handed me an envelope, and I must say I was suddenly very irritated with the unwarranted presumption of these people. In the envelope was a sheet of paper torn from a stenographic notebook and smack in the middle of it were just three words: "*Please?* Till Monday?"

"Well, Schlingel," I said, "you happen to be in luck. I'm going away for the weekend and you can sleep here with your pooch, if you like, but when I come home Monday afternoon I want you both out of here. I even want the *smell* of you to be gone by then. You understand?"

"You're a real friend," he said. "You're a friend to all of us. Flora, shake hands with the gentleman."

When I got back after the weekend, the dog was gone, but Schlingel was sitting at my desk with his big head buried in his arms as if he were sleeping or crying or something, and when he straightened himself out to face me he looked very much as if he'd been doing both! As he got up from the chair he also started to weave around in front of me as if he were drunk, and for a few moments I actually thought he was—particularly when he suddenly opened up his arms and screamed, "Kill me! Go on, please kill me!"

"I will," I said, "just as soon as I get my coat off. What happened, anyway? Did you drink that bottle of turpentine I had in the closet, or what?"

"Your manuscripts are gone!" he said in a sepulchral voice. "*My what?*"

I looked quickly toward the corner near my desk, and sure enough, the big box in which I usually kept all my papers had disappeared.

"That dog has eaten them up!" I said.

"No. Please sit down and let me tell you."

"Go on," I said.

"Please, sit down," he begged. "Please!"

He looked as if he was going to bust out crying, so I sat down on the edge of a chair.

"Go on!" I said.

"The dog *did* bother the box," he said. "She kept on chewing on the corners of it, and I was afraid she might do some harm, so . . ."

"Yes, so?"

"So I moved the box out into the hall, right in front of the door. When I got up the next morning, I thought I'd die—the box was gone. The janitor had taken it away. He thought it was just some garbage. Go ahead, *kill* me! *Kill* me, I deserve it!"

I'm not going to bother describing the next half hour to you. It is still something that brings an acute feeling of nausea to me whenever I think of it. Luckily I don't quite remember all the things I said and all the things I threatened. When I finally threw myself in deep exhaustion down on my bed, I suddenly remembered that Aron Gross, an old friend of mine, had some kind of job in the mayor's office down at City Hall at that time. So I quickly jumped up again, and after quite a bit of trouble I finally managed to get Aron on the telephone. With as much composure as an utterly distraught man was able to muster, I proceeded to brief him about my grotesque tragedy.

"I've got the manuscripts of three plays in that box," I told him, "and also six longish articles that I was just getting ready to mail out. But the worst of it is, I had an almost completed book in there too, a book I may never get around to doing again. It represents almost two full years of work. Don't you see? Please, please, in God's name, do what you can about it!"

He wasn't very encouraging. "You know how much garbage is collected in New York every day," he said. "Well, that'll give you an idea what we're up against."

"Can *I* be of any help at all?" I asked. "Please tell me what to do, and no matter how slim the chance may be I'll be glad to do my damndest."

"I'll call you back later," he said.

He did, too, and, by using a great deal of influence and by pulling a lot of wires, he finally succeeded in getting Schlingel and me aboard those horrendous garbage scows that permanently poison the air in Lower New York Bay. It was perhaps pointless and idiotic, but I couldn't just stand idly by while my precious manuscripts were being smothered in schmutz and in ashes before being dumped into the sea.

Ashes! That was the word that kept me going. I was determined to arise again, like a phoenix?

Dig?

So Schlingel and I were equipped with rubber boots that reached up to our hips, and the next morning we proceeded to sort out six and a half million tons of garbage. On the friendly advice of some kind sanitation official I even hired twenty bums at two dollars apiece to overhaul the most likely spots with us.

You can't imagine all I saw, and all I smelled, in the next two days. Schlingel, like a soul in purgatory, labored harder than all of us combined, and it came home to me again that the sincere contrition of a genuine idiot is one of the most depressing sights that this world can possibly offer. After the first day I got so sick looking at him that I finally persuaded Gertrude to lead him away.

After forty-eight hours, I also gave up.

Gone were my witty, brilliant plays that would have startled Broadway and would unquestionably have earned me a neat fortune. Forever lost were the trenchant, critical articles that were destined to revolutionize the whole literary spectrum. And, saddest of all, my nearly completed book, three hundred and twelve pages of my immortal memoirs, were, at one stroke, grimly denied to a now sadly pauperized posterity.

At last you know why the pages you are now reading did not see publication sixteen years ago.

However, posterity can brighten its face, and relax from its regrets. It is all here, including this chapter, which, for obvious reasons, was not included in the original manuscript.

CHAPTER ELEVEN

AND NOW, how about the Baroness von Freytag
Lornighofen? Well, how about her?

She was a great gal, one of the best, and when I heard a few
years ago that she'd knocked herself off in Paris I was damned
upset about it. Yes, she went out in a deadly smell of cooking
gas, and I understand her dog Pinkie went right along with
her. He always did. I suppose he's frolicking around with Cer-
berus and the Unicorn in an empty lot somewhere, while his
mistress is lying in a hammock in the shade of some asphodels
and taking herself some long, cool drinks of forgetfulness—I
hope.

She's got plenty to forget, too, poor girl. She had an awfully bad time of it the last ten or fifteen years of her life. I saw
her a couple of times in Berlin and in Paris and she always

talked about the good old days in New York—and, believe me, even those good old days of hers would have seemed pretty impoverished to a leaner imagination.

The Baroness used to be my part-time model during the early twenties, and although she was certainly no chicken even then, she still had one of the finest figures of any doll posing anywhere in New York at that time. She was tall and strong but very, very feminine all the same—an Amazon with two fine breasts and a voice like a two-edged sword to go with that fabulous figure of hers.

What's more, the Baroness was quite talented on her own account. She wrote excellent verse and was, to her own undoing, passionately and desperately in love with all the arts— and much too many artists, I'm afraid.

Only artists.

No one else need apply.

She modeled for some of us to make herself a small living, and far too few ever realized that she had more brains and more ready wit than most of the people she was modeling for.

Her eyes were the eyes of a suddenly unhooded falcon. Her hair was a smooth satin cap coming down just a little below her ears, and the color of that hair changed almost daily, to suit her mood or her current infatuation. She was wonderfully whimsical and inventive as no other woman or her day, and like all the choosen ones of this world she suffered from a terrible blemish which occasionally almost shattered the smooth façade of her bronze fortitude.

She had three teeth missing—right in front of her jaw, where it couldn't be hidden, where it was instantly visible. In her vain effort to hide it, her smile had become like the grimace of a profound ague. Endless numbers of people had given her money to repair this ruin but throughout the many years that I knew her nothing ever came of it. She needed the money for new clothes; for food for herself and Pinkie; for a new, illustrated edition of *Hunger* by Knut Hamsun; for a beautiful musical instrument she was going to learn; for a vacation near a quiet lake which would remind her of Bavaria. You see, there were just too many other desperate urgencies to be appeased with those pitiful little sums, and so the teeth just had to wait; and I believe she finally went to her grave without them.

She wrote some remarkable poems. I remember one called "Hamlet of the Wedding Ring, or, The Cast-Iron Lover." It was a pretty long affair, too, written in great anger against the poet William Carlos Williams, with whom she had fallen hopelessly in love. It was hopeless because Mr. Williams was not only a poet, he was a physician out in Rutherford, New Jersey, of all places. He was also happily married, and his wife and his two children lived with him in a fine house out in that small town. What's more, he hadn't the vaguest intention of giving up either his practice or his domestic felicity to play satyr to the Baroness' nymphomania.

A drag. A real drag.

Not that the Baroness herself gave any kind of a damn for the doctor's injudicious connubial commitments. If you're a poet and you're in love, then the world better beware! You don't throw Love over your shoulder just because you happen to be married. That's only common sense, isn't it?

But Dr. Williams didn't quite see it that way. Naturally, the Baroness was indignant. "He fooled me with that Hispanic middle name of his," she wailed. " 'Carlos'! Pfui! He hasn't any right to that 'Carlos.' It is a fraud, a deception, a no-thorough-fare. He got that name because his grandmother was Spanish; but he is *nothing! Nothing!* He is a petty bourgeois, a New Jersey Don Juan who should be running a gasoline station. But I will get even with him!"

Margaret Anderson tells in her autobiography about the

Baroness' grief and her fury at that time. I saw her frequently during this catastrophic period and I remember particularly that one day she shaved off all her hair and lacquered her head with an intense shade of bright magenta. I can tell you, it was quite startling. Well, then, in this condition she went out to Rutherford, New Jersey, and planted herself smack in the front seat of the doctor's car, which was parked right at the foot of his lawn.

We shall never know what the neighbors actually thought of that truculent pink-domed picket. All we know is that there were no unpleasant outward repercussions of any sort, because Dr. Williams was always one of the best-loved and most deeply esteemed members of that little community. After all, the citizens had managed to overlook the fact that he *wrote* books of *poetry*, and so an additional piece of eccentricity on the part of one of his incalculable friends was hardly worth calling a town meeting about.

After a couple of rainy days the Baroness was finally persuaded by some of her intimates to give up her fruitless vigil and to ennoble her classic rancor through the medium of art.

She agreed. She went home, relacquered her head to a deep green and wrote "Hamlet of the Wedding Ring, or, The Cast-Iron Lover."

And now you can understand the true significance of that poignant little title.

The last time I saw the Baroness in this country, I had an appointment with her at a Village restaurant. Surprisingly enough, she was late. I say "surprisingly" because she was quite Teutonic on the subject of punctuality and prided herself inordinately on keeping a meticulous time schedule.

When she finally arrived she simply spluttered with fury, and, judging by her disheveled appearance, she had obviously suffered a sudden mishap of some sort.

"What's wrong?" I asked. "Did somebody run you down, or what?"

Her eyes were aflame, she bridled and puffed at the world at large, and, as always when she got very angry, her German accent got the better of her otherwise carefully groomed locution.

"Dose svine!" she hissed. "Dose filty svine! Ugh, it iss unbearable. It iss dissgusting!"

"What happened?" I said. "Did you get bumped by a car? Or what?"

"Oh, no, it iss too annoying. It iss the last vord! It iss *abscheulich!*"

"In God's name, what happened to you?"

"Tree sailors grebbed me, you hear? Dey grebbed me and dregged me into a hallvay, and dey wiolated me! Dat's what heppened!"

"They *violated* you? Why didn't you scream for help or something?"

"I couldn't. Dey were choking me vit deir elbows. Dey were on top off me before I could open my mouse. You understand?"

"I'm terribly sorry," I said. "Here, Baroness, let's get you a drink, and maybe you better lie down for a couple of hours."

"Oh de dirty bums!" she went on. "Jumping on top off me, like vild enimels. But dey vill regret it for de rest of deir lifes. Hah!"

"Did you have them arrested, or what?"

"Oh, no. I ren off as fest as I could. But dey'll regret it just de same, because now—now dey'll all heff *syphiliss,* dose dirty besterds!"

As you see, a real lady, with no nonsense about her.

Before I came up to the country a few weeks ago, I stopped at her old apartment on West Eighth Street, because a couple of other friends of mine live there now. The Chumpties. That's not their real name, of course. His real name is Guido Rumpert, and she was originally called Stella Wallace, or Wall-ass, but since she's put on quite a bit of weight she's called Chubby. Collectively, the Chumpties. They are artists. What else? They generally exhibit their stuff in the Village *outdoor* shows; that'll give you an idea. Rumpty mostly makes charcoal likenesses of people who pose for him right out on the street, while Chubby specializes in portraits of cats and dogs. Once she even made a sepia wash drawing of a tame hamster. If hard-pressed, she can produce batik lamp shades and even belts and pocketbooks with peasant embroidery, and once, when things got really tough, she cooked up great batches of homemade candy which they placed on sale in all the Village tourist joints.

In short, they're an accomplished couple, and the only danger they face is fatty degeneration of the heart, because they both eat too damned much. If you go up to them for a meal you emerge covered with butter from head to foot and you can't breathe normally for hours afterward. They cook Chinese, Armenian, Greek or Hindu grub, or anything else that requires a lot of complicated preparations and endless running around for the various ingredients. The one thing I've never been served in their house is a steak. Too easy. So naturally I'm very fond of them.

I suppose I ought to mention that if Rumpty just took off his beret and shaved off his curly reddish-blond beard, he'd look like any other overfed delicatessen-store owner. Chubby, on the other hand, despite being overweight, still retains some of the looks that made her the favorite model up at the Art Students' League about ten years ago. Her tight curly almost-black hair has never been fried in any beauty parlor and her lovely pink-and-white complexion owes nothing whatever to the lockjawed, constipated chatter dished out by the Revlon girls. Chubby's just too fat, that's all.

Anyway, when I dropped in on them the other night Professor Haupt was there and Lennie Corten, a painter friend of ours, had also obviously just finished dinner with the

Chumpties. They all looked as if they were ready to be tapped for oil, and no wonder: Chubby had just dished them up an eight-course Haitian meal with a Levantine dessert made of dates, walnuts, crushed almonds and sour cream.

So they sat around puffing like a lot of landlocked whales, waiting for me to entertain them, I suppose. Actually I had gone to their apartment because Rumpty had phoned me earlier in the afternoon and begged me to come around to discuss some impending business matters with them. I had come over not because my advice in business matters could be of the slightest value to anyone, but because the idea of Rumpty mixed up in any form of commercial enterprise was too beguiling for me to resist.

Well, after they had offered me a lot of dishes I'm not allowed to eat, the big business promotion was finally unveiled by Rumpty.

"We've got a chance," he said, "to better our street location and to move over to Sixth Avenue with our outdoor display, and I wanted your considered opinion on this pretty ambitious little scheme of ours."

"Not just Sixth Avenue," said Chubby. "It's to move between *two banks*, right near Waverly Place."

"Between *two banks*," said Rumpty, "and we'd like to hear what you all think of such a move."

"Those places are all taken," said Lennie. "I know all the people who are squatting there right now."

"That is true," said Rumpty, "but one of these squatters, as you call them, is thinking of going abroad, and, for a certain financial consideration, something might be arranged."

"They can't charge you *anything*," said Lennie. "They have no right to sublease, to sublet, or to promise you a goddamned thing. I think you'll just get stuck for your money, that's my opinion."

"I've looked into it very carefully," said Chubby, "and

you're right, in a general way, but I've got good reason to think that it *can* be arranged. Besides, we wouldn't have to pay until after we're in possession. That's been agreed."

"How much would it cost you?" asked Professor Haupt.

"Sixty dollars," said Rumpty, "to be paid in three equal installments."

"*Man!* Sixty smackers, that's a hell of a lot of charcoal portraits, ain't it?" said Lennie.

Lennie Corten fancies himself a simple, down-to-earth type. As a matter of fact, he looks very artistic—crew haircut, Amish beard, fishnet shirt and stuff—and he is definitely allied to the Guts school of art, of which Boshko is the most articulate exponent. Lennie likes to put his feet up on tables, for instance, even if that happens to be the most uncomfortable position in the whole room, but he is otherwise really quite harmless. He paints landscapes which are reminiscent of Henri, Glackens, Coleman and Sloan—the old ashcan school, if you remember; but because Lennie is too young to have belonged to that original group, he contents himself with cleaning up whatever garbage has been overlooked by those old ex-Villagers.

"I'll tell you what our problem really is," continued Rumpty. "It is this: *Will* we be making a definite improvement in our prospects if we *do* decide to make such a move? You understand, the assumption we make is that to be located between two banks is going to be of definite financial advantage to us. *That* is the question—will it be profitable to us, in the long run, to be sort of vaguely associated with all those scads of rampant money in back of us. See what I mean?"

"First of all," said Corten, "that money is far from rampant. Just try to lay your hands on some of it, and see what happens. I admit that the location has a certain amount of class—the brass tablets, the smooth stone façade and all that—but it's my experience, after four years on the Street, that you can't ever figure what goes on in the heads of those dizzy squirrels that come down here to look at our pictures. You know, one of the biggest businesses down here is done by guys who stack their stuff up against trees or wooden fences. I suppose it reminds those browsers of Montparnasse or Montmartre, maybe, and yet I'd bet my neck that not one out of a hundred among those saps has ever been even as far as Staten Island."

"I'm wondering," said the professor, "whether people going to banks to deposit their money are more inclined to buy pictures than people who are just idling by, with a vague intention of *perhaps* buying something."

"Aha!" said Rumpty. "There you have it! That is the critical fulcrum of the whole problem. Very happily phrased, Professor. Very happily phrased."

"People also *draw* money *out* of banks," said Chubby. "They often stand right in the doorway to count it. I've seen them."

"Exactly!" said Rumpty, who was obviously enjoying himself. "They stand in the street *counting* their money, and right alongside of them all sorts of wonderfully tempting things are on display that for a small sum can instantly enrich their whole lives. Right?"

"I've got a funny feeling," I said, "that the people who patronize those banks are *local* people. That is to say, they're Village artists, or Village storekeepers—not exactly a group from which you have reason to expect a lot of patronage."

"That is true," admitted Rumpty. "Well, Chubbs, my darling, what do *you* think?"

"I like the location," said Chubby. "As Lennie says, it has class."

"Ah, there's my darling for you," said Rumpty, giving her an affectionate pat on the behind. "She's all for class. Well, let's do it, then. Let's move into the circle of general solvency

157

and see if the change of climate will improve *our* financial health too."

"I'd like you to remember," said the professor, "that *one* of those banks is strictly a *savings* bank, which means that people come there *especially* to deposit their funds or to withdraw certain predetermined sums for carefully calculated expenditures."

"I'm afraid, Professor," said Rumpty, rather somberly, "yes, I'm very much afraid, that your stupendously accurate deduction has just fatally pricked the scintillating splendor of our shining, big hope bubble. My darling, I'm sorry to say I think the professor is right. I think it is a foregone conclusion that the soberly thrifty clients of a savings bank are not likely to interrupt their calculated and mundane doings just to sit down impulsively on the Sixth Avenue sidewalk to have their portraits painted."

"I guess you're right," said Chubby, nibbling on a peppermint. "I suppose we'll just have to stick where we are, and maybe we'll just hang up a couple of shawls, or something."

"Right!" said Rumpty. "So it is unanimous, isn't it? We *don't* move. All those in favor say aye!"

We all said, "Aye."

"That would be quite a headline for *Variety*, wouldn't it?" said Rumpty. " 'Chumpties Nix Banks!' "

"Wait till the *Wall Street Journal* hears about this," said Corten. "It's liable to knock the bottom right out of that bull market."

And then we adjourned.

As you see, it was a typical Village business proposition, full of incalculables.

While I walked home from the Chumpties it occurred to me how crowded with memories all those streets and houses along the way—MacDougal Alley, Waverly Place, Washington Mews and all the rest—were for me, how many dear people, mostly dead now, had walked alongside me in the past, and how difficult it is for us few anomalous survivors to reproduce the easy texture of the carefree lives we once lived all along these pleasant thoroughfares.

It was at 62 Washington Mews that I first met the late Muriel Draper. She was ageless as the Pyramids, fervent as a revivalist, and as feminine as Nell Brinkley. She was as full of surprises as a Christmas stocking, too, and had a fabulously sharp wit, as many well-stuffed truffles frequently learned to their cost. She was the official hostess at that party of mine that I told you about earlier, the one which I gave to welcome George Grosz to this country. The whole idea of this get-together was to help George sell some pictures, of course, and although I was married at the time, my wife seemed just a little too young and inexperienced to handle two hundred and fifty guests singlehanded. Since those far-off days the dear girl has grown so much in poise and social stature that at this moment one could safely entrust her to run a durbar at Delhi, but we were both a lot younger then, so I hied myself up to our friend Muriel Draper's hoping that I could persuade her to help us out. I remember I had prepared a sort of tentative guest list and when I got to her place I showed it to her. She looked at it through her lorgnette and I could see at once that she seemed deeply perplexed.

"Dear boy," she said, "for what hour of the day is this festival of yours planned, anyway?"

"Around five," I said. "Five to seven or seven-thirty maybe. Why?"

She looked at me stony-faced.

"My dear child," she said, "I've just casually skimmed over your guest list and it is quite obvious to me that you're just moonshining along without the slightest reference to the *facts*."

"The facts?" I said. "What are the facts?"

159

"The facts are that you can't invite a lot of *evening* people to an *afternoon* party. That's just common sense, isn't it?"

I tell you, suddenly I felt like an absolute fool, an upstart, a clumsy pfoosher who is crowding himself into an area where his betters have for centuries been carrying wrist watches instead of sundials. Yes, until that moment I had never even realized that there were certain people abroad in the land who didn't even *materialize* until after it got dark. I instantly understood, however, how utterly right she was in her diagnosis, and I congratulated myself on my dumb luck that this great lady was willing to put all her vast experience in such matters freely at my disposal.

"And you aren't asking any *freaks*, either," she said. "Not a *single* freak, so far."

"Freaks?" I said weakly.

"Of course! Somebody who wears a silver dollar instead of a monocle in his eye, or a frying pan in lieu of a purse. You've just got to have a few honest-to-God freaks, or your guests will just stand around and bore each other to death, don't you see?"

I just want you to realize that such constructive criticism would have been entirely beyond the scope of a superannuated saddlebag like Elsa Maxwell.

At any rate, I don't have to tell you that these ghastly omissions of mine were all properly looked into and rectified by the time the invitations were finally sent out, and that party of mine eventually turned out to be the smash sensation of the whole artistic winter season. You can be sure that nobody arrived at our saturnalia until after sundown, and nobody left it until the following morning.

You can also be sure that George Grosz, the hero of the occasion, didn't sell a single one of his fine pictures.

But *I* at least profited greatly by this experience. I learned, and just in time, too, that I had been foolishly subscribing to a

160

popular but nevertheless flagrant piece of scientific fallacy. You see, I had seriously believed—I must say I'd believed it on the authority of the greatest zoologists extant—that man, the camel and the tawny pipit were all diurnal animals; that is to say, they functioned effectively in the daytime and rested from their labors at night. Well, by means of just sixteen words and a couple of significantly raised eyebrows, Muriel Draper had once and for all brought home to me the great truth that man is all too often as helplessly nocturnal as his other cousins the lemur, the skunk and the vampire bat.

CHAPTER TWELVE

EVERYBODY IN HIS RIGHT MIND knows that Communism is a hell of a way of life. We can see, all over the world, what happens to people who are unfortunate enough to fall, one way or another, under its religiously doctrinaire form of thralldom. Some of us even knew all this from 'way, 'way back and therefore never had any recanting or public breast-beating about it. So?

So I'd like to make plain at once that that still doesn't make unhampered, catch-as-catch-can capitalism into a snow-white maiden without fault or blemish. Not by a damn sight it doesn't.

What constantly brings this to my mind is the fact that the publishers and editors of *Life, Time* and *Fortune*, for instance, do unremittingly sponsor the notion that to lack faith in capitalism and all its works is tantamount to spitting at the holy source of divine wisdom itself, because man can surely never hope to aspire to any nobler spiritual plateau than the expectation of a minimum of six per cent interest on invested capital. They have made a career of ignoring the evidence that the steel companies, the automobile manufacturers and the mine owners of this earth fought brutally and savagely to maintain an inhumanly long working day, and that collective bargaining is a very recent innovation indeed. All the large-scale employers the world over had to be shoved and mauled into grudging decency by long-overdue labor legislation that each one of them resisted and fought until the very last sound of their mildewed alarm bugles had died out over the swamps of medievalism.

You can read it yourself; it's all on the record.

I know all about the Ford Foundation, the Rockefeller Researches, the General Motors Munificence, and all the other philanthropic and quasi-altruistic giveaway programs of big industry; the fact is that all these people had a dreadful past to wipe out of the public mind, and a great deal of their lavish spending can fairly be written off to new, enlightened policies in the field of public relations. Also, let's face it, a good chunk of that dough would have to go to the government in taxes anyway.

However, the sponsors and editors of *Life, Time* and *Fortune* believe, or pretend to believe, that capitalism is a naturally benign and almost instinctively public-spirited development in human affairs, and anybody who doubts this is automatically antisocial, anticivilization and antidemocratic.

I don't know why I pick on these particular three magazines, though, since the country is certainly lousy with publications that year in and year out sponsor the same nauseating, mendacious drivel.

Yesterday somebody left a copy of *Look* on my hall table,

and, as I riffled through the pages, I made myself a few random notes which I planned to expand later on in the week. But I've changed my mind about it, and I'll just offer you a few of my unedited thoughts.

This issue of *Look* contained, among other things, an interview with Bertrand Russell, some advice by Norman Vincent Peale, a biographical sketch of Pat Boone and a color portrait of Dürer's father.

As I looked at this mélange I jotted down the following comments:

Dürer's Father
Obviously a heart heavy with the guilt of having sired an immortal son.

Pat Boone
An underdone potato pancake who has happily fallen into a puddle of warm buttermilk.

Bertrand Russell
An old eagle looking compassionately down on mankind from the high eyrie of his lonely wisdom.

Norman Vincent Peale
A rancid lump of peanut butter, sweating with unmotivated optimism.

And that's about the size of it.

If you are a consistent magazine reader, the chances are you are probably involved with one of these pieces of dreck with some regularity, anyway, so I'm not telling you anything new about them.

Of course, there are a few better sheets around, such as *The Atlantic, Harper's, The Paris Review* and, I suppose, best of all, *The New Yorker*. But even this last one quite frequently stinks up the neighborhood and in recent years has fallen into a sad state of decline. I'm afraid they too are finally perishing of the familiar state of creative dystrophy that has settled the hash of a lot of their distinguished predecessors.

The New Yorker crowd, by the way, were always a pretty strange lot to work for even in the days of their greatest creative puissance. I once wrote a profile of Rose O'Neill for them, which they printed, sometime in the early thirties, and the writing of that piece gave me a terrifying glimpse into the peculiar working methods that obtained up there.

Their offices used to be at 25 West Forty-fifth Street, in that same building where I once sold covers to Mencken and Nathan, and where, later on, I did some cartoons for *The Saturday Review of Literature*.

I remember I went up to meet Harold Ross, their editor, accompanied by Alec Woollcott, a very dear and loyal friend of mine, and I must say that Ross, on first sight, was quite a shock to me. However you looked at it, *The New Yorker* was certainly a damned hep magazine, and the chief editor of this witty and sometimes even scintillating sheet turned out to be an obvious yokel. I never much changed my mind about him —not *much*. I finally decided that it probably helped him to be a good editor for a magazine with such a formidable name, since he certainly never seemed to get over his amazement at the multiple facets of this rich and astonishing city. He had other qualities too, of course, but let's not kid ourselves, he never did become part of the lively social, artistic and intellectual life that was fermenting all around him. He *met* everybody who mattered, that's for sure, but he remained the permanently astonished and insecure kid from Aspen, Colorado. As I said before, this was probably one of his greatest assets, just as later on, on *Life* magazine, the photographers from Berlin and Paris invariably brought in the best pictures of New York, simply because they never grew weary of seeing and recording new and fascinating aspects of a town to which we natives had already become all too blasé.

Anyway, I suggested to Ross that I'd like to write a profile of Rose O'Neill, the inventor of the Kewpie doll. He liked the idea, although it was obvious from the start that he didn't particularly care about *me*. I'm a real city weed and I guess I must have rubbed him the wrong way by some remark that I could certainly never have gotten printed in his magazine. Whatever the hell it was, Woollcott noticed that I had somehow bothered Ross, and so after we'd left the office of the magazine he hardly spoke to me at all.

Just before we separated on Fifth Avenue, he said, "Of course, as usual, you've made a terrible impression. Well, at least you've antagonized somebody who is even more annoying than you are. I'm sorry I won't be there to see you demoralize each other. I'll have my broker reserve a double plot at Woodlawn for you boys, unless you happen to be particularly partial to cremation."

To tell you the truth, I never got under Ross's skin at all. It was *he* who whittled away at *my* composure during the next few weeks, until I nearly puked all over him at one of our frequent meetings.

It was all about the profile, of course. For all I know, you may never even have heard anything about Rose O'Neill. Well, she was quite a talented illustrator, to begin with, and sold her first drawings to a magazine called *Puck* which flourished and even prospered during the first two decades of this century. I was told that she used to arrive at the *Puck* offices always accompanied by a nun because they accepted her first contribution when she was only a teen-age kid in a convent school. The editor of the magazine during those years was a man called Harry Leon Wilson, who'd written some damned funny books in his day; you may even have heard of one of them, called *Ruggles of Red Gap*, that was made into a fine movie with Charles Laughton in the leading role.

At any rate, Wilson later told me that he got quite stuck on young Rose O'Neill, but that he had himself a hell of a time sneaking mash notes to her under the eyes of her alert duennas. But he eventually must have managed it somehow, because he married Rosie and even lived with her for a number of years.

But that's beside the point.

What made the O'Neill career an American phenomenon was her invention of the Kewpie doll. It seems that Rose had actually been doodling away at this same little darling since her very earliest childhood, but then, quite suddenly, one day a doll manufacturer popped up from the swamps of the novelty business and offered to make three-dimensional versions of it. Luckily someone in Rose's entourage advised her to hold out for a royalty arrangement—urged her to gamble on an eventual volume sale rather than accept an immediate cash settlement.

And that's what she did. She also insisted on modeling the original Kewpie herself, since she had always been a rather adroit sculptress and had, as a matter of fact, been fooling with clay and plasticine figures long before any novelty entrepreneurs had appeared across her horizon.

The rest is mystery.

I suppose the doll manufacturer hoped to sell, in the course of years, a few thousand of these poppets to the kids around the country. If so, he made a truly stupendous miscalculation, the most profitable miscalculation of all time. America—that is to say, *grownup* America—just took this ossified hunk of peach ice cream so completely to its heart that for many, many years you couldn't enter anybody's home without finding at least one of them in possession of some conspicuous part of the family living room, of all places.

I've never been able to estimate accurately how many

167

millions of dollars Rose actually garnered from the creation of her little masterpiece, but one thing is certain, that all the sculptors in the whole world from Phidias to Rodin never managed to earn *collectively* more than a tiny percentage of the amount she finally extracted out of that dimpled bonanza.

But all this would still have been only another banal American success story. What lifted it completely out of the rut of the familiarly unique was the astonishing personality of Miss O'Neill herself. You see, she remained quite unspoiled by her phonomenal success—or, more correctly, she was already so fantastically eccentric to begin with that she never even blinked when that mad shower of mazuma suddenly decended on her. She accepted it as a logical extension of a long-familiar daydream. Rose was an honest-to-God pixie whose behavior had always been activated by a highly unpredictable if somewhat sirupy imagination, and now, when she finally had enough money to do as she pleased, she was at last able to carry out some of her farfetched and sometimes even quite deadly whimsies.

Let me tell you something about her appearance. When I first met her, she was a plumpish, fair-haired, pink-and-white bundle of tallowy undulance—a sort of grownup Kewpie with all of the Kewpie doll's inane, helpless appeal. In the many years that I knew her I never saw her dressed in anything but velvet, and most of the gowns she wore were encumbered with long, dust-scattering trains. Some of these drags of hers often trailed as much as six feet behind her, and when, in her chatelaine manner, she sometimes ambled across an autumn lawn, she would stir up as many dead grasshoppers and dried leaves as a motor-driven power rake.

So much for the rear.

In front, these creations of hers were likely to be speckled with a picturesque scattering of food and fruit stains, because most of the time Rosie's pale-blue vision was so far off scanning the distant mountaintops of fairyland that she simply couldn't be bothered to keep track of such vulgar, splashy things as mere bean soup and prune juice. This sloppy method of feeding, by the way, was something she had in common with Charles II, Napoleon III and Henry VIII. Also, like these distinguished forerunners, she was hopelessly addicted to lace fichus, feathery jabots and wide-meshed flouncy cuffs of all sorts. It stands to reason that all of this spidery haberdashery of hers used to get snagged in everything she ever touched or handled, but she always would stand very indulgently by while her adoring followers busily extricated her from the threatening tentacles of toasting forks, filigree muffin bells and three-tiered Etruscan candelabra.

She lived out in the suburbs in a house called Carabas Castle (after "Puss in Boots"), and in the cellar of this dwelling I saw an enormous steam boiler which had been especially cast for her in the shape of a Kewpie doll. When she had originally taken possession of this mansion sixteen years before, somebody, in turning on the lights, had accidentally broken off the wall switch, and so the lights had remained on during all those years, and they were certainly still burning when I looked back at the house for the last time.

Rose had a favorite cat which had six toes on each foot and which came to her room through a private little six-inch door every morning and placed a dead bird at the foot of her bed, as a greeting for the day.

One evening she decided to read us some of her poetry (not really bad, either) and, naturally, quite a crowd was gathered in her living room to share in this special treat. She was standing in front of the fireplace, in which an enormous log fire was blazing, and, shortly after she had started reading, the always alarming odor of burning cloth seemed suddenly to permeate the religiously attentive silence of the room.

Sure enough, the end of her goddamned train had flounced

'way inside that red-hot grate, and the lace on it had already begun to smoke like a sputtering time fuse. Because I was sitting quite a distance away from Operation Tail Burn, I just jumped up from my seat and began to wave hysterically at her like a demented windmill, but she didn't pay me the slightest mind. Not only that, but she looked at me rather reproachfully a couple of times and went right on with her childishly cadenced chanting.

I was absolutely stunned.

I really thought I was losing my mind.

Was it possible that among the twenty-some-odd assembled nitwits in that room, not a single one had noticed that our hostess was any minute about to go up in flames? Was that really possible?

Obviously it was.

Well, when I couldn't stand it any longer, I finally just had to yell at her myself.

"Rose!" I screamed. "Rose! Your dress is on fire! Take a look at it! It's smoking like crazy!"

She glanced calmly, almost disdainfully, down at that crackling tail of hers and with one queenly gesture swished it out of the furnace. Then, quite unalarmed, more like a Spanish dancer doing a flamenco, she stepped on the still burning frills a couple of times, looked up at me reproachfully, and quietly went on with her reading.

And that was that.

It was more than poise; it was marmoreal composure in the line of fire. I'd never seen anything like it.

What's more, I was fully aware that everyone in that room simply loathed me for that tactless piece of interruption, and later on, when refreshments were served, nobody bothered to offer me even a tuna fish sandwich.

I think I ought to point out to you that Rose didn't just quietly sit still and rake in the kale from those Kewpie dolls

170

alone. No, sir. She did a lot of illustrating for the Hearst papers, for *Good Housekeeping*, and for a lot of other women's magazines all over the country. It was a real never-never-land existence she had, and the only time I ever saw her really deeply depressed and heard her speak with accents of unmistakable sorrow was when I happened to refer to the First World War.

"I lost many dear ones in it," she said. "They went down in the English Channel, poor things. I was so prostrated at the time that my life was despaired of."

"Were they relatives, or friends?" I said.

"Kewpies!" she said. "*Bisque* Kewpies, the first ones ever made out of that wonderful material. They were made in Germany and were on their way over to me when a whole shipload of them went down in the English Channel. Those terrible British torpedoed the lot of them. It is too awful to think about. Oh, that war! I've never really gotten over it. I don't think I ever *shall!*"

I think Kewpies became so popular in this country not only because they were so nauseatingly cute but because they were quite completely bereft of gender. Almost every American home in those years had one of those pudgy pink fetishes standing on its mantelpiece, and if anybody happened to lift up its tutu there was no embarrassment involved. Those sexless horrors must have filled some deep psychic need in the hearts of American mothers, who always fear and tremble at the slightest sign of any gender awareness on the part of their children, particularly their sons. In short, Kewpie was the ideal American child—it had no genitals.

So, at any rate, I wrote my profile of Rose O'Neill and discovered almost at once that I'd made a terrible mistake in the choice of my subject. Harold Ross seems all through his life to have had a rather peculiar and special relationship to women, which naturally preconditioned him to loathe almost every-

171

thing I had to say about them. Among other things, I think, he felt rather chivalrous toward most of them, that is to say he divided them into two clear-cut types—they were either on top of a pedestal or lying under a sofa. And so he was sincerely worried that my little opus was going to hurt Miss O'Neill's feelings. When I assured him that she'd read every word of my piece and didn't really give a damn what I wrote about her, he seemed even more distressed.

"It might, just the same, upset a lot of other women," he said. "You talk very careless, you know."

And so it went.

I rewrote that wretched profile about fourteen times and Ross submitted it each time to his assorted hatchet men, henchmen and shamuses, until there was practically nothing left of the original impetus that had given it any worth. I finally wrote it out in triple space, and every frustrated hypochondriac who worked at *The New Yorker* scribbled suggestions and criticisms between my typed lines until the sheer mass of their splenetic pedantry nearly drove me wild.

But that wasn't all. I discovered later on that some of these boys had bitterly loathed each other for many years, and that they often used the manuscripts of innocent contributors to lash out at each other with satirical asides that had no connection whatever with the pieces that they were supposed to be editing. My own article was finally full of so much petty backbiting and interoffice rancor that it was practically impossible to make head or tail of the original script. These gruesome sadists eventually ignored my piece altogether and just concentrated all their pent-up frenzy on criticism of each other's criticisms.

A great little outfit to work for, as you can see.

You may think they were just cunningly trying to get rid of me, and doing it by a long-perfected system of collaborative editorial strategy, that's all. Nonsense. Unless you were al-

172

ready a well-known name before you ever came around to them, they gave the same meat-chopper treatment to everybody who happened to fall into their psychopathic bailiwick. I know for a fact that a lot of their writers finally got so used to this form of savagery they actually couldn't live without it, and a good many of these dreary masochists were ever afterward unable to work for anybody else.

They behaved even worse to illustrators. I myself heard Miguel Covarrubias tell one of their editors to go to hell, after he told Miguel to do a cover drawing over again for the third time.

No, that was just their ordinary paranoid system of operation, and no personal malice against *me* was involved. That is to say, they loathed *everybody*, including me, but not *especially* me, in any case.

Somehow I did stick it out with Rose O'Neill just the same, and, in the end, a completely devitalized, castrated and embalmed version of my piece was printed. I never had the hardihood to look at that macerated disaster in their goddamned pages. I just checked it all off as so much noodle pudding down the publishing drain and forgot about it.

I don't know how they function up there nowadays. All I know is that they're obviously encouraging their writers and artists to freely plagiarize each other. Most of the new names signed to the work in their pages are practically interchangeable, excepting maybe on the stuff about somebody's childhood among the penguins in Antarctica or the pygmies in the Ituri Forest. I still look at it once in a while because I like to read Perelman, Salinger, White, Thurber, Liebling and Wilson, and because the drawings by Arno, Addams, Frueh and Darrow are still just as much fun as they were twenty-five years ago.

CHAPTER THIRTEEN

Wʜᴇɴ ɪ ᴡᴀs ᴀ ᴄʜɪʟᴅ ɪɴ Vɪᴇɴɴᴀ, about fifty years ago, there were hardly any republics loose in the world at all. France, Switzerland, the United States and San Marino were the only ones I ever heard about; and, unless my memory is playing me tricks, there was a certain geographical condition called Andorra, where the divine right of kings had also been inexplicably usurped by mere drab civilians. But for all I know, this whole business may well be just a retroactive illusion sprung from my subsequent stamp-collecting days.

At any rate, my own country, Austria, and the kingdoms and principalities submissive to it, as well as the countries adjacent to us, were in those distant years constantly atwitter with royal baptisms, royal weddings, royal coronations and, frequently enough, royal mayhem and assassinations too. These latter, called regicides, I believe, were, to my juvenile mind, despite their common occurrence, never quite properly accounted for. I finally concluded that there must be at large in the world certain flagrantly hairy individuals who suffered sudden incalculable urges to fling matutinal bombs under the glittering carriages of passing potentates. I was even more puzzled by the fact that a few of these moody practitioners would occasionally even hurl crude, homemade explosives into the chamber pots of middle-aged princely concubines.

As you can see, there were really lively goings-on in those days, and so it is no wonder that I became an avid reader of newspapers at the age of six. What got me into the habit of reading so early were the fabulous illustrations that were featured in these journals. I just couldn't seem to learn soon enough what the hell all those astonishing pictures were all about. You see, photoengraving hadn't been perfected yet, and so these designs were all still manually executed by certain skilled master craftsmen who obviously had a deep relish for their lurid jobs. Bloodshed and calamity were their bread and butter, and I became a constant and compulsive reader under the aegis of their tantalizing delineations. When I had finally managed to master the meanings of the captions underneath their hypnotic pictures, I realized at once that a man might do worse than become just such an artist, who was professionally privileged to examine at first hand the minute, gory details of all such fascinating disasters.

That is, in fact, when I had my first intimations that this might indeed someday become a highly congenial career for me. However, I did not immediately or finally commit myself to this decision, because at that time I also had quite a strong hankering to become a lamplighter. (In my childhood street lamps were lit every evening by a municipal lamplighter, who went on foot from post to post and ignited the gas mantles with flaming torch affixed to the top of a long bamboo pole.) But very shortly afterward I did definitely decide to become

175

a professional artist, and this happened while I was staying for a couple of months with my Aunt Katharine at the Kurhaus in Deutsch Altenburg.

I had wandered over to the Koppelberg all by myself one late summer afternoon, when I suddenly came upon a rather strangely attired little group. A plumpish, bearded man wearing a beret and a velvet jacket was standing in front of a portable easel and painting away with seemingly frenzied concentration. I suppose he was in a hurry to get as much work done as possible before the light finally failed altogether. Although I'm sure he could quite plainly hear me approaching, he never even bothered to give me a glance. At any rate, when I came closer I could see a couple of gypsy-looking characters sitting under a nearby tree, obviously posing for him. These picturesque derelicts had long, droopy black mustaches, in addition to which they had also been rigged out with the superfluous bravado of some discarded military uniforms— Zouave uniforms, I think.

I'm sure you've seen just such pictures endless numbers of times in your doctor's waiting room, and you've probably wondered how in hell they ever got to be painted, and by *whom*.

Well, now you know. I saw it done myself. But that wasn't all I saw. Oh, no!

Just before the sun actually went down behind this tableau, a servant in livery appeared from behind the bushes, doffed his hunting cap, and I heard him address that bearded hunk of bacon as "Maestro."

(Remember, I'm only fifty-nine years old, so Louis XIV was dead and buried, and this all must have happened after some kind of automobile had already been invented. I just want you to keep these things straight in your mind.)

And then I heard this servant say, "Is it all right to clean up now, Maestro?"

"Yes," said the genius, "but I want you to be particularly careful about the sable brushes, Loisl. They were just a little stiff this morning."

"I'm terribly sorry," said the servant. "I'll be extra careful with them." He took the dripping palette out of the painter's hand and then delicately, I should say reverently, proceeded to lift that crappy picture from the easel. I was only just a kid, but even I could see that that picture simply stank.

Well, at this point the gypsies finally got off the ground, and as they approached the painter they also took off their caps, and the older one even coughed apologetically a couple of times before he dared to address him.

"What time do you want us tomorrow, your worship?" he said.

"Oh, at twelve-thirty," said the artist. "I don't like to get up too early, you understand. It always ruins my whole day. Maybe we'd better make it one o'clock. You see, I'm going out to a big party tonight and I may not get home till God knows when. I'll tell you what, let's play it safe and meet here at two-thirty. All right?"

"Two-thirty it is, your excellency," said the older one.

"Have a pleasant evening, your worship," said the younger gypsy.

"Thank you," said the artist as he turned away from them.

The models slowly started down the trail, but neither one of them put on his cap again until they were almost out of sight. All in all, it had certainly been quite an elaborate little display of respectful deference confronted by self-assured grandeur.

But the most lasting image I carried away from there was of the painter himself, now silhouetted commandingly against the surrounding countryside. Even in my simplicity I felt that despite the ineptitude of his painting he had nevertheless placed some sort of yoke on the neck of the disorderly mon-

177

ster. He was an artist. His large beret, almost a tam o'shanter really, his flowing bow tie and his silken beard, all gently agitated by the soft summer breeze, gave an impressive aura of picturesque authenticity to his occupational presumption. His calm and aloof posture was in particularly significant contrast to the servile Loisl, who was still groping around on his hands and knees, gathering up the scattered artistic debris from the moist evening grass on that dark hillside.

So I'm sure you'll not be surprised to hear that that final vision decided me.

Yes, I said to myself, this is certainly the sort of life I'm particularly qualified to adorn. Maestro, eh? Very good. Yessir, I liked it, and as I stumbled down the path into the deepening darkness I liked it better and better. I thought it was going to be a fine life. I had confidence in it. I was sure I'd be good at it, too. And so the fly was cast. I would definitely angle for the fattest carp of all: I would become an artist!

Looking back now, after all these years, at that fateful encounter on the Koppelberg, I'm just as glad that I made that particular choice that summer evening. I discovered some-time later that the artist whom I had accidentally observed at his labors was married to Adelina von Krupp, the daughter of a billionaire munitions manufacturer. Still, in the end, I proved to be a lot better off as an artist than if I'd decided to become a lamplighter. Those boys couldn't even qualify for a Ful-bright scholarship nowadays, and, as you can plainly see, the poor picturesque bastards eventually wound up nowhere, ex-cept maybe in the writings of J. M. Barrie, God help them.

If I remember correctly, it was during that same year, in 1908, that Francis Joseph, the King-Emperor of Austria-Hungary, the one with the muttonchop whiskers, celebrated the sixtieth anniversary of his ascension to the throne. I don't think the Hapsburg business had ever been so long under single executive management, and it naturally became the occasion for some truly stupendous festivities. All of Europe and Asia was pleasantly agitated by this piece of occupational longevity, and all the kings and kinglets of the world happily forgathered in Vienna to help along with the royal hullaballoo.

We kids hardly went to school at all during that year, and if we did go, once or twice a week, it was just to do some concentrated piece of choral work on some themes by Haydn or Schubert or one of those boys, because it stands to reason that the whole goddamned country was planning to sing itself into hysterics over this joyous occasion.

There were lots of other interesting things going on too. A friend of my father's told me many years later that some of the oldest whores in Vienna used to work in double shifts during that memorable time, and that after the last regal customer had finally gone home half a dozen of the most influential pimps got together and opened a bank of their own. One of them, Franzl Nepomuk, was even elected to Parliament—on the Conservative ticket, but he had the full support of the Socialist Workers' Party and of the Catholic Centrists too. For once, true merit had completely disarmed all forms of political sniping; Franzl just made it on the unanimous vote of all his contented and grateful clients. That's real history. Austrian history, if you please.

It was certainly a very unusual time. Even on normal occasions Vienna was always loaded with military personnel, and you must remember that soldiers didn't wear any khaki uniforms in those days. They all looked as if they expected any moment to appear for the Ballet Russe. So you can just imagine what must have gone on with all those Army men during this crazy gala. I understand that Vienna's twenty-six thousand servant girls were in a permanent state of smiles, tears and pregnancy, and that the birth rate was increased by forty per cent in 1909.

I remember that the Shah of Persia arrived one day and

Francis Joseph went to the station to greet him dressed in the costume of a Persian prince. The Shah, in his turn, had decked himself out like an Austrian cavalry officer. *Noblesse oblige*, dig?

Anyhow, this piece of royal *mishugass* at once set the fashion for all the other crowned heads who came along, and if you had the time you could watch all these demented transvestites pulling in at all the different railroad stations during various parts of the day, kissing each other, swapping medals and rattling their hardware, until it all looked and sounded like a whirling toy store that had been hit by a tornado.

You can be sure I hardly ever missed even one of these extraordinary meetings, and my poor mother, who had an absolute phobia about crowds, nearly had a nervous breakdown by the time all these crowned blubberheads had finally assembled.

Then came a new and official decree: The citizens of Vienna were commanded to put two lighted candles in all of their windows which were at all visible from a public thoroughfare.

Let me tell you, I'm certainly glad I was there to see it. It was fairyland itself. I never saw anything that was visually anywhere near as stirring until I witnessed the illuminated fountains at the World's Fair in New York City. I don't mean the goings-on at the Aquacade, which were good too; I mean the undulating water display, with the colored lights playing on it, which was performed every evening right in front of the French restaurant. It was the best thing at the fair. It was absolutely superb.

But, back to Vienna.

You can figure it out yourself that all those candles in people's windows were bound to start off an endless number of fires. All through the night the fire horses kept galloping up and down the streets, and the racket made by the clattering samovars they were dragging around over those cobblestones simply drove everybody wild. Everybody except me, I guess. I just adored it all. The fire engines, the alarm bells, the sparks flying from under the horses' hoofs, the people jumping out of windows in their nightshirts were like so many wonderfully added pieces of stage business in a show that was pretty near perfect to start with. I lost ten pounds during the first week of the public illumination, and of course my folks in great alarm sent for our doctor.

"He needs absolute quiet," he said.

"But, Doctor," said my poor mother, "he just wants to go everywhere and to see everything. He goes to bed at two-thirty and he gets up every morning at six. What can we do with him?"

"Take him to a theater or a concert, maybe, but nothing that will upset his nervous system. I strictly forbid it," he said.

So my parents got some seats for the first performance of *Der Rosenkavalier*, which was to be conducted by Richard Strauss in person at the Hofoper.* Since this opening was scheduled for the evening, I'm afraid my folks weren't exactly fulfilling the doctor's orders; but luckily they hadn't the vaguest idea how to raise a child, and, besides, I would certainly have fought like a savage if they had suggested taking me to a mere matinee.

Then a really bad piece of luck hit me: I got a terrible earache—got it around two o'clock in the afternoon of the very day when we were supposed to go to the theater. It was no ordinary pain either. It was as if somebody had inserted a good-

* Please, please don't bother writing me that this date is wrong. I know all about the official statistics on this subject, but when I did a piece on *Rosenkavalier* for *Vanity Fair* in 1931 I verified with Richard Strauss himself that, although the opera had its premiere in 1911, a preview of it was given in honor of the King in 1908.

sized corkscrew into my eardrum and was trying to pull the left side of my brain along with it. But I just had to keep my trap shut about it or else there certainly wasn't going to be any show that evening. I don't know how I finally managed to make it. All I remember is that I took about half a dozen aspirins before we finally started out, and that my mother had to dress me twice, because I perspired all through my clothes the first time. Of course my parents wanted to stay home, but I gave them such a desperate sales spiel that at last I managed to change their minds. That evening, obviously, cost us all a great deal even before the joy of it was properly under way. When we were finally seated in the opera house, my pain, luckily, left me, or it well may be that I just couldn't spare any further attention to it, considering all that was going on around me.

Once, years later, I saw a bum movie about the Congress of Vienna, with Lilian Harvey, and believe me, it was almost exactly like that. Everybody was dolled up in fancy dress with at least one red sash across their frilled shirt fronts; loaded down with swords and epaulettes and decorations of all sorts; and bowing and heel-clicking and hand-kissing enough to dazzle the most blasé of worldlings. I was embedded in such perfumes, such hair oils, such pomades and hairdos on all sides that I thought I was suddenly going to rise right up to the crystal chandelier with the wonderful odor and ecstasy of it all. It also seemed to me that the men who were pouter-pigeoning it all around me were even more startlingly decked out than the women. The women showed off a lot of bouncy bosoms and bare shoulders and stuff, that's true, but the men were the ones who really had the most daring explosions of gold and silver trimmings all over their duds. It was sheer heaven.

There was one depressing note in this glittering assembly, however: *me*, and my folks. We looked like a nest full of molting dormice, and I must say I had never before realized that my old man was such a complete failure. He didn't even wear a silk rosette in his buttonhole, or have a feathered cockade in his hatband, or nothin'. *He* was a real false note, and no mistake about it.

The minute the show started, the pain in my ear woke up again. It throbbed like crazy and I suddenly felt some tears running down the side of my nose. But it was dark and nobody noticed anything. I can't tell you how much I dreaded the coming of intermission. On previous occasions these used to be my favorite times in the theater, because, in Vienna, people stowed away enormous wads of grub during every entr'acte and this was always my big chance to wolf a lot of contraband stuff that I was never allowed to eat at home. I think I often liked to attend a lot of plays especially for the exciting food interludes that were offered at least twice every evening.

But not this time. I nearly died during that intermission.

Later I must have fallen into a kind of protective stupor or something, because I can't remember much about it. All I know is that when the opera was finally over and Strauss was up on the stage holding hands with the bowing principals, I suddenly slipped from my seat and passed out cold.

I woke up in the office of Dr. Brieger, a friend of my father's who lived right near the opera, and that good man diagnosed my condition as middle-ear inflamation.

"It is fiendishly painful," he said, "and I don't see how the child was able to stand it for all those hours."

"He just didn't want to miss the excitement tonight," said my tearful mother.

"Well, we'll have to lance it immediately," said Dr. Brieger. "I'm sure he'll be a good little trouper about it."

He was wrong, of course. I screamed bloody hell when the time came, and when my poor parents finally carried me home through the noisy, festive streets I was just a collapsed bundle of whimpering disaster.

Twenty years later, to the very day, I was back in the

Vienna Opera House to hear *Der Rosenkavalier,* with Richard Strauss conducting again. He had gotten quite a lot older in the meantime and so he was directing the orchestra sitting down in an armchair. Well, I was there, all the way from New York, to help him celebrate the twentieth anniversary of his work, and my wife was there too, but my children, better brought up than I had been, were both properly asleep at our hotel.

It was a wonderful if somewhat less picturesque evening than the last one, and when we finally got back to the Bristol my wife and I were still harmonizing some of the enchanting melodies from the evening's production. When we arrived at our room, however, we found that we had nothing to sing about, because my older boy, age eight, was sitting up in his bed and tearfully complaining about a bad earache.

In the middle of the night we had to rouse the hotel physician, who examined him with Teutonic thoroughness and finally told us that the kid was suffering from an acute inflammation of the middle ear.

Fortunately I'm not particularly superstitious, so I never attached any special significance to this silly coincidence. It was just a drag, that's all.

While I was busy writing these last few lines about *Rosenkavalier,* my own ear suddenly started to hurt again after an interval of fifty years. So I knocked off for a while, applied a heating pad and even took a nap for a couple of hours.

But the pain continued.

Dr. Merton Hoskins, a neighbor of mine here in Framingham, just left me, after having given me a stiff dose of penicillin.

And what do I deduce from all these goings-on? What meaningful conclusion have I drawn from this astonishing, almost symphonically repetitive emergence of the earache theme in juxtaposition to the *Rosenkavalier* leitmotiv?

Only this. That the knowing monitors of *The New Yorker* magazine may never dare to offer their sophisticated clientele any stories that form neat little patterns or have vulgar O. Henry finishes, but *life*, much more carelessly edited, just obviously doesn't give a good goddam.

Speaking of themes, just listen to this little tone poem for a moment.

I was reading a book in a hospital bed down in Kentucky one afternoon, and I was having a terrible time of it, too, because this book had obviously been rebound, and rebound so badly by an ex–dope fiend of some kind that I was barely able to flatten out the blasted pages. Every time I tried to read the beginning of a line, I just had to crack apart that ossified glue and lean on it with both my hands. A real nuisance.

Well, I was just about to fling the whole arthritic contraption up against the wall, when I suddenly noticed something crawling across one of the half-opened pages.

It was an ant.

I'd never seen such an ant before in all my life. It was a measly little pale-brown specimen of creeping failure. Decrepitude and pauperization ambulant on six feet, that's what that creature exemplified.

But there he was, making some kind of bitter living for himself, and making it the hardest way possible, too, simply because he happened to be one of the world's outstanding snobs.

I *knew* he was a snob, because the book that I had been trying to read was Maeterlinck's *The Life of the Ant*—and I was sure he lived his ghastly starvation existence merely because he wanted to dwell in the aura of his distinguished relatives.

You know, the ones who build bridges across raging rivers, who go to battle armored to their deadly pincers, who lay pipelines across aqueducts, and some who even keep herds of insect cattle in thrall and milk them for their progeny and make cheeses from the overflow.

I had read all about those accomplished operators, and so I could easily guess why my shabby visitor had taken up his residence in that forlorn outpost.

What's more, I had originally asked the librarian to bring me Fabre's *Life of the Ant*, which is an infinitely better book, but I was convinced that this little stowaway had purposely chosen the Maeterlinck volume because the sentimental Belgian had written far more romantically and floridly about all those accomplished ancestors and relatives of his.

I had that ant dead to rights.

Still, I got out of bed and went next door to consult my neighbor, a nice Puerto Rican boy called Miguel Pereires, about it.

You see, in the wretched state of my health, it had suddenly come to me that I might possibly be just imagining this whole thing, and I wanted to make sure that something *alive* was really crawling across that paper.

Miguel, who in private life was a skillful commercial artist, took the volume out of my hand and stared at it for a moment.

"It's a live ant," he said. "Wonder what made the damned fool camp out in such a spot, where there's nothing to eat."

"He's starving," I said, "because he's just too stinking proud, that's why!"

And then I showed Miguel the title of the book and explained my deductions in the matter.

"Well," he said, "you're damned lucky, at that. You might have been reading *The Call of the Wild*, by Jack London, and that's full of wolves and huskies and stuff."

"Yeah," I said. "That *would* have been something, wouldn't it? You get a chance to land yourself in the bug ward here by just taking the wrong book out of the library. By the way,

Miguel, don't tell anybody about this ant, will you? The head psychiatrist has his eye on me anyway. I made the mistake of asking him whether he dreamt in black and white or in Technicolor, and it seems to me like he hasn't been sleeping any too well lately."

"And you better get rid of that book, too, before anybody spots it on you," said Miguel. "They're liable to think *you* planted that beast in that binding."

"You're right," I said. "They might even think I'm training it to bring me in some weed [marihuana] from the farm. I wanna get out of this joint someday. Remember, *I* haven't got any famous relatives to live with down here. This is a great place for an ant, maybe, but not for people."

"Definitely not for people!"

We agreed on that.

CHAPTER FOURTEEN

WHEN I CAME HOME from Lexington for the last time about five years ago, I was free from opiates for about ten months before I settled down to do some work. I decided to do a sort of picture book with a little text to go with the illustrations and I thought I'd call it "The Human Dilemma."

I made some twenty-odd drawings and wrote the stuff to go with them, but somehow or other the juice seemed to fade out of the whole idea even as I was going along working on it. I think I know what happened to me at the time. I had originally planned to do about two hundred and fifty of these vignettes, but as the memory of Lexington faded from my mind and as my good, quiet home life placed a benign obliterative cloud over the ten shattering years of my addiction, the true acid and bitterness required for such a job was somehow lacking in me.

At any rate, I have included those twenty-three original sketches in the following pages because I think they do represent a fair and accurate measure of my mind at the time when I made them.

Here they are.

THE LATECOMERS

They came to America as refugees in the ugliest sense of that
   word.
Now they are grateful citizens.
They have a tendency toward terrace restaurants and manifest
   themselves in large groups near parks and lakes and public
   reservoirs.
They drink American refreshments that taste as if iodine had
   been diluted in sugared Seltzer water.
They would much prefer fresh raspberry juice, but would consider it disloyal to the country to follow such an inclination.
They fancy themselves completely acclimatized.
But, in their secret hearts, they believe that the pianos in the
   United States have a more nervous
   action than the European ones
   and that under consistent pounding
   they tend to become skittish.

THE ENTREPRENEUR

"Minky" Taubman got his nickname after prohibition was re-
pealed and he dealt for a while in stolen mink.

Later he branched off into printing pornographic pamphlets
for teen-agers.

When one of his authors wrote a play, Minky backed it and
made more than money—he made Broadway.

He is now a producer whose plans for the next season include
an all-Negro *Peer Gynt*. He doesn't care particularly for
Negroes, and he doesn't like people who do, but he thinks
it's an angle.

He is rarely ever seen without a hat, because he once overheard
someone remark that Minky's head of virile hair actually
resembled an oversized pubic toupee.

His girl friends are barely nubile blondes who run off with
jockeys or A & P clerks and finally are reputed to be
engaged to George Jessel.

THE GIRLS

Now their festivals take place in health-food stores—a just
 retribution for years of unhampered gluttony.
They once had a houseboat on the Nile and yawned their
 dreary hours all through the Vale of Kashmir.
They've buried seven husbands between them and embittered
 the lives of endless unfortunate in-laws.
Their seed, however, goes on.
Their duplicates in other garb will patronize the Pitti Palace
 and the Pyramids and speak reverently only of their own
 interior rumblings and gastric misadventures.
Their arthritic talons are safely clutched around paying dividends.

195

CURED

He spent seven thousand dollars to have his psychiatrist tell him that in all his life he had never loved anyone and nobody had ever really cared a rap for him.

THE HEIRS

These are the unfortunate children of distinguished parents.
They have committed no crime except that their names instantly evoke the colorful images of their talented begetters.
These offspring generally have a deep sense of wrong which emanates from them like a bad smell, and people finally come to resent their very existence.
It is as if they were
living, and embarrassing, evidence of their sires' fallibility —a proof of their essential weakness, their tawdry oneness with the rest of humanity, a humanity which begets only children and nothing else.

THE VESTALS

.

These are the dedicated souls, the ballerinas who are ashamed
of working in Broadway musicals for the bread of their
dancing teachers.

In a world without shape or reason they maintain an iron self-
discipline.

They are the eternal ladies of the ensemble who work as others
work only for great fortunes or for stardom.

They are the shock troops of Art with a capital *A*.

Unfortunately, they are as severe with others as they are with
themselves.

They are humorless and almost sexless, but they are on familiar
terms with Mozart, with Debussy and with Schönberg,
and, surprisingly enough, a flock of them dressed in classic
gauze tutus is a truly wondrous thing to behold.

THE TYCOON

This is a self-made man—
God help the rest of us.
He has poisoned a few rivers with deadly chemical refuse and
    smothered the world with ball bearings.
By the mere lifting of an eyebrow he can create a famine in
    orange marmalade.
He prides himself on his gift for facts and figures.
The only fact he has never bothered to figure out is
How many thousands of people it takes to make
    One Self-made Man.

AVANT-GARDE

They are ultramodern painters.
They work in Duco on reinforced hairnets.
They spill the paint classically out of cans, but use no brushes.
Wearing leather shorts, they plant their rumps honestly in the
    color and spin in the pigment until the results seem to
    justify their autographs.
Nothing can go wrong with this process, since all these works
    are frankly called improvisations.
One critic who viewed their finished labors said:

> *The sensitive hands that wrought these masterpieces can be
> discerned in every touch of these whirling syndromes of
> emotion.*

KITTY

It stands to reason that she's always dieting, but her husband
    is a bookie and they eat at odd hours.
This also explains her blood-red talons and her midwinter tan.
She's a generic type who refuels at Lindy's and Reuben's and
    various good chop suey houses.
She patronizes little specialty shops.
She plays a tough hand of bridge or poker.
After her husband dies of coronary thrombosis, she will open
    a specialty shop of her own called Chez Kitty.

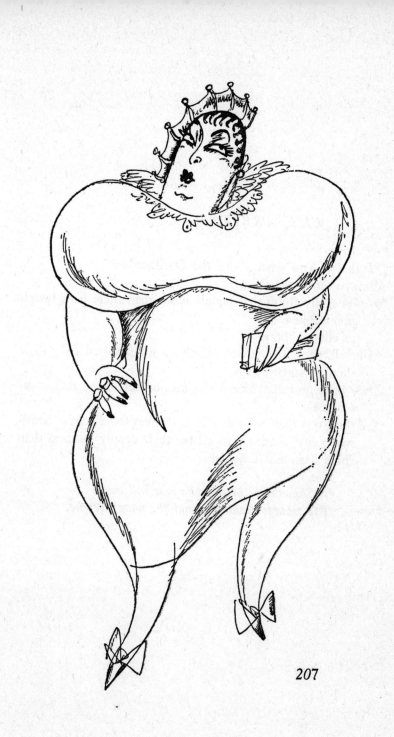

207

THE ARBITERS

"Yeah?!!? And what about the Dardanelles?"
Well, what about them?
So you really think that people wiser than these park bench
    philosophers are
    in charge there?
After all, these loquacious oafs have mismanaged only their
    own personal affairs.
They have no international victories or defeats on their con-
    sciences.
Are the great ones who deal in waterways and juggle conti-
    nents any better equipped for their deadly business than
    these harmless dimwits?

Sometimes these cogitations still amaze
The troubled midnight and the noon's repose.

209

FORSAKING ALL OTHERS

This is a young married couple in Greenwich Village.
The boy is on the right.

THE BOOKWORM

She will not wear glasses, because she doesn't want to look
schoolmarmish.
She is a librarian.
She reads omnivorously with practically no results.
She is deeply devoted to her profession and is never at a loss
in this special field.
She files books on nudism under "Costumes."

213

THE POWERLESS ATOM

Sixty years ago Soapless Barney was a little boy.
The century didn't advance, it rolled over him and left him
flat.
Freud, Ford, Morse, Einstein never lived for him.
Now that the Bowery has changed its cozy character by
emerging into cold daylight, Soapless wonders what ever
became of Teddy Roosevelt, who was a really great man
and would never have allowed such crazy things to go on.

215

INVESTMENT

This is Potato Head.

Between orphanages, reform schools, houses of detention, hospitals and penitentiaries, he will, in the course of fifty-one
years, cost the state almost as much as Boulder Dam.

It is one of those investments a democracy must necessarily
make on the off chance that he might at any point of his
life show a talent for some sport or, far more likely,
become a successful
politician.

217

THE PHOENIX

He claims to have been cradled in a theatrical trunk and to
   have played Puck with E. H. Sothern and Julia Marlowe.
After years of retirement in the Minnetonka Hotel at Eighth
   Avenue and Forty-third Street, he was revived by televi-
   sion as an elder stage man—an introducer and commen-
   tator on its dramatic regurgitations.
He is content—not proud, but sweetly and good-humoredly
   grateful for being a revenant.
His comeback is more remarkable than most people suppose.
   Wardens of various state prisons around the country
   could testify to this.
He began as Tommy Tucker in a Christmas pantomime at
   Elmira State Reformatory in 1912.
Through various trespasses against the public welfare, he
   worked his way into the Missouri State Prison version of
   Beauty and the Beast in 1917.
He subsequently toured sixteen other jails and houses of deten-
   tion and finally scored his memorable hit as Macbeth in
   the great production of that play in Sing Sing.
An unusually critical audience, most of them well qualified
   to judge mayhem and murder,
   pronounced him a "cool cat."

218

CINDERELLA

This little twelve-year-old is being psychoanalyzed.
She has four fathers and speaks three languages badly—including English.
A typical product of an expensive modern school, she will never learn to spell properly or to add a column of figures with ease.
After her own fifth marriage, she will either star in summer theaters or edit a page on home economics and child care for some women's magazine.
She will probably do both.

LOWER DEPTHS

These people are great dancers.
When they dance the Mambo, it is hard to believe that they
    sleep ten to a room . . . that they earn less pay for
    more work than anybody else in the country.
A man dancing can forget that the rent isn't paid, that the wife
    has missed her period, that another installment is due on
    the television set.
These passionate dancers are Puerto Ricans—so poorly off in
    our midst, so badly cheated on all sides, that even the
    Negroes in their ghastly slums now, at last, have some-
    one to look down on.

SOMEBODY'S MOTHER

Before she was married, she read somewhere that a woman
    should bear her pregnancy proudly—"Let her carry the
    fruit of her love like a Greek vase."
The man who wrote this piece of advice was second mate on a
    tramp steamer and hadn't seen a pregnant woman in
    eighteen years.
But *she's* carrying on.

225

THE LITTERARTY

These boys have to bleed quite a lot of ink to make themselves,
and their hysterical wives, and their privately unschooled
children, a good living in the fashionable suburbs they
all infest.

They don't write any ordinary books.

In the crap that gets published under their names, in magazines
that are thoughtfully riffled by the literary cognoscenti,
they deeply deplore the decline of Crabbe Robinson and
are shattered by the public inattention for the works of
Jean Paul Friedrich Richter.

Their major work, if any, will be a complete re-evaluation of
Rasselas in the light of the latest psychoanalytic findings.

227

HANDMAIDENS OF THE MUSES

The wives of long-haired musicians are loaded with anecdotes
about Toscanini.
They are good homemakers, nevertheless.
Most of them are adept sight readers and can furnish reasona-
ble piano accompaniments.
Some of them even play chess.
Only their wardrobes seem to have been derived from
unusually artistic jumble shops.

THE BOYS

Gerald and Otto have been on their first visit to Cherry
    Grove, Fire Island, and have returned greatly reassured
    and strengthened.
They were happy to find that ancient Greece is not altogether
    in eclipse, and that the Philistines are not completely in
    charge everywhere.
Gerald is planning an evening jacket with a brocade lining.
    Otto will quite frankly join a ballet class. Before long
    they will wear hairnets and paste sequins on their eyelids.

THE HUCKSTERS

Here are some pretty standard maps of typical advertising
and editorial executives who infest the upper echelon of
creative stupidity in our midst.

They have made the country crotch-conscious and invented
the underarm insecurity gambit.

Most of them are unacknowledged alcoholics who firmly
believe in their mission.

What makes them drunkards and potential suicides is their
inability to hide from themselves what their mission in
life really is.

233

FATSO

He drives a cab and tells all his customers that his wife just
    came home from the hospital with a brand-new baby.
He isn't even married, but this piece of crude poetry nets him
    an extra ten to twelve dollars a day in tips.
He doesn't do this just for the money.
He's been "Fatso" ever since his kindergarten days.
Cadging for affection, he once ate sixty egg sandwiches and
    drank twenty-two Cokes.
The ten dollars he won for himself just about paid for the
    food.
He wants to be taken seriously, for a change.
That's all.
How would you like to walk around the world looking like
    an inflamed armpit?

CHAPTER FIFTEEN

THIS MORNING I wrote a letter to my friend Taylor Caldwell, up near Buffalo somewhere, and before I was able to mail it off to her my Margie made me a clean copy of it and left it on my desk. This is what I had written:

DEAR, DEAR FRIEND,

You are surely the world's most prompt and satisfactory correspondent, and your letter did get to Fire Island after all. It is very nice here. Not as nice as it used to be in '33, or even in '42, but the sea is the greatest, and the scrub foliage always makes me feel good, because it somehow manages to make some kind of living where life is pretty hard for greenery of any sort.

I'm just rewriting Chapter Fifteen, which is mostly about

love, and I must say I'm rather enjoying it. You see, I'm so eternally proud of Adam's fall, because that's where all the meaningful, worthwhile things in life really began; and every time I think of it, it gasses me all over again.

Just imagine what a dreary life he must have had as a kept man—as a "doll" man, as my Haitian friends in 1938 used to say. No work, no worries, no nothin'. Well, I'm glad, for my sake, he didn't settle for that. Maybe that's why I'm such an ardent feminist, and why I've always felt so chivalrous toward women—because, by repute at least, *they* started the whole strange shebang that set this wild world going. In fact, I'm sure that the odious, stultified climate of Eden just bored poor Eve right out of her senses. You see, I know that women aren't at all the docile, contentedly humming house-keepers that we would like to think they are. We've just desperately tried to reduce them to that status for our own comfort and convenience, but inside them they're always churning with every form of wild frustration.

You know, I love Bertrand Russell—in fact, his lucid mind is one of my great delights—but I disagree vitally with him on several very important points. He thinks that the whole saga of mankind is not of the slightest significance in the light of interstellar space—in the light of the quadrillion galaxies that twinkle and roar all around us. Well, maybe so. *I* just don't believe it. I believe that *man*, who invented *love* (and I most devoutly believe that *man* invented it), has profound significance for the whole universe. Indeed, I believe that through *this* manifestation *alone* he has, in fact, made all the rest of creation significant.

You dig?

Eve gives me a real bang. What a cool cat *she* was. She brought about the necessity for work and, incidentally, the pride in "workmanship," as Veblen says. She invented *nudity*, and that was surely one of the most significant disclosures

237

that ever happened to mankind. When I'm finally mature enough, and skillful enough, I'm going to paint myself an Eve. I don't think anybody who has ever painted her, excepting only Gully Jimson perhaps, ever truly understood her. I'm absolutely convinced that I'm the first one who properly grasps her blinding beauty, her complex nature and her true worth.

I'm going to do it after I finish this book maybe. It will take lots of thinking, lots of prayer and lots of preparation, but it might easily be my masterpiece at last. It will certainly be no waste of time even to *fail* in such a worthwhile enterprise.

Oh, if I were only ten years younger!

What plans and projects are slumbering in my heart, what stupendous dreams are nurturing in my lurid subconscious —dreams that I am too ill to permit into the frontal lobes of my awareness. G. B. Shaw was quite right, one little life isn't long enough to learn anything properly. How in hell am I ever going to complete all the work that is now stewing inside my noggin? How am I ever going to tell everybody about my tremendous joys, my awful hangups and my minute misgivings, and how can I ever get around to giving a proper account of the miracles of love that were showered on me in this supposedly worst of all possible worlds?

As you know, I never joined or subscribed to any organized religious faith, because the extant orthodoxies never quite manage to rate God *high* enough for my taste. Get it?

This is just a minute splinter of my mind at the moment, dear friend, and I'm sure you can imagine the rest. One thing you can't suspect, of course, is my bitter sense of guilt about all the time I've wasted in my short, short life. I don't mean that I frolicked around in night clubs or spent my days carousing with a lot of mindless nobodies. Not a bit of it. I just wasted my time daydreaming and moon-gazing on the

238

scintillant, deceptive wings of dope, that's what I did. That is indeed my great, unforgivable sin. Ten years of morphine addiction lie heavily on my heart, and believe me, my frenzy for work at this moment is just my desperately anxious attempt to nullify that ghastly, unrectifiable deficit.

Please write soon. Your letters brighten my days, and I'm sorry that fate waited so long before she finally managed to bring the two of us together.

May heaven be kind to you and yours.

Love,

ALEX

I have a strange feeling at this moment that practically everything I have written so far, really, just led up to this particular chapter, because in it I'm going to tell you something about my various beliefs. My beliefs about the universe and my beliefs about mankind.

You see, I'm quite convinced that the world I live in is by no means an accident. Even a badly written novel is no accident, so how could this elaborately fascinating and exact creation be the result of mere happenstance? Such thinking defies all the intrinsic logic of art, and naturally I can't subscribe to any such drivel. On the other hand, I can't quite make it with a deity that is so inconceivably grandiose and puissant as to have willed all this vast and minute magnificence into being and yet is busy all day long throwing banana peels in *my* path, so that I may slip and fall from grace simply because my eyes were momentarily averted from the bright highway of salvation. That's what I call reducing God to the petty role of a choleric top sergeant. Surely that doesn't make any sense. I can't settle for an all-forgiving and compassionate social worker who's got nothing but *me* on his mind all the time, either. I just can't believe that I'm really that important, don't you see? It doesn't really make any sense to me no matter how

239

the hell you try to explain it. It just seems that I'm stuck, brother, that's all.

Well, it couldn't matter less, since I'm perfectly happy to accept the wonderful gift of life even without an ecclesiastically certified endowment policy. I take reality on trust. I'm convinced that man fulfills his role on this earth adequately if he just does as little harm as possible. That's surely a plus in my book.

I also believe that food and lodging ought to be freely provided for everyone, at all times, regardless of seeming merit. (I know that that's neither Capitalism nor Communism. Well, so much the worse for the both of *them*.) You see, I'm convinced that merit is a very relative matter and always subject to geographic and cultural deviations.

Just think of the hard-working, virtuous people involved in public relations, for instance. I can easily imagine a time and a period where their various greasing activities would be considered not only dangerous and antisocial but perhaps definitely inspired by the devil himself. So please let the public-spirited press agents of the world not cast the first ping-pong ball in my direction. (A ping-pong ball with a very confidence-inspiring trademark on it, no doubt.)

Think of the stupendous, nerve-shattering lies that the advertising fraternity launches at us every day of our lives. If you just remember that some of its most august practitioners are good family men and devout churchgoers, it will give you some idea how difficult it is to decide who is, and who is not, out of step with the eternal harmony of creation.

Another thing: The human body hasn't undergone any mutations in many thousands of years. Well, it is my sincere belief that it isn't going to have any more in the future either. The only mutations that are still in store for mankind are going to take place in the *human brain*, and these mutations are definitely up to man himself. *He's* got to take over now, that's the way nature intends it, and high time, too. Remember, our ancestors have done pretty well, considering—and by ancestors I don't mean Pythagoras or Leonardo, I mean the great, sacred, anonymous, human genius who invented love.

Lacking any accurate data on the subject, I generally give credit for this stupendous discovery to Orpheus. Remember him? He's the cat who so loved his wife, Eurydice, that after she died he went down into the nether world to bring her back.

Actually, love, *personal* love, is a comparatively recent emotion in the strange history of mankind. There are still places in large areas of the world, to this very day, where a man never gets around to loving anybody at all. In fact, even in some reputedly civilized countries men never get any further than just loving their oldest sons and practically nobody else. I'm not planning to get involved at this point with the ghastly history of parent worship and ancestor worship, since common sense will tell you that these grotesque travesties on love were certainly inaugurated by some powerfully cunning parents 'way, 'way back in the dim dawn of family life.

What I'm talking about here is a *man*, who, by free choice, picks himself a *woman* and finds in his relationship with her a body-and-soul-satisfying answer to most of his earthly yearnings. This, of course, means a complete collaboration on both their parts which should be ideally sustained by an unlimited capacity for passion, for friendship, for imagination and for gratitude. *That's* the mark to shoot at. And believe me, friend, if you're settling for a lot less than that, all I can tell you is, you're being gypped.

I myself have had large chunks of this comfort all my life, excepting only the first few years of my blasted dope hegira.

Well, anyway, I notice that mankind is beginning to suspect that it is getting short-changed somewhere along the line, and I don't mean just in a materialist, Marxian sense, either. No. A

241

lot of people want their children to have better and more complete lives than they themselves had, but because the poor saps don't know any better, and don't know how to go about it, they think it's all going to be solved by getting their kids better bicycles or larger TV sets, or by providing them with some other form of shoddy gadgetry. It can't be done that way. I'm afraid it can't even be done by sending them to a lot of expensive schools, although a good education can certainly be of some help to them. It all has to start in the home, where the *father* is single-mindedly devoted to his life partner, and the *mother* is graciously and joyously offering all the rich gifts of her nature on the altar of their common devotion.

Now, don't misunderstand me. It certainly is not going to be solved by just a boring ritual of soul-destroying domestic pretenses. The goddamned women's magazines are just dead wrong about that too. Their Home, Heart and Hearth advice columns are just so much balderdash, because their drivel is primarily geared to a lot of consumer angles whose blatant, vulgar use of the advertising pages forms the major part of their real concern. You and I know that "togetherness" isn't even for the birds. You and I know that it just means bigger refrigerators, more powerful vacuum cleaners, and running hopelessly into debt for a lot of mechanical junk that we can all do beautifully without.

No, fellas, we've just got to have a new deal all around. The kids don't get a break, because the home in too many cases is just an armed camp full of hypocrisy and self-interest. The old lady most of the time just tries to chisel as much money as possible out of the old man, and too often she uses the kids only for her own silly, show-off purposes against her friends and neighbors. Pop, in nine out of ten cases, is the pathetic money drudge who barely knows his dependents beyond an occasional authoritarian reproof. Chances are, neither one of them has learned to live with himself, let alone anybody else, and their nobler emotions come into play only if some member of the family suddenly falls ill or dies.

And that's about the color and the shape of it all around, excepting only that every once in a while into these dreary and totally arid circumstances a *freak* is born, somebody who in biological science is called a "sport."

In too many cases for my own comfort at this time, such a creature turns out to be neither a boy nor a girl, and I suspect that these disasters happen so frequently nowadays simply because the emotional climate in the home is so completely phony that a halfway sensitive organism seeks instant flight from its own seemingly hopeless gender limitations. It stands to reason that it does this in the vain but instinctive hope of finding a better adjustment in a world too bewildering for the ordinary, established emotional routines. I'm quite sure that that is why we have such a plethora of pansies and lesbians in the arts, for instance. I think that these sensitive young creatures, born into a disturbed and hostile environment, make a frantic search in any direction that promises at least a minimum of grace and color along the gray, turbulent routes of their existence.

And, what, finally, is the love life of such a sexual anomaly? I tell you, it is destined to be pure disaster. If you don't believe me, read Marcel Proust, who managed to write a truly great masterpiece about these poor, defrauded emotional cripples. Of course, in the end they pretend to prefer their disastrous condition to anything else. How else could they make it? In fact, they finally comport themselves as if their sexually better-oriented contemporaries were just a lot of retarded Philistines. But I have been friends with a lot of them over the years, and I can tell you that it's just another kind of bankruptcy sale. Pansies don't naturally fall in love with *other* pansies. That would be too abnormal even for them. No. Pansies really care, mostly, for *normal* men. Well, what good does *that* do them?

243

They can't possibly get at normal males unless these men happen to be down on their luck and have been in the habit of whoring for just such depraved appetites in the past. And that's about the size and the area of their possible romantic involvements, unless they're willing to indulge their furtive needs with some *other* frustrated fairies.

See?

Not such a big deal, after all, is it?

I know, of course, that my little analysis here doesn't account altogether for *all* the perversions that are rampant around us nowadays, but it certainly explains a lot of the messy, botched existences that happen to have crossed my own life path during the past twenty-five or thirty years. What I actually resent most about a lot of homosexuals is their dull pretense that they belong to an injured minority, like the Jews and the Negroes and the Puerto Ricans in our midst. They seem to feel that they ought to have proper pansy representation in Congress, pansy policemen, pansy juries and pansy firemen, that their special condition ought to entitle them to certain legitimate tax deductions, and that our unfair world should be compelled to recognize and to appreciate their unique prerogatives and potentials. These cats don't act like *sick* people, they act like *superior* people, and if you tend to denigrate their status they instantly bring up ancient Greece, the sonnets of Shakespeare and the poems of Oscar Wilde.

Well, fellas, let me tell you, there's been an awful lot of talent around in this world that wasn't sexually inverted, so please don't bother quoting your statistics at *me*. Just quote them to each other.

But the squares aren't having such an easy time of it either, and that's what's *really* upsetting me.

Just think about love for a minute.

Think of what a hard climb it had, coming as it did from the primordial ooze, until it finally managed to get all the way up

244

to Tristan and Isolde. As you know, in the beginning life was monosexual, when aqueous, single-celled creatures fructified themselves and begot their amorphous progeny by simple fission. Later, for reasons unknown, it took *two* specimens to accomplish the same results. Offhand, it seems to me like a needless complication that I certainly hope did *somebody* some good. Anyway, life continued to get more and more complicated, until finally even rutting seasons and elaborate courtships were added.

Very good.

We know that, for its own unguessable ends, nature kept adding a whole network of decorative circumstances to the procreative pattern, until a truly bewildering filigree of preparational punctilio embroidered the comparatively simple act of purely physiological self-perpetuation.

In short, as you can see, it's been quite a long climb from the amoeba to Romeo and Juliet, not to forget all the romantic noise that has accumulated through the millenia from the swooshing of a bivalve to the Song of Songs which was Solomon's.

Just think of all the music, all the painting and all the poetry that have come to festoon the amorous doings of mankind since the beginning, and you will learn to stand in proper reverence before the miracle of the Maidenform Bra.

Well, there you have it—all the juice and gravy of it finally served up on a foam-rubber titty, ready for instant consumption by love-famished mankind. Yes, it took an awful lot of talent and a truly stupendous amount of imagination and ingenuity to levitate nature's simple procreative patterns to the heights where they now rest. Frankly, I'm quite dizzy from the climb, and all I can conclude in these perilous times is that men had better be careful of their precious emotional reservoirs, because many animals in the past have been known to lose the use of certain limbs, and certain special faculties even,

245

if for one reason or another the wellsprings of their need had somehow dried up from lack of proper functioning.

So, you better hold on to your gender, boys!

Actually, when I look at some of the unhappy marriages in my own acquaintance I can't help wondering why in hell these people ever decided to get hooked up with each other in the first place. Most of the men are chronically rude and unshaven, and unless company is expected the girls drag themselves around in sleazy, faded wrappers, their heads revoltingly studded by curling devices, and most of these monsters lie around all day scratching themselves shamelessly, like a lot of hibernating iguanas. Nobody makes even the slightest attempt to keep a shred of illusion alive in the mind of the unfortunate partner.

But the minute such people have an evening date with someone *outside* their homes, the ladies will start shaving their legs and their armpits at three o'clock in the afternoon, the *caballeros* will douse themselves with banana butter and camel sweat until innocent houseflies fall dead onto the carpet at the mere smell of them, and then, finally, wearing their best duds and their most artificial smiles, their nerves on edge with frothing vanity and venomous distrust, they step out into the evening to make a grand impression. An impression on whom, for God's sake? On other monsters like themselves, I suppose!

You see, I myself am the product of a truly happy married life. My mother, as I've probably already told you, couldn't cook and couldn't sew and was probably the worst all-round housekeeper of her day. Nothing could possibly have mattered less.

Five days a week she would get up in the morning shortly before my father, and she would sit down with him at the breakfast table, all smiles and charms, her face shining with great good will for the new day. Of course, my father always had to cook his own breakfast, because you couldn't trust my

246

mother anywhere near a stove so early in the morning. Even later in the day it was always a major hazard, and we considered it something of a miracle that she never actually burned down the house while we were gone.

At any rate, after my father had finished his breakfast, she would take him to the door and give him an affectionate kiss—no mere peck on the cheek or nonsense like that, because she had plenty of time—and after my father was gone she would climb right back into bed again for a little more sleep. She'd finally get up sometime around eleven o'clock and eat whatever had been left from his breakfast, fortified by a little cold cereal and milk maybe.

Well, this little tableau repeated itself for the better part of thirty-five years without evil consequences for anybody. After she died, he was, of course, quite inconsolable.

"I miss her most of all at breakfast," he said to me. "It started my day off right, don't you see? No matter what was on my mind or no matter how bad the weather, she was always even-tempered and cheerful. My mornings will never be the same again. Never! She was a truly noble spirit and no one can ever really know what she meant to me."

He was wrong, of course. *I* knew, because I'd just had the dumb luck to be her ever loving son.

And what did I learn from all this?

I learned to pick up my wife's occasional stray hairpins and to kiss them secretly before replacing them on her dressing table. I learned to appreciate women for what they *were* and not to reproach them for the things that they were *not*. I didn't make a fetish out of my own punctuality just to keep them constantly aware that they had only the sketchiest notions of the meaning of time. I didn't make a big production out of it if ever they happened to forget their gloves in a theater seat, and, most important of all, I never talked to a woman as man to man.

247

Women are *not* men—and thank God for *that*.

They have their own special gifts and unique virtues and I learned to look for *them*.

Just think about it for a moment.

Women are still subject to the monthly lunar mystery, aren't they? So why don't you lay off your old, corny gender superiority and learn to *live* with them happily and gratefully, like a *man*.

Grow *up*, why don't you?

CHAPTER SIXTEEN

Someday I plan to tell you in great detail about
my long and memorable visit to North Africa. It will take quite
a lot of overhauling of the old memory box to do justice to that
very strange interlude in my not exactly humdrum existence,
but, for one reason or another, I haven't yet managed to reduce
it to any verbally negotiable terms. We lived in a place called
Marsa *Résidence*, a little north of Sidi-bou-Saïd, near the ruins
of ancient Carthage. We managed to fester there for quite a
spell, too, before we finally ran into some difficulties with the
local population and the ruling French authorities. All this
came toward the end, of course.

At any rate, we had rented a house not too far from the
beach at Marsa, and in the beginning at least only my wife,
my two children, my friend De Hirsch Margules and I took up

residence there. Later on, Miguel Covarrubias, his wife, Rosie, and, still later, George and Böschke Antheil also joined us. For various reasons not relevant to this tale, this sojourn in Tunisia proved one of the most turbulent parentheses in the strange, upsy-downsy story of my life.

Anyway, there we were, living high on the mutton in the land of couscous, assisted by three ruinous, inefficient and unspeakably slovenly servants called Machmoud, Soliman and Kafeer. These three lads were truly unique specimens, if only because, in their own web-footed, trachomatic and squint-eyed fashions, they managed to exemplify all the irritating chicanery, perversity and willfulness that can possibly be encompassed by three totally debased human hearts.

One morning quite early, about six-thirty or thereabouts, I decided to go to the beach for a matutinal swim. The rest of the household was still sleeping, which means that when I got down to the sea I had about thirty miles of Oriental landscape all to myself. As far as I was able to determine, none of the Arabs around us ever went near the sea. They used to wash their mangy camels in it once in a while, but, by and large, they managed to leave it pretty well alone.

You might as well understand at this point that, since all violently athletic demonstrations have always thoroughly nauseated me, this particular hunk of the Mediterranean was especially well suited to my peculiar tastes, because it was for miles and miles almost uniformly shallow at all points and warm enough to cook supper in.

Altogether delightful!

So this morning, after I'd waded out quite a piece and was just about to lower my rump into the refreshing embrace of the tepid chicken soup, a screaming little native girl came tearing along the beach, flailing her arms in violent distress and obviously asking me to help her. I quickly sloshed back to shore again, and as I came closer I could see the kid was completely awash with tears and almost hysterical with grief.

"What's wrong?" I shouted. "What are you scared of?"

The dirty, tattered little girl (she must have been about seven or eight at the most) made a desperate attempt to control her sobs, and finally, through her incoherent gibbering, I managed to gather that something had gone terribly wrong with her mother.

"She's very *malade*," she said in pidgin French. "She's crying for help, but *papa* isn't home. There's nobody home but us children."

Now, let me explain something about this waterfront layout that will add materially to your understanding of what was going on in that part of the world during those years.

You see, hundreds of ancient Carthaginian and Roman houses that used to stand here many centuries ago, at the water's edge, had in the intervening years either sunk or tumbled wholly or partially into the sea. Yet many of these often elaborate dwellings had nevertheless remained in reasonably habitable shape—habitable for people who had no other habitation, I mean, and also when you remember that throughout most of the seasons the climate here was uniformly benign. By the way, the people who lived in these antique ruins were rarely the local Arabs from the township itself, but rather a lot of displaced semi-mendicants from farther south—nomads who had somehow gotten stuck in this corner of North Africa, or jugglers, acrobats and snake charmers who earned a few coppers displaying their dismal skills in the nearby city of Tunis. A few Sudanese fishermen and their families lived there too, and I discovered later that some refugee Italians who had managed to cross the Mediterranean by some makeshift means had also come here to escape the benign paternalism of the great Benito.

At any rate, my little girl friend, whose name, I discovered, was Fatmah, led me up to an enormous, side-tilted Roman cistern, and when I peeked inside its murky interior I discovered what, for local purposes, was a perfectly well set-up household. Fatmah, by the way, had taken my hand as we walked along the beach, and she was still clutching at me as we arrived at the entrance to their cave.

There were four other kids inside the shelter, two boys and two girls, and Fatmah was evidently the eldest among the lot of them. At the sight of me the children all stuck fingers into their mouths but nevertheless smiled at me with dark-eyed, embarrassed trustfulness. Although all of them were uniformly dirty, they were also quite uniformly handsome, and I couldn't remember when or where in my life I'd ever seen a more good-looking bunch of children.

And it was then that I heard somebody groaning near the back wall of the cistern, and when I approached closer I could see an enormous woman stretched out in seeming agony atop a pile of dirty goatskins. Her forehead and lips were tattooed and her poor bloodshot eyes were swimming in tears.

"Do you speak French?" I asked her.

"*Un peu* [a little]," she said.

"What's wrong?" I asked her.

Instead of answering me she gave an inhuman, soul-shattering howl, whereupon all of her children at once set up an improvisational concert of hideous bawling the like of which I've heard only at some pretty advanced modern music festivals sponsored in America.

I stood in petrified bewilderment, surrounded by that horrendous racket, until the lady of the house, seemingly exhausted by some of her major efforts in the howling department, finally settled down to some less alarming but still anguished ursine groans. I approached her again.

"What's wrong with you?" I asked. "Where is your husband, anyway?"

Her French was even less than *un peu*. Nevertheless I managed to gather that her husband had gone 'way up the beach somewhere to fish, and that she herself was just about to give birth to her sixth child. She also made me understand that she had somehow managed to give birth to all her other children without any pain or melodrama of any sort, and she was not only bewildered but deeply ashamed of these sudden incalculable birth pangs.

There was another complication. The good lady, obviously a devout Mohammedan, had terrible difficulty in talking to me in her travail, because despite her suffering she was desperately trying to keep her face veiled from my infidel gaze. The few casual glimpses I did manage to catch of that visage of hers made me think that it was rather public-spirited of her to keep it out of sight. But I quickly concluded that that wasn't really her aim. No, even in this extremely trying moment of her life she was still being to the last degree conventional.

Of course, the minute I heard that a human birth was imminent I commanded the assembled brats to get a kettle of water boiling. Actually I didn't have any special purpose in view for such a large body of hot water, but I'd seen enough Dr. Kildare pictures in my day to know that this procedure was obsolutely *de rigueur* on such occasions.

The kids, happy to be of use, at once dragged an enormous copper caldron from under the house and, with the heart-breaking efficiency of the very poor the world over, instantly set an effective fire going under it.

Anyway, at least this had the immediate good result of temporarily getting rid of the children. And high time too, because the woman had just started to howl again. She seemed to be in dreadful agony, poor thing, and when I impulsively reached toward her she grabbed my arm with such frenzied force that I nearly tipped over on top of her noisily fermenting protuberance.

Seven more bitter screams came out of that tormented soul, and God knows I shall never live long enough to forget them. Those screams actually curled the scalp under my hair. When

I thought I couldn't possibly stand any more of it, she suddenly kicked up her crazy, tattered skirts, and the both of us reached blindly for the struggling life between her enormous, sweating loins.

At this point too I could really have been a lot more help to her if only she hadn't half the time been so busy arranging that goddamned veil around her face.

It came to me then, once and for all, that morality is largely a matter of time and geography. I have since learned that in Japan in the old days, for instance, the disclosure of the back of a woman's neck amounted to a hopeless compromise of the lady's person, and that if you happened to be even innocently present during such a disclosure you simply had to marry the gal. It certainly meant a shotgun among the shoguns. In the old days, I mean. Nowadays they wear bikinis in the supermarkets and dry their spare brassières on top of their parasols while strolling along the Ginza.

Aren't people wild?

Here was this poor suffering mammal, racked with insane birth spasms, and while I was practically creeping up her uterus all that the dizzy doll was really worried about was that I might catch a forbidden gander at her tattooed map.

Just try to figure it out. You'll get dizzy too.

Luckily for both of us she'd had a hell of a lot more experience with childbirth than I'd ever had, so once the kid actually stuck its silly noggin into this vale of woe she had the rest of the program taped pretty cool. She even smiled at me reassuringly once or twice. When the infant was finally lying, all of one piece, between her shanks (looking like a mummified midget) I dramatically jumped to a wall rack and took possession of a huge kitchen knife. As you have probably guessed, I meant to employ this deadly utensil to cut the umbilical cord. As a matter of fact I even found some use for all that boiling water, too—I plunged the knife in it and sterilized the blade.

But when, brandishing my medical dirk, I approached the blushing mother, that strange woman's face suddenly clouded over and she made quite unmistakable signs for me to beat it. I figured, Maybe the dope doesn't understand me. Maybe she thinks I'm about to cut myself a couple of slices out of the kid for a souvenir. Who can tell what morbidly inclined riff-raff she had already come across here on this beach in Africa. Maybe she had some friends, or even relatives, who'd think nothing of broiling themselves some newborn-infant cutlets for a luncheon snack (with no rancor or bad feelings involved, you understand, just a little local gourmandizing, that's all).

I attempted to reassure her with smiles and with blandishments, but the silly woman seemed to want no part of it. I must tell you the truth, *I* was no longer in a condition to be reasonable either. An unaccountable clinical frenzy seemed to have taken possession of me. I pointed sternly to the dangling navel cord, and I must say I was getting so irritated with her that a couple of times I nearly smacked her across the belly with that goddamned knife. As I kept on gesticulating she only seemed to become more and more alarmed by the minute, and I couldn't help wondering whether the woman was perhaps far gone in feeble-mindedness, or whether maybe the birth shock had somehow rattled her loose marbles out of their sockets. Who the hell can possibly know what goes on in such an organism? After all, the rest of the kids were obviously all disattached from her rump, so what could she possibly have done before?

I must have become pretty exasperated by then and I'm sure that my manner was certainly peremptory and perhaps even threatening, because she suddenly gave in. She lowered her protective arms, leaned back, closed her eyes, and just settled down to making idiotic, whimpering, animal noises to herself.

She was pooped. But, by God, I'd had just about enough of it too for one morning, and so with one deft whack I cut straight across that obsolete life line. She gave a shudder, a little squeak—and the matter was done. There were two of them now.

The moment it was all over, I suddenly felt very good about the whole thing. I felt so good that I even took time out to wash myself in some of the hot water that the kids had prepared. When I was finally ready to leave their domestic dungeon, the proudly coy mother was full of snaggle-toothed affability toward me. She opened her bodice, took out an alarming udder and settled herself cozily on the doorstep to serve her boy (it was a *boy*), his first alfresco breakfast.

When I got back to my house everybody was up and about, and before they all dispersed to their various esoteric activities I filled them in on the morning's happenings.

Of course they didn't believe any part of it. Then, after a while, after I'd repeated my little adventure about six times, Miguel allowed that maybe such a thing had really taken place, but even so he judiciously minimized my share of it. He figured out that the story was very likely based on nothing more substantial than mere market place gossip. *Somebody* had been *born*, that much was finally admitted by everybody, but I nearly spit blood trying to convince them of my heroic part in the proceedings.

Now, get this straight, nobody actually disbelieved me. It was just part of a general procedural technique in our house to denigrate all happenings that the whole group hadn't personally witnessed in a *completely sober* condition.

Well, I was to be utterly vindicated before night had fallen, by a denouement so altogether fantastic that nobody could possible have anticipated it—not even I, and I generally anticipate the looniest.

Listen to this. About four o'clock in the afternoon a friend of ours called Breyito dropped in, and we were all sitting around the dining-room table having coffee when one of our

256

boys, Machmoud, the most dishonest and foul-smelling one, came in to announce a visitor.

"Sidi Halef ben Omar to see you," he said to me.

"Halef ben Omar? Never heard of the guy. What does he want?"

Machmoud bared his gums down to his tonsils and said, "He's the man whose newborn son *you damaged so badly this morning.*"

I jumped up as if I'd been nudged by a tarantula. "What in hell are you talking about? Who *is* this guy, anyway? *Where* is he?"

The door flew open and a wild-eyed, wild-haired Sudanese warrior entered the room, flourishing the same kitchen knife that I had used in my adventure in obstetrics down near the beach that very morning.

I'm afraid I've misled you. The man didn't *enter* the room, he exploded into it, like Nijinsky in *Scheherazade*, only this guy obviously had murder on his mind. Also, he wasn't a warrior, he just *looked* like one, with that goddamned knife and all. You must also remember that Arabic, under the most gracious circumstances, is a pretty turbulent guttural-type language, so the vituperation that now poured out of this guy's mouth was like freshly molten lava hitting an ice cap. I tell you that the whole house simply rocked with this madman's indignant splutterings.

Now, the only ones present who could possibly have understood him were Machmoud and Breyito. Machmoud, however, was so enchanted by this sudden calamitous interruption that he was of no use to us at all. He leaned up against the wall absolutely groaning with ecstasy and held his stomach tightly with both his hands, as if the joy that was agitating his sordid innards might momentarily explode his carcass and spray his indecent entrails all over our ceiling.

For a moment or so, while the flood of abuse was at its very

257

height, Breyito just stared stonily at the gesticulating figure of our incalculable visitor and quietly went on smoking.

I think I'd better explain Breyito. He was the local renting agent who had found us the house we were living in. He had, of course, in keeping with local tradition, cheated us mercilessly, but at the same time he had also done us certain small kindnesses, for which we were somehow beholden to him. On our first taking possession of our dwelling he had appeared on the doorstep carrying some traditional bread and salt as a token of welcome to the new house. True, the bread was mildewed and the salt was pretty moist and unusable, but it was a nice gesture all the same. He later presented us a small bill for these grimy comforts but we preferred to remember the hallowed symbolism implied by this offering rather than the mercenary footnote that trailed after it.

On this solid foundation he had become our patron. He occasionally dropped in for a friendly cup of coffee and also, incidentally, to abscond with some of our loose packages of expensive American cigarettes. He was reputed to be half Jewish and half Arabic, and, as far as I could determine, he was suspected of unimaginable deviousness and guile by both these ethnic groups. He was about five feet tall, ageless, scragglybearded and given to wearing all sorts of ill-assorted cast-off clothing, including our own. He also always wore a red woolen skullcap, with an enormously long black tassel which used to bounce playfully up against his lean buttocks. He spoke a wonderful brand of French that undeniably enriched that sober, logical tongue with nourishing and unexpected adjectives from four other languages. To tell you the truth, we all rather liked Breyito.

I must further apprise you that the moment the infuriated intruder landed in our living room, I had instinctively taken a crumpled ten-franc note out of my pocket, because I had discovered long ago that in all these tropical countries the presence of a little money was likely to work instant miracles of

258

good will when everything else had already failed. I say this not in distaste or criticism of those dear populations. Actually, I felt quite the contrary about it—I always love to live, and to be, among people who are quite frankly bribable.

In fact, I realized with great misgivings and finally even with absolute horror that the Nazis under Hitler were a truly deadly menace to the world at large when I discovered that you couldn't possibly bribe them. "That's the end of civilization," I said to someone at the time. "These bastards are all raving lunatics—and, what's more, they're absolutely incurable."

Now, then, as I kept flourishing my little ten-franc note under the nose of our furious Sudanese visitor, I observed with a sinking heart that he wasn't paying the slightest attention to my conciliatory gesture.

We're lost, I thought. He ignores money. An *Arab* who ignores *money*. He'll make mincemeat out of the lot of us. Obviously another crazy man.

And then finally Breyito intervened. He intervened by bellowing even louder than the vessel of boiling wrath, and when, in the nature of things, the Sudanese had to pause for a moment to catch his breath, Breyito suddenly raised his own voice to absolutely frenetic heights of indignation.

Well, whatever the hell he was screaming, it certainly seemed to have almost a magical effect on Halef ben Omar. After a dozen bloodcurdling guttural hemorrhages out of Breyito, our guest looked quite subdued, and even a little sheepish. The harangue kept right on, and about a minute later Halef even reached out absent-mindedly and took the ten-franc note out of my hand.

After that, in a somewhat more subdued voice, Breyito still continued to admonish the man, until I could see the sweet spirit of reasonableness and conciliation spread its benign veil over the features of our Sudanese time bomb.

You realize, of course, that not one of us had the vaguest

idea what the whole bloody hullaballoo had been about, and so we nearly died waiting for that idiot Breyito to finally cop out to us.

You've just got to try and picture the whole crazy scene for yourself. Soliman and Kafeer, who had joined Machmoud up against the wall, were like a daffy background of epileptic marionettes, laughing, gibbering and gesticulating among themselves. George, Miguel, De Hirsch, our wives and my two children all sat like petrified figures in some frozen tableau of ultimate astonishment.

Breyito, in the role of grand interlocutor and admonisher, reached, even at the dizziest height of his righteousness, only just about as far up as the Sudanese lunatic's navel.

Navel. Of course.

You've probably guessed it by now—the whole goddamned rackety explosion had been brought about by that kid's navel. What else?

Later, after I'd added another ten francs to Halef's baksheesh and he had, after many apologies, finally sought surcease from his grief in the ample bosom of his household, Breyito explained it all to us.

It seems that the subdivision of Mohammedanism to which Halef subscribed still had a good many pagan rituals and customs accruing to it. Well, one of the most important of these primitive excrescences had to do with the birth of a child. The Herrata, the tribe of which Halef was a member, considered it of the utmost importance for the future welfare of the newly born infant, that the umbilical cord be *bitten* through *by the officiating midwife!!!*

Bitten!!! Get it? And I had used a profane kitchen knife. No wonder the father was ready to murder me with the same sordid implement. According to him, I had flagrantly trifled with the spiritual and physical welfare of his offspring by refusing to bite traditionally through the brat's umbilical cord.

"So—what finally happened?" I asked. "How come he suddenly took the dough and copped himself a walk?"

"That's not all," said Breyito. "He's also going to make you godfather to the child, and he's going to name him Alexandre ben Halef."

"How come?" I said. "What did you tell him that made him finally see reason?"

"I told him," said Breyito, putting my pack of cigarettes into his pocket, "that he is not the *only* religious man in the world, that you too have certain traditions and laws that you sincerely believe in and live by, that you too have sacred principles, even if he is too ignorant to know anything about them."

"Well, what in God's name did you tell him? What did you say my religion was, anyway?"

"I told him," said Breyito with a small smirk of self-satisfaction, "that you were a devout *vegetarian.*"

It goes without saying that later I had to fork over a somewhat more substantial sum for the party that had to be given to celebrate the glory of the newborn son. Even years afterward I used to get letters from Tunis, alerting me to various joyous and commemorative occasions in the life of my godchild which entitled him to certain tangible contributions on my part.

Still later, when he had already grown to be fourteen or fifteen years old, he got into some trouble with the local gendarmes and I was asked to subscribe for an expensive lawyer in his behalf. And finally in the mid-forties sometime he seems to have skipped bail from a particularly lurid rape charge that had accrued to his criminal dossier. Indeed, rumor had it that he was rapidly maturing into something of an outstanding scoundrel, even for this part of the world, and I'm sure his parents ascribed most of his misdeeds to that unfortunate morning when I had so impetuously carved my way into his life line with a common kitchen knife.

I might also add that at some unspecified date in his nefarious career he did me the singular honor of calling himself Alexandre Kinch, which was probably as close as he could spell himself into euphonious consanguinity with my own name.

Some time in 1946 I happened to be in Libya on a job of some sort, and I decided to pay a short visit to a few friends of mine in Tunis. When I crossed the border a sloe-eyed, perspiring customs official suddenly looked at me rather reproachfully.

"Anything wrong?" I asked.

He pointed at my passport. "Your name is Alexandre Kinch?" he asked.

"*King*," I said. "K-i-n-g. *King*."

"I see," he said. "You are, however, related to Alexandre Kinch, are you not?"

"He is my godson," I said.

He folded my papers and handed them back to me. "Are you planning to stay long in Tunisia?" he said.

"Just about a week," I said. "I'm planning to stay with some friends in Aouina."

He gave a deep sigh. "Please," he said, "don't play the midwife for anybody this time. It is obviously not your most auspicious talent."

CHAPTER SEVENTEEN

In the last year I've become something of a television * personality. It is a very depressing medium for a sensitive man. I don't say that *my* chores in it are depressing. Not at all. I do exactly as I please before the cameras, and I

---

* Note to Posterity: *Television,* a means of projecting moving images and sounds over large areas, enjoyed a frenzy of popularity, particularly among children, during the forties and fifties of the twentieth century. This potential art form perished prematurely in the late sixties of that same era. Its operational destiny, aesthetic as well as financial, eventually fell under the exclusive aegis of some softheaded businessmen who fancied themselves great creative entrepreneurs. The end was inevitable. It languished on in deep doldrums for several decades, until finally even children were completely repelled by its idiotic, repetitious and stupefying monotony. By 1969, only the absolutely childish were still sometimes beguiled by it.

have never been censored or seriously admonished by anybody. You see, as my friend Lazarus says, my program is as refreshing as a breath of stale air in a vacuum.

But then, let's face it, I'm something of an anomaly in the business. I have no written act, no prepared routine, and nobody has the slightest idea what I'm going to say. That's the chief reason I like the Jack Paar show so much—because it has some unpredictable elements that very frequently carry a real nubbin of pleasant surprise at least.

But television, by and large, is nothing like that. It is actually so depressing that I can barely manage even to think about it. On the other hand, it may very well be the most accurate mirror for the aspirations and hopes of our present-day world. That's probably what gets me *down* so about it.

And the people that work in this gristmill?

Oh, my *God!* The *people!*

The guilty, the gifted and the gentlehearted were always ill at ease on this earth, but nowadays even the moneyed, the mindless, and the mediocre are having an awfully tough time of it. It doesn't make any sense. I have the funny feeling that the worst job anybody can ever have is to be a salesman. On television *everybody* is a salesman. They're not just selling merchandise either, they're selling *time* itself.

Can you imagine it? For zeptilennial centuries, time has been running on for nothing, creating worlds and oceans, and landscapes, and animals, and even men, and horse chestnuts; nobody ever charged anybody a single penny for it. Now they're selling time by the fraction of a minute. It stands to reason that such a hunk of salesmanship certainly involves a lot of finagling, and a lot of blatant lying too, and it is equally clear that this activity must represent some sort of gargantuan hoax on all mankind. That's why everyone involved in it is sort of furtively smug—keeps licking his chops in secret corners, as if he'd just eaten the family canary. That actually describes it.

They act as if they expected at any moment to be caught red-handed, their mouths full of feathers.

The big shots and the middling howitzers and the beebee guns in the television battle all act like a bunch of secret weapons for which nobody has bothered to invent any ammunition.

I understand them all much better now since I've decided on this. Nobody seems sure that their crazy machinations will go on indefinitely. They actually seem to behave as if they were just waiting for somebody to call their combined bluff and tell them all to beat it.

And *then* what???

At one blow, they'll have to return their country houses, their Jaguars, their Chris-Crafts and even their wives and children, probably, and turn them in for a much cheaper brand. Everybody!!!

There's real insecurity for you.

I saw something of the same desperate spirit out in Hollywood years ago, and believe me, those boys sure were quite right to be distrustful of *their* good fortunes. Yes, their dumb luck finally ran out, and nowadays they're exhibiting automobiles and tractors in those vast emporia where the great Thalbergs and Selznicks once held unchallenged sway.

Well, these characters in television give off the same acrid stink of insidious fear that once used to get up into my nostrils at Hollywood and Vine back in the thirties and forties, not so terribly long ago.

You know what happened to me once? I had an interview with Louis B. Mayer, the head of M-G-M and the highest paid executive in the country at that time. I was working on *Life* magazine then, and because I was the possible source of a lot of free publicity for his studio old Louis B. took me to lunch. He was very affable to me too, although he was reputed to be a pretty aloof and even tough hombre on certain occasions. Encouraged by his benign manner I decided to ask him a really leading question.

"How come," I said, "that the French, and the Germans, and the British, make so many good films, and here in Hollywood we turn out so much trash?"

Mayer put his hand on my arm, and a sweet conciliatory smile buttered his soft features. "You are very severe on us," he said. "Very severe indeed. After all, we *do* make *some* good pictures, don't we?"

"Oh, once in a great while," I said. "Hardly worth talking about really."

He pressed my arm a little harder. "But you must admit, Mr. King, that we *do* make *some* good pictures. Don't we?"

"Oh, yes," I said, "*some*. Very, very few, that's for sure."

"But we *do* make them," he insisted. The pressure on my arm increased and I realized that his seeming sedentary pudginess was largely deceptive.

"Once in a great while you *do* make a fairly good picture," I admitted.

"Well," he said, releasing my arm, "I just want you to remember *this:* We don't *have* to!!!"

And there is the spirit that animated Hollywood during the days of its greatest prosperity and puissance. They could go on turning out crap indefinitely, because the market was so voracious and unlimited for it. And yet, out of sheer good nature, just to indulge the fancy of some favorite director perhaps, they *did* make a good picture once in a while too. But they didn't *have* to. They did it out of sheer altruism, that's what it amounted to, and *not* because *bad* pictures weren't salable.

You dig?

Well, those days are gone. Louis B. and his kind are now one with the tyrannosaurus and the pterodactyl. But the same noble and public-spirited impulses that once activated the movie industry are now freely rampant in the television business. The same smug *laissez passer* attitude is presently digging the grave of another human enterprise that might, who knows, under more enlightened guidance even have aspired to become a fresh, new art form. Meanwhile, you can find all the old Hollywood cynicism on tap all over Madison Avenue and nobody seems to have learned a goddamned thing.

And, then again, maybe what animates all those hand-tailored moles isn't cynicism at all. Maybe it's just plain stupidity. They just don't know any better, so naturally they can't *imagine* any better, and the few enlightened characters that do happen to stumble into their bailiwick are afraid to speak up, for fear of losing their jobs.

There is, in fact, something corrosive and debilitating about the TV shenanigans and it seems to affect nearly everybody who gets mixed up in it. Actors who have earned honest reputations for their skill and integrity in the theater, for instance, tend to behave rather sheepishly, and even apologetically, when you happen to run into them at television rehearsals. It is as if you were catching them in the midst of a rather shady transaction, some character-destroying swindle, that they'd only briefly gotten mixed up in for the large amount of loot that was involved.

There are exceptions, of course. And I don't mean the eternally untalented male and female idiots, creatures of accident, most of them, who claim to see a "challenge" in television. A challenge to what? To their chronic ineptitude? To the patience of mankind? To their goddamned dumb luck, or what?

Well, whatever the hell it is that they're doing, they can all drop dead, for my part. I'll stay in it as long as it amuses me, and if the whole crazy racket folds up tomorrow morning I can't imagine to whom it could possibly matter less.

It is Saturday night in New York as I am writing these lines,

267

and if you look in the paper to see what is going on tonight on TV you'll learn that you have your choice of Guy Lombardo, Sammy Kaye and Lawrence Welk. That's the musical fare for the evening. Last year you could also have tuned in on Perry Como. (He's been moved to another night since then.)

Now, just take Perry Como, for instance, or take Dinah Shore, for that matter. Or, better still, leave them both alone —because I'm sure you'll survive somehow without them. *I* manage to do *magnificently* without them. So, you see, it *can* be done.

And yet these two mildly gifted middle-aged vaudevillians are probably the highest-paid entertainers on the air today. I wouldn't really mind them so much if only the poor things weren't constantly being coaxed, coached and cajoled into telling jokes, or being funny.

Being *funny!!!*

For God's sake, it's enough to make the angels in heaven weep for sympathy with all of mismanaged mankind. And, what's more, I think what makes these people, and a few others like them, so popular with the general public is the fact that the rest of TV entertainment is even worse. These characters at least have some amusing guests once in a while. They keep swapping them back and forth between them all the time, of course, but even so it is better than nothing.

But undeniably their chief virtue lies in their popularity with their sponsors, not to forget the sponsors' wholesome wives and their apple-cheeked children. And believe me, no artist who has ever performed in the world before this day has ever had to meet such incalculably high and such profoundly exigent standards.

Let's talk some more about this nonsense.

We all know that Leonardo da Vinci and Michelangelo had to work for some pretty eccentric Renaissance bosses. So did a lot of other artists over the centuries, but it must surely be obvious to the meanest intelligence that even the Hollywood dopes who ran their businesses right out of this world were undeniably superior to the chronic fatheads who now have the final say-so in television circles. *When*, in the history of recorded time, did a man who had, for example, launched a nauseating synthetic sandwich spread have the power to dictate a compulsory entertainment program for millions of his helpless fellow citizens?

For almost twenty-four hours a day, somebody is always prating on the TV screen about the especially soothing virtues of certain splinter-free toilet papers (they call it *tissue*, of course), and the man who originally compounded this public-spirited commodity is, in the very nature of things, the absolute assthetic arbiter for endless programs that are going to come thundering into your living room for the next few years.

By the way, what the hell *is* all this constant yapping on the tactile suavity of toilet paper all about, anyway? What, in heaven's name, did people use until now? Corncobs? Or pine cones? Or What?

But never mind!

It is my belief that America's unique contributions to world culture are democracy, jazz and plumbing. (I don't mean these are its *only* contributions. I just maintain that these are its truly *unique* ones.) Well, you can hardly hear any decent jazz on television from year's end to year's end, simply because some of the lentilheaded sponsors' wives just don't seem to care for it. And how did I happen to obtain hold of this particular piece of inside dope? I *heard* one of these dizzy, lymphatic dolls talking to her husband, an important soap sponsor, about it. That's how.

"Stanley," she said, "you know I had lunch with Gertrude and Paul yesterday, and they both can't understand why you're paying out your good money for all that jazz racket. Nobody I talk to can stand the sound of it. Why don't you get something light and soothing, with a little romance to it, that everybody enjoys? After all, *you're* the one that has to pay the bill, aren't you? I really don't understand why you let those agency people lead you around by the nose. Honest, Stanley, it's about time you put your foot down."

She's quite right. Stanley ought to put his size fourteen foot down. Right on top of her neck, too. And he ought to kick the stuffing right out of her with his other two feet. But you know damned well that no such thing is going to happen. He'll just go down to his agency the next day and get the guy fired who had the idea to hire good jazz musicians in the first place.

So you'll say, But they do occasionally get around to sponsoring a real jazz jamboree with a lot of famous names and stuff, don't they?

Yes, they do. They launch some kind of frozen-assed Spectacular, and they even hire Louis Armstrong, and Dizzy Gillespie, and George Shearing, and then they get hold of Milton Berle to act as master of ceremonies for the shindig. (Believe me, I didn't invent this little eisteddfod, because *nobody* could have invented it. It all really happened, on a bitter, sinful night some months ago, and I myself took in the better part of five minutes of it.)

Isn't there ever anything *good* on television? Is it *all* just a lot of hopeless trash? Oh, no. Once every six or eight weeks you're liable to get something rather decent, I think.

I did enjoy a series of wonderful programs that were televised from tape—interviews with Edith Hamilton, Sean O'Casey, Robert Frost, Wanda Landowska and others. And believe me, it made me absolutely sick with regret when I realized what a valuable tool for the benefit and improvement of mankind television might have become, if only it had landed in the hands of people who had had a decent, human regard for its profoundly significant potential.

Man! That Landowska interview, for instance, was absolutely the wildest. You may, for all I know, never have heard of her at all. She's dead now, the dear soul, but she happened to be the greatest living harpsichordist in the world at that time. She looked it too. Her face was completely spiritualized from the impact of the musical beauty to which she had constantly exposed herself for many, many years. She had a large, wonderfully commanding nose that was judiciously balanced by a substantial bun of hair and by a long velvet train which generally trailed regally behind her. These combined effects, sustained by a highly deliberate and stately manner, gave her the appearance of a medieval duchess who had just stepped out of her golden frame in some secret gallery in Verona.

She was Polish, of course, and still had a strong Slavic accent which added immeasurable nuances of charm to the precise method of her locution. In the course of this program she played some compositions of Bach (to whom her life was dedicated), and, if I remember correctly, she even played the same piece over again, because *she liked it so much.* (Can you imagine what a sponsor would have done about *that* one?)

At any rate, the interviewer, obviously a sensible and musically cultivated man (not Milton Berle, this time, nor Tennessee Ernie Ford either), asked her about her colorful and adventurous life and wondered whether, out of the fund of her many experiences, she could perhaps recall some particularly cogent examples whose application might prove useful to some of the young, aspiring listeners in the large television audience.

"Oh, yes," said Miss Landowska, "a great many things have happened to me that have been very useful to me as object lessons in my own life, and it might perhaps be helpful to young people if I told them something about it. Particularly in the old days, when I was young and very impetuous myself."

She gave a sweet, reminiscent smile and proceeded. "Many, many years ago I gave quite a number of recitals in Czarist Russia, and my dear husband traveled with me there also. And then one day a very wonderful thing happened. I had a letter from the great Tolstoi, asking me to come to Yasnaya Polyana, his place of residence, and he asked me to please bring my harpsichord with me and to play for him. You can imagine how thrilled I was by this invitation. So, I immediately canceled all my other appointments and we set off at once to go to the home of Leo Tolstoi. But it was the middle of winter, a real Russian winter, and we sometimes found it pretty hard going across the many deserted and forlorn country roads. We were traveling in two sleighs—my husband and I in one, and some of our small baggage and the harpsichord in the other. And then, late one afternoon when we had nearly arrived at our goal, the horses, all of them, suddenly stopped dead in their tracks. Curiously enough, neither of the drivers seemed upset or even took notice of it. In fact, both of them took time out at that moment to refill their old, evil-smelling pipes. I sat still for a while wondering what was going to happen next, but after about ten minutes of this completely meaningless halt in the midst of this snowbound wilderness, I suddenly became very indignant. I really couldn't stand it any longer, so I threw aside my fur lap robe and jumped out of our sleigh."

Miss Landowska gave a soft chuckle in memory of that long-distant youthful leap and continued.

"Luckily for me, I have a big nose. I suppose you have noticed that I *have* a big nose. Well, it was very fortunate for me at that time, because when I jumped out of that sleigh I sank straightway into the deep snow, and if I didn't have such a big nose, then that would have been the end of me. I was saved by my nose. But I was young then, and very angry, and

272

even angrier now, because I was wet all over, and so I screamed at the driver and scolded him for all he was worth. And I must say the driver took it all very calmly. Finally he removed the pipe out from under his icicle-covered mustache, touched his hand respectfully to his fur cap and said, 'Madam, the horses stopped of their own accord. *I* did not stop them. Believe me, when *horses* stop, it is best not to go on. They know. In a little while, God willing, you will see they will start moving again, and with heaven's help we shall get you safely to your destination before dark.'

"And that is just how it all came about. In an hour or so we arrived at Yasnaya Polyana, where a warm supper and warm greetings were all awaiting us. I must tell you that this experience has been of inestimable use to me all the rest of my life. Whenever, later on, I happened to be struggling desperately to accomplish something within a certain time, and when, perhaps, strange unforeseen obstacles arose before me, and when these irritating delays seemed absolutely foolish and exasperating to my tormented patience, I would suddenly pause in my wild charge toward my imminent goal and remember the horses on the road to Yasnaya Polyana. I remember that it is sometimes quite childish and willful to try to rush the gates of opportunity. I found that when the time was ripe the gates would miraculously open of themselves."

That's what I heard that great and gifted lady say on television one afternoon. Of course, it happened to be Sunday, when most people are either sound asleep or wading around knee-deep in their funny papers. It was not really "choice" time in the television business, and so they let us have the program as a sort of good-will giveaway.

You see, they too, like Louis B. Mayer, "didn't really *have* to do it, but they *did*."

And now let me tell you my final parallel between Hollywood movies and TV.

273

Some years ago when the big studios were still riding high, a director out there read a short story, in *Harper's*, I think, and he liked it so well that he sent word east to the young man who had written it. This guy's name was Merle Sedgwick. I knew him. Sedgwick had never in his life earned more than seventy-five dollars a week, and so when the studio out on the Coast offered him two hundred and fifty he was perfectly enchanted, of course. So he went out there very happily, after we'd thrown him a farewell party in the Village.

And then when he arrived a quite common thing happened. The producer of the proposed film wanted the ending of the story changed. He wanted the boy and girl to get married in the end, and even to have a couple of children. The original plot had them just vaguely drifting apart.

The director told the author about the proposed alteration, but surprisingly enough Kid Sedgwick refused to make the change. The director reported this unusual behavior to the producer.

"How much does the guy get here?" said the producer.

"Two fifty a week," said the director.

"Give him five hundred and tell him to get his ass into gear," said the producer.

But Sedgwick was still stubborn, and he refused again.

The director reported this also back to his boss, and the producer, getting pretty irritated about the whole thing, said, "Give the idiot a thousand, and I don't want to hear any more about it."

A thousand bucks a week is a lot of money, but Sedgwick just couldn't see himself changing that story of his even for such a princely fee. "I'm sorry," he said, "but it somehow knocks the guts right out of my whole yarn. It just doesn't make any sense to me that way. Don't you see? I really couldn't do it."

"Is that final?"

"That's final."

So the director reported back again, and this time the producer got good and sore. "Fire the son of a bitch this minute," he said, "and get somebody to work for us who'll listen to reason. And one more thing—don't ever get me any more *cheap* writers."

You get it, don't you? The producer meant, "Get me only people who start at fifteen hundred or two thousand, then we're sure to have no trouble. A guy who gets that kind of money is in no position to argue."

It's the same in TV. They pay those shmoes such large salaries because then they can't afford to have any kind of guts. Their guts are in escrow up in the payroll department and that's where they stay for the duration.

If you think I have been too severely critical, and perhaps even unfair, in my appraisal of the role of the sponsors and their advertising errand boys in the world of TV, I'm hereby appending an excerpt from a newspaper article that I hope will help to exculpate me in your eyes.

This piece was printed in the Sunday edition of the New York *Times* and was written by their distinguished television critic, Jack Gould.

Read, and marvel.

How advertising agencies operate in television—their strict supervision of shows and the business factors that influence or limit the choice of programs that the public sees—was explained by agency executives testifying at a hearing held in New York last week by the Federal Communications Commission.

* * * * * * * * * * *

What was made abundantly evident was that advertising agencies, which never solicit billing on the screen, in practice may be virtually the actual producers. The Theatre Guild, David Susskind and Desi Arnaz may take the public bows, to judge by the testimony, but they don't make an important move without an approving nod from the agency men.

In the case of most shows in which they are active, for instance, the agencies said that they review all scripts in advance, scrutinize dialogue and story lines and have their "program representatives" on hand to check each day's production work.

The Theatre Guild, one of the more independent institutions of Broadway, agrees in the case of television to let B.B.D. & O. sit down and jointly review what dramatic property to do, the wisdom of the casting and "each revision" of script, Mr. Foreman testified.

The agencies readily acknowledged that considerations of advertising dictate limitations on subject matter.

Mr. Seymour testified that "on dramatic show after dramatic show" the advertising agencies delete material deemed contrary to a sponsor's interest. "An advertiser cannot afford to lose any segment of society," he said. Any political mention is prohibited in drama supervised by his agency, he added.

Mr. Clyne, speaking for clients of his agency, said as a matter of company policy a sponsor does not want to leave a viewer "sad and depressed" about the one-tenth of one per cent of the country that knows desolation and misery. The sponsor is not in "the business of displeasing" and wants to leave with the viewer "a pleasant and favorable impression," he said.

* * * * * * * * * * * *

Mr. Foreman added that even a relatively small volume of critical mail can make a sponsor "apprehensive." He recalled an experience of seeing the head of a very large corporation personally reading each letter received. Because of the nature

276

of their business in dealing with the public advertisers are "extremely sensitive," he said.

The agency executives agreed that the policies of sponsors did not usually lead to difficulties with most writers, producers and directors. The creative folk are "hep," Mr. Pinkham observed; they know the headaches to avoid. One result, Mr. Seymour reported, is that script conflicts have become fewer and fewer.

Mr. Pinkham noted that a manufacturer of non-filter cigarettes wanted the villains in a drama to be shown smoking a filter cigarette. Similarly, he said, a filter manufacturer wanted the villain to be depicted as preferring non-filters. An aspirin company, he noted, would not stand for a drama that showed a suicide committed by swallowing too much aspirin.

Despite the high degree of agency participation, the executives stressed that in their opinion *their companies often improved programs in terms of theatrical effectiveness and that their supervision did not dampen creative spirit.**

Well, how about it? You like it?

In conclusion, let me say that television, more than any other falsifying medium abroad in the world today, has most thoroughly distorted man's sometimes noble and always tragic posture in the universe. I'm afraid it has reduced us all to a pathetic role which seems by now to have become quite unrectifiable.

If a visitor from Mars arrived here after mankind had already perished, and all he found were just a lot of old television tapes, he would certainly get a most sinister picture of what sort of animal had once dominated this sad planet.

On the strength of overwhelming evidence, he would have to conclude that Homo sapiens must have been an evil-smell-

* Italics mine.

277

ing, dandruffy, overweight monster whose chest or bosom was in perpetual need of clinical attention. It would also be obvious to him that this creature's overly hairy legs ended in feet that were covered with disastrous calluses, bunions and corns of all sorts. And I can't imagine how the visitor would explain to himself the fact that there was an unaccountable physical hiatus between man's sordid navel and his chapped, unsightly knees. The silence on that vital area alone would certainly puzzle him to the point of distraction.

I am not a man from Mars, but, by merely listening for a few years to the depressing and suggestive commercials on TV, I myself have finally arrived at a pretty grim image of my poor dilapidated fellow men.

Depressing, isn't it?

CHAPTER EIGHTEEN

E VERY ONCE IN A WHILE somebody sits down and
writes himself a fat book to prove the great social usefulness
of the advertising business. You can't really blame them for
trying, since the long-suffering but nonetheless quite hep
American public seems to have become more and more aware,
in recent years, that the advertising business has finally turned
itself into a soggy, overripe fungus prospering jubilantly on
the body of modern industry.

The champions of this racket always maintain—indeed, it
is the basic fulcrum on which all their loaded arguments seem
to pivot—that the advertising fraternity has almost single-
handedly brought about our high and enviable standard of
living. These boys have alerted us, so the authors claim, to all

the wonderfully good and useful things that are available to us nowadays to make our lives so much dozier, cozier and rosier all around.

Mebbe so.

I just have a funny feeling that their chief business is to waken a lot of needless appetites in the hearts of the general public—appetites which eventually are bound to lead to a lot of vanity-buying, vulgar ownership competition and a top-heavy load of worrisome debts. I strongly suspect that those public-spirited lads actually often tell us about a great many things that we *ought* to want, just because some big-time gambling gents have their goddamned warehouses loaded with some of the crap they can't get rid of. See what I mean?

Well, whatever the merits of the situation, when I was a much younger man I never bothered to examine the true values involved in the case, and, since the young are notoriously heedless, I even tried a couple of times to grab myself a fast buck in the lush advertising pastures. I really don't know why I bothered, since I was making a good enough livelihood for myself and my family as a book illustrator. The books that I illuminated with my drawings were mostly classics that I myself had read and loved for many years, and it was absolutely ideal work for me, too, since none of my publishers ever advised, edited or censored me in any way. Nevertheless, as I'm telling you, I occasionally had eyes for the advertising pages of newspapers and magazines, knowing for a certainty that that was where the real mazuma was actually spent and garnered.

So, by the time ten or twelve of my illustrated books had hit the market and my name had become pretty well known to art directors all over the country, I let it be gently bruited about, through certain discreet and influential friends, that I was not above making the needed obeisance to the god of commerce and his officiating potent high priests along Park and

Madison avenues. And, in due time, the long and impatiently awaited call finally came to me.

In the life of an imaginative young man every urinous lamp-post and sordid fire hydrant looms like a possible turning point in his career, and so the call I received one morning from Shreeve, Hamilton and Dekker was, of course, the big turning point. They roosted up on Park Avenue, sure enough, and the following day I landed in their cool, characterless offices with flushed cheeks and a palpitating heart. Mr. Arthur Dekker, a junior member of the firm, was ordained to be my destiny on that particular morning, and in due time he proceeded to grease me up and grease me down with the vacant, meaningless amiabilities that are eternally current in such circles.

"I *love* your work," he said. "I think you're *just* the man for the job I have in mind."

"Thank you," I said. "Did you see my *Hairy Ape*, or *Anna Christie* perhaps?"

"No-o-o," he said. "I'm sorry to say I haven't. I *must* send out for them this very afternoon."

He made himself a quick note on a pale-blue pad and turned back to me with all his headlights ablaze.

"Perhaps," I said, "you've seen my *François Villon*. It was just published last week."

"No, not that one either."

He added another title to his list.

"But never mind the past," he said. "Why don't I just show you some of the copy we have tentatively laid out—subject to your approval, of course."

"Fine," I said.

And then he showed me the copy. There were about four large pages, on which some layout man, who was certainly on their staff and was following his harassed life somewhere around that building, had made a few quick but wonderfully deft sketches. I was absolutely stunned. I couldn't understand why those idiots didn't just use *his* drawings, with their skillful, evocative verve, instead of hiring a completely ignorant outsider like myself.

Well, it was none of my business, I thought, and if that's the way they wanted it, it was certainly not my job to enlighten them.

But at this point another worm of uneasiness had started to gnaw away at my vitals. This advertising campaign of theirs had surely something to do with a Caribbean or Mediterranean cruise of some kind, and why in hell they'd gotten it into their ossified noggins that *I* was the boy to embroider their goddamned traveling doilies was more than I could possibly imagine.

Well, I'm not going to torment you much longer. It was indeed a cruise, a series of cruises, in fact, that they were about to publicize, in full color. And, what's more, they had a lot of money to operate with and were determined to hire a lot of "serious artists" to distill the necessary *spumone* out of it for them.

That's where *I* came in.

"This, Mr. King, is addressed directly to the higher-income brackets," Mr. Dekker told me. "This is no ten-day goulash along the eastern coast down to the banana republics. No, sir!"

His voice was like the Voice of Judgment on that great day when All things shall at last be set right: when not only shall the goats be separated from the sheep but the beetles shall be divided from the cockroaches, and no mere mediocre bank balance shall be allowed to sail into glory under false colors.

"It is something quite unique in the whole concept of pleasure travel," he continued. "It establishes a new level in vacation exclusiveness and expense. First stop is Honolulu. Everything is paid for. Native feasts, tips to the waiters, gifts for the folks at home, moonlight serenades for the ladies, leis—everything."

"Sounds great," I said. "And what exactly have you in mind for *me* to do?"

"You'll *visualize* all this rampant luxury," said Mr. Dekker. "You'll bring the *atmosphere* and the *smell* of all that ambient potential *romance* right into their living rooms." He got up and put his hand on my shoulder. "I know it's a big responsibility, but I have every confidence you'll pull it off for us in style."

He didn't notice that I had aged twenty-six years in the last five minutes and since he was so totally unobservant I thought I'd quickly risk another question. "How, for instance," I said, "do *you* visualize this whole pudding—this *situation*, I mean?"

He got absolutely glassy-eyed with inspiration. He looked like a love-drunken heath hen at the height of its mating season.

"I?" he said. "I see it all very clearly."

"Yes?" I said. "Go on!"

"I see the top deck of the S. S. *Pansylvania* completely awash with moonlight. . . . I see forty or sixty couples dancing against a background of lifeboats, silhouetted against the calm, pale-blue Pacific. . . . I see Romance like a tangible emanation coming right out of that vision and tenderly embracing the spectator who looks at that full-color ad."

He is a great man, I thought to myself. He's either a very great man or the biggest bonehead I've ever met in my life. Whatever the hell he is, he is sure to own this building, and maybe the whole street, before he's much older. He sure is *going* places, and it ain't just to Honolulu on the S. S. *Pansylvania*, either. He'll be in Washington in somebody's Cabinet, if we don't watch out. This character is dynamite.

I finally left him to his dreams and went home, a broken man. You have to understand that I had always picked myself books like Rabelais or *The Brothers Karamazov* to illustrate. That's the direction my general tastes had always taken, and what in hell had given this daffy wizard the notion that I would be good at executing his ice-cream mirage was more than I could imagine.

I forgot to tell you that they were prepared to pay anywhere from thirty-five hundred to five thousand dollars for this drawing, but I don't suppose I have to tell you that I was certainly going to *try* for it, if it killed me.

First I held a council of war. I called Covarrubias, Johnnie Held and Al Hirschfeld and asked them to give me their well-considered advice about how to handle this booby trap.

"Forget it!" said Al. "And if you *insist* on monkeying with it, do it all just a little above eye level. Like a semi–bird's-eye view, get it, so you get a titivating glimpse of the girls' cleavages. You might even have one of the couples necking in one of the lifeboats."

"The lifeboats are *covered*," I said. "And, besides, all these people are high in the chips, brother, and by the time you've accumulated a pile big enough for that kind of a cruise you're no longer young enough to leap in and out of lifeboats."

"Nonsense!" said Al. "If you make any of the jokers on that cruise older than twenty-four, they'll just laugh you right out of that office."

I realized, of course, that he was dead right.

Nobody in an American ad is ever out of his, or her, early twenties unless it's an ad for some premature retirement fund. And even those inventions used to puzzle me like all hell. The couples in those ads would always be sitting in some landscape, or in some boat on a lake, with rambler roses in the foreground, orchids and palms in the near distance and the high plateaus of the Himalayas as a backdrop. *She* was generally a semi-motherly type. I say *semi*-motherly because you couldn't possibly imagine her in the sort of compromising condition that is bound to occur when a woman gives birth to something. Much less was it possible to visualize her involved in the disorderly machinations that must inevitably have taken place to result even in a minor pregnancy. Her hair was curled and coiffed like coiled aluminum, and she had been caught by the artist or photographer in the act of knitting some sort of incalculably pure piece of gossamer wearing apparel for a nixie. The husband had just at that moment nailed an enormous speckled trout (two and a half feet long at the most conservative estimate) and this trout was grinning toothily from gill to gill, obviously enchanted to have been captured by such a neat and eminently solvent couple.

Years ago the legend beneath this tableau used to read: "Retire at *Fifty* on a *Hundred and Fifty* a Month!"

I notice that the ante has been raised a good deal since then. Things have gotten a lot more expensive in the interim, don't you see?

I wonder what ever became of that original couple when inflation started to set in. Where in hell can they possibly be now?

Washing dishes in some nearby diner, I suppose.

All these dismal musings, naturally, landed me nowhere. I just had to get down to limning my great cruising masterpiece if ever I expected to rake in all that rich, loose advertising kale.

I'll skip three bitter weeks and just tell you that it was pure, ever suffering hell. You see, solvent people nowadays are so goddamned unpicturesque—*that* was my chief trouble. All those barbered, Brooks-tailored men, all those sanitary, carefully groomed women, just gave me the absolute willies. Let's face it, it was a lot easier for artists in the old days. The beards, the mustaches, the ruffs, the cuffs, the swords and the lutes were simply the greatest. Rembrandt and Van Dyke had a cinch; Holbein and even Ingres never knew what a portrait problem *really* was. They should have come to *me*. And I had to do eighty of these monsters. That's more people than El Greco painted at "The Funeral of Count Orgaz."

Man!

Well, it was finally done. I mean I *did* it. My household was completely demoralized when it was over, and I went to a

Turkish bath just to make sure that all the remaining poison was properly sweated out of me.

The following day I went up to the advertising agency to submit my creation.

I was admitted at once.

Mr. Dekker, who had called me several times during the weeks of my labors, had a flower in his buttonhole. There was a festive, almost bridal air in the making. There was only one other person present, an elderly factotum who pretended to be busy in the far corner of the room. I wondered how many years this poor creature could possibly have worked in this soap-bubble factory, since he still wore black bombazine sleeve protectors on his withered arms.

At any rate, the mantel was cleared and I unveiled my opus.

Mr. Dekker stepped back, put a hand on his chin, cocked his head sideways and squinted critically at my picture.

"Ma-a-a-arvelous!!!" he said. "Absolutely ma-a-a-arvelous!!!"

He said it as if the word had six syllables at least. I can tell you, I nearly fainted with joy. *So*—I'd made it, after all. With all my misgivings and everything. Who knows, I thought, I might even have an unsuspected knack for the hideous crap. Talent *is* a mystery, isn't it? Well, I was glad. I was *damned* glad. Now we could build that additional porch on our country house. The kids' camp was coming up pretty soon, too. Well, there'd be plenty of moolah around for everything. But still my greatest satisfaction came from the surprise that I'd *had it in me all the time*. Forgotten were the dismal three weeks, the painfully deferred nervous breakdown, the Turkish bath and everything. I was on top of the world—and I just loved the view.

My rambling thoughts were interrupted by a cough. The old has-been, or never-was, with the sleeve protectors had broken the spell.

"Chrisholm," said Mr. Dekker, "get yourself some Ludens. You're bothering everybody." He looked stern during this piece of admonishment, but instantly turned a smiling face back to the picture.

"It's great, Mr. King," he said. "Great!" Then he stepped just a little closer.

"There's just one little thing I'd like you to do for me."

"Yes?" I said. And believe me, I loved that man so much at that moment that I would gladly have leaped out of that window for him, although it was an unusually windy day.

"I'd like you," he said, "I'd like you to take those dancing people—those couples—"

"Those *forty* couples," I said.

"Those *forty* couples, and turn them all a little to the left."

I'm not good enough a reporter to tell you what happened immediately after that. The words "crazy son of a bitch" seem to recur constantly whenever I try to recall that dismal event, but then again I may be wrong; I may have used some other, more accurate terms.

When I finally landed out in the hall again, several decades later, I instantly tore my drawing into small fragments and flung them into a large metal trash can that was standing in one corner. As I turned away to go to the nearest elevator, old Mr. Chrisholm with the sleeve protectors suddenly appeared before me. He waggled his silly head from side to side and I could see that he eyed me with stern disapproval.

"You made a terrible mistake, Mr. King," he said.

"*You're* telling me! I made the mistake of coming into this goddamned building!"

He took hold of my sleeve, and because he was an old man I didn't bother to sock him one.

"You see, Mr. King," he went on, "your mistake was really a very simple one." He picked one of the pieces of my picture

287

that was still sticking out of that garbage can and held it up before me. "You should have made a hairy, masculine man's hand, right here," he said, pointing straight at a girl's arm.

I shook myself loose from him. "You're nuts!" I said. "That's a *woman's* arm you're pointing at. Why would I put a *man's* hand at the end of it?"

"Ah!" said Mr. Chrisholm. "But if you had only done it! If you had done that it would have been an *obvious* mistake. Don't you see? Your drawing was really very good. Just about what he wanted, in fact. Indeed, it was so good you ruined your chances. If you'd only painted the wrong hand on that arm, he would have jumped at it at once. He would have been flushed with triumph that he'd spotted that terrible error just in time. And then you would have quietly taken the drawing back to your studio and you would have erased that flagrant error with a razor blade, and in less than twenty minutes you would have repainted it properly. Right? Everybody would have been happy. But you see, Mr. King, you unfortunately submitted a picture in which there was *nothing* for him to *edit*. You're a very young man, Mr. King. I advise you strongly to mend your rash ways while there is still time."

I have a fine parable about a wise old man that I heard in Paris around 1926. It came to me from a guy called Nathan Wirt, who was compiling and translating some tales and legends from the Yiddish. One evening at the Café Dôme, surrounded by a lot of pansies, lesbians, show-offs and nitwits of all sorts, he told it to me. It goes something like this:

It seems that under the Czars, when the Jews certainly had a very tough time of it, it sometimes happened that by unimaginable industry and frenzied perseverance some Jewish families still somehow managed to acquire a great deal of money.

Now, then, this story has to do with a grand old patriarch from just such a rich family, whose name was Reb Eliezer Kalman. Reb Eliezer was a deeply religious man, who, not only because of his great wealth, but rather because of his astonishing worldly wisdom as well as his compassionate nature and his kindliness, was deeply respected and loved by the whole Jewish community. Indeed, the repute of this great sage had gone abroad even among the Gentiles, and it was therefore common knowledge that occasionally local dignitaries and people affiliated with the provincial government would call at the Kalman home in the local ghetto, to discuss certain knotty personal and official problems with the wise old Jew.

It was a tradition in the Kalman family that once every two or three years Reb Eliezer would go abroad to visit the commercial fairs in Germany and make large purchases of various sorts of merchandise, such as tobacco, woolens, soap, linen and other commodities, which were later dispensed at retail in the stores owned by the members of his considerable flock. It was also an old established custom for him on these occasions to take along one of the younger boys of the Kalman tribe, preferably one who was at least thirteen years old and had therefore been confirmed and, according to Jewish tradition, had officially matriculated into manhood.

And so it happened that sometime in the late eighties of the last century, Reb Eliezer was again making ready to go to Germany on one of his extensive shopping tours. This time he decided to take along his favorite grandchild, a bright and sensitive boy called Chonon.

Well, you can just imagine what this prospect must have meant for the child. First of all, to be all alone with his adored grandfather would already have been happiness in abundance for him, but to be permitted to see all the strange world of the Gentiles, to marvel at their houses, their gardens, their great rivers and cities, was a promise of such unalloyed bliss that his little heart was filled to overflowing with the mere expectant wonder of it.

At last the day arrived when they were to start out on their journey, and the miracles began the very moment they boarded the train. The stern conductor with his belted and buckled uniform was unbelievably courteous to the old man and he was even particularly affable to his little grandson. The travelers had a compartment completely to themselves, and, since the conductor knew from previous experience that Reb Eliezer paid very generously for good service, all strangers who sought admittance to their private refuge were instantly and unceremoniously expelled.

So they had ample room to stretch out for a rest whenever the spirit moved them, and all through the trip they remained undisturbed at their frequent prayers, as well as during their pretty lavish meals. Indeed, the old man had even brought along a large bottle of prime vodka, and during one of the conductor's many friendly calls he was offered a good-sized sampling of it. Chonon noticed that at the end of the voyage he got the rest of the bottle, too, along with a good-sized stack of green and blue paper money.

Meanwhile the country landscapes and the whizzing telegraph poles rushed madly past the befogged windows, and the young boy actually savored the magic of the voyage rather warily, for fear he would suddenly wake up in the morning back at home in his feather bed. But there was one sure piece of glorious certainty he could plainly feel in his pocket; it was a silver ruble that his grandfather had given him before they had embarked. This ruble was to be spent at his own discretion at the great fair at Danzig, where he was going to be free to indulge his purchasing fancy in any direction he chose. That had been the agreed stipulation at the very outset.

Because it was Reb Eliezer's habit to travel only in the daytime, it came about that late in the afternoon, after they had already crossed into Poland, the conductor dropped into their compartment to help them pack and move their belongings before they were to descend from the train at nightfall. The old man had made this same trip scores of times through the years, and he generally stopped over at the same familiar kosher hostelries, where in the past a great deal of thought and care had been exercised by the various managements for his peace and comfort.

Now too, when the train finally pulled into the station, the landlord and a few servants from a nearby hotel were already smiling their welcome and waving exuberantly to Reb Eliezer from the platform.

And then, just as the old man and his grandson, assisted by the conductor, were stepping carefully down from their coach, a venerable old Jew with an enormous white beard approached Reb Eliezer, touched him gently on the arm and said, "Peace be with you."

Reb Eliezer turned toward him, took a quick but searching look at the aged patriarch, and said, *"You can kiss my behind!"*

Then he quietly took his grandson's hand and without a glance backward walked cheerfully into the welcoming arms of his host.

To little Chonon it seemed as if the railroad station had suddenly been struck by lightning. His ears still roared with the ugly, repulsive words that his grandfather had just uttered, and, stunned by the impact of that inexplicable piece of unmotivated rudeness, he suffered himself to be dragged along quietly to the hotel.

You must remember that Chonon had never before in his life heard anything but prayers, words of wisdom and statements of kindness come from the lips of the old man. As a matter of fact, in the past, with the facile imaginative gift of a child, Chonon had always freely associated his grandfather with the revered patriarchs of the Old Testament.

291

In his bewildered state Chonon silently endured the fulsome greetings and endearments of the fat, rancid-smelling landlady, and when that undulant bolster smacked a wet, hairy kiss on his mouth he hardly even troubled to wipe it off.

Later, when he sat staring blindly at his filled supper plate, a wild resolve was finally born in his heart. He would run away. He had a whole ruble in his pocket, and that money would surely last him for food and shelter until he could find himself some sort of work. He certainly could not possibly continue on a journey with the foulmouthed horror who had so shamelessly disclosed his true and sordid nature that very evening.

Luckily Reb Eliezer, with the postprandial somnolence of the elderly, had noticed nothing at all amiss with his grandson, and so when Chonon asked him for permission to go down into the street for a while he readily gave his consent.

"Don't go too far away from the door," he said. "And don't show your ruble to anyone."

"I won't," said Chonon, as he quickly made his way out of the hateful apartment. In a moment he was down the dark staircase, and as he stepped out into the street he took a deep breath that was very much like a sob. He wondered in which direction he ought to strike out to reach the nearby town. Just as he was trying to reach a decision, he noticed an elderly Jew coming toward him along the wet pavement. As the child was about to accost the stranger for advice, he suddenly recognized him as the same old man who, only half an hour before, had been so brutally offended by his grandfather at the railroad station.

So Chonon smiled up at him apologetically and wished him a good evening.

"Good evening, my boy," said the old man. "A very good evening to you indeed." He leaned down toward the child most benignly, and it was obvious that he bore not the slightest rancor for the insult that he had so unaccountably suffered just a little while ago.

"Tell me," he said to Chonon, "is that your grandfather taking a nap upstairs?"

"Yes," admitted Chonon, somewhat shamefacedly.

"And his name is Reb Eliezer Kalman from Poltchock, isn't it?"

"Yes, it is," admitted Chonon.

"And he is going to Danzig, to the fair, is that right?"

"Yes, that's right."

"And what is your name, little boy?"

"Chonon."

"Chonon! Oh, so you must be son of Sarah Leib Graschitzer and Leibish Kalman—is that right?"

"Right."

"And how is your Aunt Rachel? Did she give birth yet?"

"Yes, she had a son, he should live and be healthy."

"And your Uncle Saul, did he move his saddlery to Twelk, or is he still in Velish?"

"He moved to Varonoslava."

"Varonoslava? What is he doing in Varonoslava? There are three saddlers there already!"

"He's bought one of them out," said Chonon.

"Very foolish!"

The old man had spread his two arms apart and placed his large hands solidly on either side of the child's head, flat up against the wall of the house. Poor Chonon felt completely hemmed in by this maneuver, and he was beginning to feel suddenly quite warm and uncomfortable.

"Tell me," said the old man, "your sister, Surkeh, is she still going with Heinoch Libitch from Blatchitchka? Or is she going to marry Moishe Essig from Prentz?"

"I really don't know," said Chonon. "I don't think she's going with anybody right now."

293

"Nonsense!" said the old man irritatedly. "A girl of twenty-four hasn't got so much time to make up her mind."

"I think I must be going," said Chonon. He felt a large bead of perspiration crawl out from under his felt hat, and a moment later the drop ran down the length of his nose, reached the tip, trembled there for a ticklish while . . . and fell to the ground, going *pfut*.

"Another thing," said the old man. "That partnership between your Uncle Tevye and Avrohom Twerk—did that break up because of bad business or because their wives couldn't get along with each other?"

"I don't know," said Chonon.

His clothes had become a sticky mess, and he simply longed to throw them all off and to lie down in a cool bed in a dark, quiet room somewhere.

"And that cousin of yours, Yalkeh Panitzer," said the old man, "did *she* throw that prospective groom of hers over, or did *he* finally decide to find himself a girl with more dowry?"

At this point Chonon suddenly raised his flaming face, and, looking the old man straight in the eye, he shouted, "You know what you can do, mister? *You can kiss my behind!!!*"

And, ducking deftly from between the encompassing arms, he rushed back into the hallway and up the stairs with a heart so glad it came near to bursting. As he climbed the steps, blinded by tears of joy, he kept repeating over and over again to himself, "How great is the wisdom of my grandfather! May the blessing of the Lord be with him always! *He* didn't have to go through all this awful *narrischkeit* with this terrible man. *He* just took one quick look at him at the station and said, *You can kiss my behind!* and he was rid of the tormenting monster once and for all. Oh, how great is the wisdom of dear old Grandfather. May the Lord keep him and preserve him, for the joy and profit of mankind, forever! Amen!!!"

CHAPTER NINETEEN

IT IS SUMMER AGAIN, and this year I happen to be living out on Fire Island for a spell. The sea is almost too majestic and wonderful to bear for any great length of time, but by and large the general circumstances of my life here are very conducive to work. I came out here chiefly because Sam and Dorshka Raphaelson had us staying with them for a weekend a while ago, and it seemed a very pleasant idea to have two such dear friends as near neighbors in an emergency. I mean a *social* emergency, of course—in case we wanted company and got a sudden longing for a little civilized conversation, for instance. You see, I find it very difficult to make any new friendships, mostly because the people I run into nowadays are full of imbecile ideas which tend to upset me. I'm too old and too busy with my own affairs to spend precious time explaining the error of their ways to a lot of guppies that fate has accidentally dumped into my corner of the aquarium.

One of the biggest hangups for me is the fact that almost everybody nowadays subscribes implicitly to the notion of endless progress. It is advertising and bad schooling that have put that piece of silliness into their noggins, and nobody ever stands still long enough to examine the merits of this particular hoax.

Just think about it for a minute. A man called Harold Frobischer crossed over Niagara on a tightrope sometime in 1874. When he got to the middle of the falls he stopped, fried himself an egg and ate it. Then he safely continued on over to the other side. Well, it seems to me that Hal Frobischer definitely set a period to *something*. He certainly settled, once and for all, any further progress in the field of tightrope walking, don't you think?

After the last Beethoven quartets there was no further progress in quartets; that's for sure too. And after they built the cathedral at Chartres the future of any cathedrals still to be built certainly looked pretty dim. I'm afraid even Corbusier isn't quite making it.

Well, how about plumbing?

Plumbing, maybe. Although the Romans did pretty well in that line too. Still, I'll allow plumbing, just as long as you'll promise not to talk to me about the superiority of plastics and plywood over more decent substances.

Whatever progress we have made is essentially a progress in trifles that has, as far as I can see, in no way elevated the human spirit to any new heights of grace.

The human mind hasn't improved any in nearly twenty thousand years, and what so utterly depresses me is that every vacant-eyed idiot who carries a transistor radio noisily past my window down to the beach (of all places) considers himself the topmost pinnacle of civilization.

That's why I find it rather difficult to set up new human companionships. I have to stick to my old friends and I'm afraid they are equally stuck with me. It isn't that we decry the modern age and its works, we just happen to know where it really gets off. We don't believe that a lot of pointless running around and having a life full of trivial gadgets is going to appease the loneliness and the restlessness that haunts the human heart today.

Most people I meet seem to disagree with this. It isn't as if they had ever thought seriously about it, they just accept the carefully fostered current fallacy that nobody ever had it so good and was so triumphantly well informed and wise as we are.

When you consider for a moment the caliber of men who once guided the destinies of this country, for instance, your mind must be appalled by the obvious deterioration that has taken place in this important area alone. Just think of Jefferson playing Mozart on his harpsichord, at Monticello. Think of him secretly walking at night into the vineyards of France and Italy to cut off some plant slips from the growing vines to bring back to this country, because he wanted to improve the quality of American wine. He loved fine furniture, fine foods, good conversation, and was, all his life long, at ease with beautiful women. He could ride a horse, shoot a bird, trim a hedge, and, what's more, he was never afraid to be witty among the wise, or wise among the witty. His letters and his speeches are masterpieces of erudition and his prose style is a high example of human clarity.

Nobody ever wrote *his* speeches for him.

Think of the tragic grandeur that lived in the heart of Lincoln. Just recall his robust humor, his brilliant gift for memorable utterance, his passionate and fearless commitments to his ideals—and then make a shamefaced comparison with the men who have taken his place since he died.

So, at least from where *I* sit, the world isn't getting better and better every day. It's just getting a lot more complicated. Don't misunderstand me. I don't want to give up electric lights and go back to candles; I just maintain that the 300-watt bulb doesn't illuminate a more intelligent or better-mannered world. Because we, and our neighbors, don't stink from sweat doesn't make the dry-cleaning business into an august fraternity for human progress or the underarm-security people into a new priesthood.

If it comes to stinks, what smells worse than an icebox container made of plastic? It stinks even when it is brand-new. After you've used it for a while you don't even dare to bring it up to your nose, it gives off such a revolting potpourri of stale odors. There must be a hundred things you use every week that some imaginative manufacturer has unloaded on you that are utterly shoddy and in every way inferior to anything your grandmother ever had to put up with. They've been improved until they are practically useless. The ballpoint pen is a good example. Remember the good old fountain pens we used to fill about once a month? Well, boy, they're coming back at five times their original price—because people are willing to pay almost anything to get rid of their "improved" ball-less horrors.

And so on.

But man goes on inventing, because the compulsion of the times are upon him and everybody wants to grab the shining golden ring on the rackety carousel that leads them nowhere. They're too busy reaching, to see that they really ain't going anyplace. They miss their neighbors, the scenery and even the music, because their frenzy to grab that treasure blinds them to the knowledge that, if they do manage to secure it, all it ever entitles them to is just another ride on that same merry-go-round.

Talking of inventions reminds me of the time I went back to Austria in the late twenties.

I had landed with my wife and my two kids at a small town called Kleinsee, near Innsbruck, in the Tyrol, and after we had put the children to bed at the hotel that evening the two of us went out to see some of the local color. There was some kind of entertainment scheduled to go on at one of the Kleinsee inns, and although I knew from experience that it would turn out to be a dreary, pseudo-peasant type of clambake, we decided to attend all the same. It turned out just as bad as I had expected, but the company that sat all around us was well worth the price of admission. They were all guzzling beer, of course, and they were doing it in family style and in truly awe-inspiring dimensions. They drank the stuff down without even bothering to make any swallowing motions—their Adam's apples just hung there in suspension while the foaming stuff sloshed into them in an absolutely terrifying cataract. It really defied belief.

My wife had ordered a glass of wine, and since I had never been able to drink alcohol of any sort I asked the waitress for some mineral water.

Consternation, of course.

She consulted the innkeeper. There were wrinkled brows and clacking tongues, and fifty pair of furtive eyes strained curiously in our direction. Our whole neighborhood had turned into a buzzing hive of whispered conjectures.

At last a busboy was dispatched into the cellar, and after fifteen tense minutes he returned, triumphantly carrying a bottle of mineral water. The cork was mildewed and it was covered with cobwebs like a bottle of particularly choice wine, and, amid the bated breath of the assembled company, it was ceremoniously opened and I took a drink.

A sigh of disbelief shook that community, as every member of it now leaned forward to take a reassuring swallow of his own beer. They took an even bigger swig than usual, too, just to wipe the image of my water performance out of their minds.

Remember, there were children present in that room, children who were no more than six or eight at the most, who hadn't ever *had a drink of water* in their lives. You see, local belief has it that water is very dangerous for you.

It gives you goiter.

At any rate, at our table a little fat man who looked like an underdone breast of veal had been watching my abstemious maneuver with particular, almost tactless, attention. At last he could contain himself no longer.

"Please, excuse my accosting you," he said, "but are you people possibly Americans?"

"I was born in Austria," I told him, "but I've lived in America for many years."

A smile of understanding dribbled across his carelessly assembled features. "Ah, well," he said, "that explains it."

He turned to the room at large and relieved everybody's mind. "This gentleman here," he said, pointing at me, "is an *American*. They have prohibition against liquor in his country, and he just doesn't want to break the law, that's all!!"

You could see that everybody was enormously relieved. They showed their relief by taking on another load of the briny, just to reassure themselves that such barbarous laws were not yet visited upon them.

But the evening was far from over.

My friend at the table, whose name was Waldemar Schindl, had graciously decided to take us under his patronage. It was actually something more than patronage, he had somehow managed to glue himself onto us like some submarine mollusk that attaches itself with deadly intensity onto another, more mobile living organism. He asked us an endless number of impertinent questions, and just as I was getting ready to bop him one with my aged bottle of mineral water he suddenly got quite confidential. I mean to say, his little pig's eyes emerged almost completely from behind their epicanthic folds, and his mouth, which looked like an inflamed rectum, moved altogether to one side.

"You see," he whispered to me beerily, "I am really an inventor!" He leaned far back to study me for a while. He wanted to see what sort of effect this stunning disclosure would have on me.

"Really?" I said. "Invent anything lately?"

He came closer again. "I've got an invention up at my workshop," he said, "that will absolutely revolutionize modern industry."

"I'd like to hear about it someday," I said, "but we're leaving for Paris in the morning."

"You shall hear about it *tonight*," he said, "before you are two hours older!"

My wife yawned fortuitously at this moment. "I'm rather tired," she said. "Please, let's go back to the hotel."

When we rose to go Waldemar Schindl got up too. As a matter of fact, he even took my arm. "You can't abandon me now," he whispered. I looked at him as if he'd lost his mind, and I noticed with chagrin that his eyes were unmistakably filled with tears.

All right, so the son of a bitch was just distilling some of his oversupply of beer. But still, the creature was actually crying. In public, too.

"I must take my wife back to the hotel," I said. "Our children are there alone."

"I'll go with you," he said. "It will take no time at all for me to show you my model after your lady has left us. Please! You're an American who speaks my language. You come from a country where new ideas are welcomed and rewarded. Here in Austria it is like being in a dark sack. I don't know where to turn or whom to go to. Please! Please! A harassed human soul is pleading with you."

Well, you can imagine what happened, can't you?

After my wife had gone into the hotel, this persistent idiot dragged me back to the inn, where he had parked his horse and wagon. It was a bitter winter night when all this took place, and I tell you, Austrian winters are really something special. In the Alps, too. At any rate, the wretch lived away off the hell and gone, high up in the mountains somewhere, and by the time we landed on his domestic glacier I was absolutely numb.

There was a low-slung farmhouse on one side of this plateau, and right across from it, separated by a kind of paddock, there stood a barn. There were no lights visible anywhere. If my guide and mentor was afflicted with a family of any kind, this deponent knoweth not.

At any rate, we climbed off the wagon and Waldemar steered at once toward the barn. Luckily there was enough light to see what the hell we were doing, and so I noticed that he first produced an enormous key from underneath a stone. This weapon he now inserted into a vast padlock, and, after wrestling with this contrivance for about half a minute or so, he finally opened the creaking gates to his sanctum.

The minute he opened those doors an icy blast hit me so hard that I nearly toppled over. And there, at one blow, I was also made aware of another one of his sordid little secrets. All the cold in those blasted mountains was obviously stored right here in his sinister barn, and it was only lent, or leased, on long-term notes probably, to the rest of the countryside. Refrigeration just isn't the word for it. I was absolutely ossified when I finally staggered into that cave.

He lit a petroleum lamp and I could see he had rigged himself up quite a handy workshop, where a man might easily repair a flintlock, or even a dormer window, come summer.

"Sit down here!" he said, pointing at a barrel with some padded sacking on it. He walked to a bench that stood right close to me, and even in that light, and in that subarctic tem-

302

perature, it was obvious that this bison was deeply moved.

"Here is my invention," he said, and he took a burlap bag off something that looked like a badly made cast-iron bird cage.

"What is it?" I said.

"You'll see for yourself." He was breathing so much and so hard that the vapor he exuded practically obliterated his dopey face. Because I have a mind that is forever lost among metaphors and analogies, I couldn't help thinking that his head was so enshrouded by clouds of stupidity that it resembled a rather foggy sunset on the Matterhorn.

"Here," he said, "press these buttons!"

I leaned forward, and now I first noticed that there were about ten or twelve buttons sticking out of this contrivance of his. So I dutifully pressed the one nearest to me. The whole machine gave an enormous heave, and suddenly a long hunk of wire leaped out of it and one crooked end of it got caught in the fabric of my tweed overcoat. He had hooked me for sure.

Waldemar jumped up, deeply irritated by something. "It is wrong!" he shouted. "It made a mistake! It needs more oiling, damn it!"

He unhinged me, bent the wire in the opposite direction and carefully replaced it in its slot. Then he got a quart-size oil-can and sprayed freely and indiscriminately all over his booby trap with it.

"All right," he said. "Now try again."

I pushed up my sleeve a little and took another whack at it. This time the hook or whatever the hell it was struck out viciously in the opposite direction and got itself snarled in a sheet of paper that I hadn't even noticed before.

"Try the next one!" he ordered. "Try two or three, one right after the other! Don't be afraid!"

I did just as he told me, and each time one of these metal prongs would whip out and make a hole in that paper.

303

And, then, suddenly, with a shock that nearly sent me tumbling off the barrel, I realized what that poor old chowderhead had really done here. He had—all by himself up here in this moonstruck eyrie—*re-invented the typewriter.*

So far he had only ten keys working for him, but he had left himself plenty of room for all the other letters of the alphabet.

I started to sweat like crazy under my freezing clothes in that icy room, because I realized if I ever made the fatal mistake of telling him that the typewriter had already been invented—that they nowadays even made them so clever they were silent, and electrified—this inebriated troll would unhesitatingly push me off that cliff. I already saw my wife and kids, harnessed to some local Sherpas, looking frantically all over those goddamned mountains for me.

"It seems to work very well," I said. "What exactly is it?"

"It is a machine that *prints,*" he said humbly. "It will print instantly anything you want to say. You understand? No more handwritten filing cards—it will all be done by this machine."

He put his hand on his inky lawnmower, and a fat tear rolled down his cheek. He didn't wipe it away, either. It was his great moment.

Finally he pulled himself together. "You arrived in my life just in time," he said. "I nearly gave up. But now you and I are partners. Fifty-fifty, that's my proposition. I can afford it. There will be plenty for everybody. You'll take my plans to America—they are all ready, there, in the corner. Twice the original size. I made the blueprints myself and, believe me, it was very tough, because I had only a small handbook to teach me! But it was worth it. It is all over now. I'll show those fatheads all around here! I'll show them!"

He was a dreamer whose dream had come true. I nearly bawled, myself.

304

He laid two enormous rolls of blueprints on me, and he even insisted on nailing a couple of wooden slats to each of their ends, to keep them from getting wrinkled.

An hour later when I tottered into our hotel room with that load in my arms, my wife awoke and sat up in bed.

"What is it?" she asked drowsily.

"It's all right," I said, "you can go back to sleep. The typewriter has been invented!"

I have never dared to visit that part of Austria again. If that schlumpf was ever drafted into the Army since I last saw him, he was bound to run across some kind of typewriter, and he must have been damned sure that I had cold-bloodedly robbed him of his invention.

Imagine, if he went to a movie even and saw a typist using such a machine, he'd be sure to cause such a goddamned riot in the place that he'd be bound to wind up in a strait jacket at least.

May heaven ever preserve me from inventors.

CHAPTER TWENTY

M Y WIFE AND I are living out on Fire Island for
the summer, as I've indicated in an earlier chapter, and all the
vacationing kids out here make me think of my own first
summer in the United States.

It was hot in New York in July. My folks had just acclimatized themselves to the city, so they had no intention of
going away anywhere, but my mother had the feeling that I,
at least, ought to get a little fresh air and have a look at some
greenery. So she began to shop around for a likely spot to
send me to. Also, she had a notion that I spent far too much
of my time with adults.

"He ought to be with children his own age," she said to my
father, who heartily agreed with her.

And then one day she did come up with something. "I've

found a nice place here, near Philadelphia," she said. "It was in the *Staats Zeitung*. They have swimming, wienie roasts, canoeing, and horses (optional) and it is only two hundred dollars."

So the next day she went to the bank, drew out the money and handed me the two hundred dollars. By the end of that week I was ready: all my clothing name-taped, a twenty-six-blade knife in my pocket—the works.

I landed in Philadelphia at three o'clock in the afternoon, which meant that I had missed the camp bus by half an hour. Luckily right near the depot there was a shooting gallery, and I decided at once to try my skill. I had been a very good shot back in Austria, but even after the first dozen tries I realized that I had somehow lost my touch in the crossing.

By six-thirty I had managed to shoot away nearly twenty-eight dollars of my money, but I had acquired about a hundred wire bottle openers, which the management had bigheartedly issued to me as a consolation prize.

It sure was a stumper.

At any rate, I decided not to give up. I was never a quitter, and I was sure that if I had a decent meal and a little nap, maybe, I'd do a lot better. Also, my madness did have a certain point. A sign on the wall of this emporium announced that if you had five perfect scores in a row you got ten dollars. So, you see, I still had every chance in the world to rectify my deficit.

I had a bite in some nearby beanery, and by nine o'clock that evening I had lost nearly seventy-five dollars. That night I slept at a Y.M.C.A., but I was back at the gallery by opening time the next morning, which was at ten-thirty sharp.

I'm not going to bore you with this silly story any longer than I have to. Just let me tell you that within the next three days I had gone through most of my two hundred dollars. But I did have three enormous paper bags full of bottle

307

openers. Luckily I had put aside my fare back to New York, and that's where I landed late in the afternoon of the third day.

I hadn't the vaguest idea what I was going to say to my folks. I just put one foot ahead of the other and marched home from Penn Station. We lived in Yorkville then, and it was a hell of a long walk, with all my baggage and stuff, but I finally made it all the way up to our block. As I remember, it was a rather pleasant evening as I hit Eighty-eighth Street, and because I was at an age when worries don't rest very long or very consistently in the heart I even began to whistle a little.

My mother must have been sitting right near the window, because I suddenly heard her say, "Karl, I think I hear Alex coming down the street!"

"Impossible!" said my father. "Alex is in camp in Pennsylvania."

"I tell you," said my mother, "that's Alex's whistle! I could recognize it anywhere." And she leaned out the window to prove her point.

All I can tell you is, they were simply delighted to have me back. It's understandable, too. They were fresh immigrants, I was an only child, and they had certainly been very lonely without me.

But the next day my father, the more organized member of my family, called me into his room, closed the door and looked at me as he fancied a responsible parent ought to look when questioning his irresponsible son.

"How did you like the camp?" he asked me.

"To tell you the truth," I said, "I never even got there. You see, when I got to Philadelphia the bus had already left, so to while away the time I went to a shooting gallery."

My father got interested.

"And how did you make out?" he asked.

308

"Pretty good, considering," I said. "You want to see what I won?" I didn't even wait for his answer. I ran right out of the room, and a moment later I came back with my three bags full of bottle openers. With one grand flourish I emptied my paper cornucopias all over his table and even onto the floor.

At this point the door was wildly flung open and my mother stormed into the room. She came at once to my side, put her arms protectively around me, looked reproachfully at my father and said, "Karl! I don't want you to *torture* the child."

And that really was the end of it, too—excepting that in future references to this particular summer my folks would always say, "That was the summer Alex went to camp."

CHAPTER TWENTY-ONE

Iɴ ʜɪs ғᴀʙᴜʟᴏᴜs "Ten O'Clock Lecture" James McNeill Whistler, the distinguished American painter, starts out by saying, "Ladies and gentlemen, *art* is upon the town, to be chucked under the chin by the passing gallant."

What he meant when he wrote it, in the late nineties, was that art—and the artist—had become fashionable again, that society and influential people in general were patronizing it and were willing to give it a condescending nod of recognition.

Well, on a somewhat different level, art, or better still, the creative process, has suddenly become a subject of interest and large-scale speculation to vast numbers of people in America, who seem to have but recently discovered that this elusive phenomenon could someday turn out to be an important national asset. Who knows, we might even learn, through proper inquiry and application, how to employ its formidable potentials against the growing ascendancy of the Muscovite mystique in the world. Who knows?

At the time of this writing, the Army, the Navy and the Air Force are sending their emissaries all over the country to sit in on a lot of investigative congresses where qualified experts from all sorts of academic bean kilns are busily analyzing the origin, the nature and the possible *control* of all our national creative talent.

Gives you a vague idea!

Unfortunately for all these well-intentioned gents, they're confronted by one big hangup right at the outset. You see, talent, as I've already told you elsewhere, is not only a totally undemocratic commodity but it completely defies all existing forms of scientific or even rational analysis. What's more, I'm willing to make book that it will continue to elude the most painstaking researches of the unctuously befuddled medicos, the long-distance-conclusion-jumping psychoanalysts, the stultifying imbecilities of the educationalists, and that it will just go on being the glorious, unpredictable will-o'-the-wisp of destiny that it has always been.

When I said, a moment ago, that it was an *undemocratic* commodity I didn't mean that it couldn't flourish in a democracy. I just wanted to make clear for the record that it was not accessible to personal worth or popular franchise.

You've just got to get used to the idea that a few things on this earth are incalculable and uncontrollable, thank God, and that some people are convinced that the most important of them will go on defying the investigative curiosity of the microscope, the telescope and even the test tube forever.

Tough, ain't it?

Particularly tough for the dopes who want to bottle it, package it, label it and have it ready on tap whenever it is required. What must rattle them even more is the undeniable fact that a good many of the critters who *are* afflicted with talent seem so little worthy of having it—from the standpoint of investigative committees, I mean, or from the standpoint of a lot of clean-cut, well-laundered citizens who own stock in General Motors and have in many other ways proven themselves as reliable members of the community.

And now I want you to pay very strict attention, because *here* is the crack that lets in all the varmints. You see, the Beatniks * in our midst pretend that at this juncture of the world's confusion *they* are the ones who have actually managed to catch the great truth by its elusive pubic hair.

By and large their qualifications are really pathetically meager. They are like a lot of egos on the half shell flying through space backward. Their untidy, undisciplined cavortings attract a good deal of attention, particularly among the young, unsettled elements in our midst, for the simple reason that the so-called respectable members of modern society have certainly nothing to offer them by way of guidance that they can possibly make any sense out of. Also, the Beatniks' attitude to life helps to solve one of the most burning problems of adolescence, the problem of sex. The Beatnik dolls do sleep around pretty freely. There is a drawback to this piece of lagniappe too, though (there always is to everything). These chicks may roll around in the hay with you rather readily, but afterward you'll be compelled to listen to them read you some of their gruesome poetic fermentations. They're all artists, remember?

That's *tit* for *that*, and no getting away from it.

* Second Note to Posterity: *Beatniks*. A form of particularly unattractive Bohemianism. The members of this group tried to codify their just and relevant criticisms of current social standards and mores by throwing overboard, as superfluous ballast, every shred of civilized balance and self-discipline that had accrued to mankind in the past twenty thousand years. Beatniks also subscribed to the belief that the growth of talent is materially aided by certain natural organic fertilizers, such as sweat and dirt. They were further convinced that physical untidiness and mental confusion are particularly suited to form ideal nesting places for the ever rampant creative urge. Actually, their real, unexpressed sentiments were these: "Why do some bastards have so much money? Why do some sons of bitches have so much talent? *We'll* show 'em all! We'll stop washing and grow beards!"

312

When you bother to examine their dingy published confessions, it becomes obvious that it is these "chicks," as a matter of fact, who invariably wind up with the stinky end of the stick in all that free-wheeling existence of theirs.

I myself am, of course, an ardent feminist, but unfortunately nature is not. Not yet. *I* want women to have complete equality all along the line, but at the moment *they* still have to give birth to children. And so, if you examine the Beatnik dossier dispassionately, you'll discover that their slovenly dolls are chronically knocked up and eventually have to pay for the whole goddamned jazz-and-jukebox revolution—out of their own unwashed hides.

Another thing: Almost all of the characters involved in this antiplumbing antipasto have a history of serious mental derangement on their records. In fact, a good many of their chief spokesmen are either clinical psychopaths, overt pansies or full-time dope fiends, and a few of the really top Marats and Robespierres among them have even managed to be all three.

So why does anybody pay any mind to them at all?

It's really not too hard to understand. Just remember that the Beatniks have a pretty large target to spray with their critical marihuana juice.

All they have to do is point out that our world is being run by a lot of heartless, conscienceless Madison Avenue crap salesmen, and that not only do these supermerchandisers go on unloading their worthless filth on a debt-laden and fear-haunted population, but they have also gone into politics and have recently begun to manipulate even Presidential elections.

We might as well honestly admit that the Beatniks certainly have a case. The only trouble with it is that when you come to look at it closely you find that their own schmutz-mirage isn't a goddamned bit more attractive. Less attractive, if possible.

And that's about where the situation rests as of this moment.

313

CHAPTER TWENTY-TWO

As you have been reading these pages, it must have come home to you by now that I am just a great big dragging anchor of nostalgia, hopelessly enmired in the pleasant, squidgy muck of my memories.

And why not?

For quite a few years now I have been expecting to die at any moment, and so I've naturally fallen into the habit of living each day as if it were my very last one. I find this state of affairs not at all depressing. As a matter of fact, I recommend it highly as the best possible way that one can live. It automatically enriches each day's happenings and colors the most commonplace circumstances with the wonderful clarity of *finally* seen events.

When I observe a toddling child lowering its inquiring face into the petals of a buttercup, and when it lifts up its head again and I notice that its nubbin of a nose is covered with the rich, golden dust of the sweet little flower, my eyes sometimes fill with sudden tears of gratitude because I am still privileged to witness the recurrence of this eternally miraculous event. But if I felt that I had another ten or fifteen years of life left, who knows with what piece of important silliness I might have been occupied at the time of this enchanting happening?

Yes, I have learned to live at peace with the constant imminence of death, but not because I'm such an amiably resigned character. Quite the contrary; I'm not one bit resigned. I'm more avid for life right now than I ever was in all the years before. I just don't let time run through me as water runs through a sieve. I can't afford it.

And it is this same sense of imminence which makes it possible for me to immerse myself so completely in the rich sediment of my past, while the rest of foolish mankind all around me goes on behaving as if it were going to live forever.

Fortunately for me, I was never, even in the years that are gone, an unobservant or permanently preoccupied person. That's why I have such a large fund of significant and colorful memories to draw on now.

Some while ago, for example, when I was down in Haiti, living at the Hotel Oloffson, of course, I noticed when I came down to the dining room one evening a middle-aged married couple and their daughter sitting at a table that was generally my own favorite roosting spot at mealtimes.

They were newcomers to the Oloffson and, as invariably happens in any country where French is spoken, I gave them a slight bow as I took a seat right near them. Later, when I heard them speaking German to each other, I deduced that they were probably refugees from the Nazis who had merely come to Haiti as a stopping-off place while they were waiting to obtain their American entry permits.

The next day I found out that this was exactly so. I talked

315

to the head of the family in the social room, where he had come to write a few letters, while I was trying to tune in on some of the mad Caribbean newscasters. He told me that his name was Einstein and that he hoped that their period of waiting in the tropics would be a short one.

They proved to be a very cultivated and charming family, and I must have talked to them and even dined with them at their table for nearly a week before I discovered that Mr. Einstein had a brother in the United States called Albert. I also learned something of their recent history. Mr. Einstein had been in the woolen business back in Germany, where his ancestors had originally settled about three hundred years before.

"When the skies became more and more threatening under the Nazis," he told me, "we reluctantly packed up our most essential movables and left for Italy. Many people in our town actually wept when we shook hands with them for the last time, because, believe me, no one had ever before thought of any of us as dangerous aliens. We naturally went to Italy, since we had visited there frequently in the past, and we were sure that the Italian character was not readily subject to blind regimentation, as that of the Germans most certainly was. Even though they had Fascism at the time, it was inconceivable to us that the individualistic Italians could ever be successfully turned into the obedient ciphers that were the basic prerequisite for a Hitlerite world. Well, we were obviously wrong. When we landed in Italy with all our bags and our trunks, we encountered a climate of such overpowering fear all around us that we had to make plans at once to get out of there too."

By the way, I soon discovered that the Einsteins' "most essential movables" encompassed just a modest amount of personal clothing and that the chief bulk of their luggage consisted of their most treasured books and their favorite musical recordings.

One evening, while I was again taking my dinner with the family, a stranger appeared on the hotel terrace, and a few moments later the headwaiter brought him over to our table.

This newcomer was such a snappy dresser, he had on such a straw kelly with such a multicolored band wound around it, that I instantly concluded that he too had but recently come from the old country. I was right, of course. He was a fellow refugee who had originally met the Einsteins on the boat that had brought them all to Haiti.

Well, the young man came to announce some very good news. His immigration visa to enter the United States had arrived that afternoon, and so he had come to bid his old fellow travelers goodbye. There were warm handshakes and good wishes all around, and, after the young man had left, a mood of inevitable thoughtfulness and understandable sadness fell upon my table companions. After all, these poor dear people had certainly little qualification for a nomadic life, and I suppose they couldn't help but wonder when their own day of good fortune would finally come.

"Tell me," I said, "how is it that your young friend is allowed to leave here before you? Didn't he arrive on the very same day as you all did?"

"Oh, yes," said Mr. Einstein. "We all came on the same boat. But, you see, *he* has a very powerful uncle in the United States who has somehow managed to speed up the issuance of the entry permit for him."

"Really?" I said. "What is his uncle's name, anyway?"

"His name is Irving Garfunkel, I think," said Mr. Einstein. "He owns a drugstore in some place called the Bronx, and I understand he has considerable influence with a lot of important people there, don't you see?"

I saw only too well. Here was this little Bronx druggist who had managed to use his drag in certain circles so that the red tape on his nephew's immigration permit was cut to a minimum. He did this just as naturally as any of the rest of us would have done it. I have no gripe against him.

But I had also seen quite a number of items in the daily press, that very same day, which told of Albert Einstein's being invited to the White House as a guest of the President. You see, the atom bomb was just beginning to be compounded around that time, and Mr. Roosevelt had fallen into the habit of frequently consulting with the scientist on various aspects of this new two-billion-dollar research project.

I particularly want you to take note of the fact that the great Albert dearly loved his exiled brother and his family and wrote them long, sympathetic letters all through their Haitian hegira, and yet, quite obviously, he never once mentioned to the President of the United States that he had such close and dear relatives languishing in the nearby tropics.

You know perfectly well that if he ever *had* mentioned it Roosevelt, a warmhearted and impulsive man, would have issued an emergency passport of some kind and would have brought the refugee Einsteins into this country at once.

But Albert never brought it up, and I'm sure that his brother never entertained any such thoughts either, because it just wasn't their style of behavior. In other words, the world might have deteriorated a great deal in their time, but *they* hadn't.

A little while later I even met the great Einstein himself. I met him in the course of some journalistic chore that I happened to be doing, and he proved a most generous and long-suffering subject indeed.

One day when I again landed in his study over at Princeton, I brought along with me a particularly dopey photographer, who tortured and irritated the scientist with so many requests for new poses and false gestures that I finally thought we were both of us going to be tossed out on our ears.

While this character was reloading his camera, Mr. Einstein looked at him earnestly for a moment and said, "You are one of many children, aren't you?"

318

"Yes. I have nine brothers and sisters. What makes you ask?"

"I guessed it," said Mr. Einstein, "because it is always hard to survive and to get proper attention in such a turmoil of children. Members of large families are accustomed to insensitiveness from their early environment. They don't expect to be seen or to be heard unless they climb right into your lap and put their fingers into your mouth. I suppose it is probably the ideal training ground for a news photographer."

Later, on our way home, my cameraman seemed somewhat moody and subdued. Finally he said, "I think that cat was razzing me—wasn't he? Well, where the hell would I have been today if I hadn't stuck my elbows into everybody's ribs?"

"He wasn't razzing you," I said. "He just dug your background by the way you were acting."

"I thought he was a mathematician," said the photographer. "I didn't know he was Sherlock Holmes too."

"A really brilliant man is always Sherlock Holmes too," I said. "He has eyes and ears in every pore of his body. That's what makes him so different from everybody else. In fact, I think that *that* is exactly what *makes* him a man of genius."

A while ago, when I told you about visiting Haiti, I said I was "living at the Hotel Oloffson, of course." Well, I'd like to elucidate that a little. I haven't the vaguest idea who runs the place these days, but when *I* used to visit it there were still some real Oloffsons around: Maman, for instance, who cured me of dysentery in twenty-four hours with some special tea that a *hungan* (witch doctor) had originally prescribed for her; Maman's brother, who was a weather prophet, and his assorted wives and children and their various friends and hangers-on; and it was all these people that made the place such an absolute delight for me.

Later on someone else took over, and I even heard from some of my friends who visited the island that Haiti had changed a lot since my day. "Mechanized!" they said. "Just like the rest of the world. Mechanized!"

319

Still, once when I had to take a trip to Paramaribo on business of some kind and the boat I was on had to stop over at Haiti for six hours, I decided to get off and to visit the old hotel, just for the hell of it.

Well, it was all exactly the way I'd left it: poinsettias, bougainvillaea, royal palms, the whole stage set, completely intact. I got so moved I even rented my old room, just for five hours—room number fifteen, with two walls missing, right up in the crowns of the trees.

Great!

I took off my clothes and stood under the shower, right out on the terrace of that fine old room fifteen, and from where I was standing I could see the bed covered with a long bridal canopy. It was mosquito netting, of course, but I was in a great mood and that's the way I chose to see it. While the water was sloshing all over me, François, the houseboy, suddenly stood in front of me.

"What is it?" I asked. "It's still too early for dinner, isn't it?"

"No, not dinner yet," he said. "You have a letter, which just arrived for you."

"A letter? You must be crazy. Nobody knew I was coming here. I didn't know it myself until about half an hour ago. There must be some mistake."

"No mistake," said François. "Look, it has your name on it."

He held up the envelope, and there, sure enough, were my name and the address "Hotel Oloffson"—and, what's more, there was even a goddamned stamp on it!

"I'm coming right out," I said. "Put it on the bureau."

I dried myself quickly and took the crazy letter over on the bed with me. It was a decent enough envelope, not too fancy, I mean, but it did have just a little smell of perfume about it. I tore it open, and this is what it said:

320

CHER MONSIEUR ALEXANDRE KING,

I am a young widow of twenty-three with a child of seven (not living with me), who, for certain reasons, is now staying in Haiti. I live in room number six, of this Hotel, and when you passed my door I happened, accidentally, to notice you, and was deeply struck by your kind, sympathetic face.

I have, *cher monsieur*, a heart full of grief and puzzlement and I long to unburden myself to someone with a worldly and disinterested attitude. May I hope that you will lend a kindly ear to my little history? I shall be in my chamber between four and six this afternoon.

My sincere greetings,
CLOTHILDE DE LAUSANNE.

Only my name was beautifully written, in red ink. All the rest of the letter had been mimeographed. Yes, I thought, Haiti has certainly become mechanized. I could just picture this doll rattling off those letters on the mimeograph machine in her room, and I wondered what kind of American sharpy had managed to unload that fine little apparatus on her, anyway. I also wondered whether it was manually operated or electrified.

Don't worry, I'll tell you the rest of the story too. I took Clothilde to dinner, and she proved not only charming but even rather good-looking. She was more than twenty-three, that's for sure, but, whatever the hell age she was, she had managed her years very discreetly. After dinner she took me to the boat, where I happily granted her a small loan. (I was on an expense account anyway, and I just entered it as miscellaneous.)

Before we parted she wept very prettily, too, and I tell you it just isn't possible to duplicate that kind of personal service anywhere.

321

What in heaven's name does the New York Chamber of Commerce have to offer a passing tourist to compare with that?

Nothing!

I have many other memories of Haiti, since I've been there so often, but most of the others are pretty depressing because the poor country certainly hasn't had a decent government in *my* lifetime. The land itself is beautiful beyond belief, and the population is charming, hard-working and docile. Up to a certain point, of course. Then, suddenly, "the buttons burst on the breeches of their patience!" and they become indignant —which means that they go around to the Executive Mansion, grab hold of their President and string him up on the nearest lamppost, like a smoked lox.

In recent years their misleaders have been growing more cagey and manage to skip out just in time. While still in office, though, they generally ship their misappropriated funds to the United States, where it is invested for them in Bronx and Staten Island real estate. There is a boom coming in these parts, that's for sure, because the disgusting brutes who get to be top dogs in the Caribbean area have the best financial advisers extant in this hemisphere.

So you better climb on their real-estate glory wagon while the going is still good, fellas. The rats always had a nose for safe harbors.

CHAPTER TWENTY-THREE

I DON'T BELIEVE that at any time during the past forty years I've spent as much as a single week without gratefully and affectionately remembering the Austrian poet Peter Altenberg.

Nowadays very few of my fellow countrymen ever read him at all, and most of the old-timers have a special and very unpleasant attitude whenever his name does come up. Their faces are generally crinkled into superior, tolerant smirks, as if they knew all about him and what they knew automatically made them into select members of an esoteric fraternity of inside dopes.

But that is really the least of it. When I say their faces are crinkled into superior, tolerant smirks I mean that actually they are tolerant of the *poet* but feel themselves mountainously superior to his childish, sentimental lucubrations.

323

Altenberg knew all about this attitude on the part of many of his readers, and he mentions it quite frequently in his work. Remember, he was completely hep and he said on one occasion, "These people all had my thoughts and my ideas long before I did, they just never bothered to put them down on paper!"

Now, then, because during my strange life I've somehow shed a good deal of ballast, it happened quite often that I didn't even have a single one of his books left among my possessions. You can readily understand that a man who has had four wives must, in the nature of things, have left a good deal of portable and insupportable property with each of his ex-partners. Not so much as a consolation prize, but, occasionally, rather as a temporary bandage for a slightly wounded vanity. Also, let's face it, a couple of these dolls just held on to my books, my masks and my gramophone records, because they saw no very good reason why they should give up any belongings to furnish an attractive household for the next impending bride.

It's just common sense.

The point is that, what with one thing and another, there have been long periods in my life when I didn't have any Altenbergs around at all. Years ago it hardly mattered, since I could always pick them up readily enough in any of the foreign-language bookshops around town. But lately there seems to have been an absolute blight on all of his stuff, and for the past five years I've been able to round up only two of his thirteen published volumes.

And, now, suddenly, like an unexpected blessing, the mail has brought me a package containing his complete works. Not *altogether* unexpected, as it happens, since Peter Schwed had told me that Altenberg's German publisher had promised to forward this treasure to me.

It was certainly an overwhelming joy for me to hold these dear pages at last in my hands again. Just think of it, here I'm sitting in this silly, makeshift summer cottage cluttered with a lot of modrun lamps and characterless furniture, the floor covered with Sandran, and in my hand I hold the beating heart of the poet who, more than anyone else in the world, taught me to look for and to love elegance, poise, imagination and simplicity.

As a matter of fact, I think he would have dug it. He had a welcoming, roguish eye for certain of life's more blatant incongruities. You know, while I'm writing these lines I'm wearing a black satin housecoat that belongs to my wife and a pair of fur-lined slippers that seem to have been designed for use in Siberia. Altenberg would have been gassed by all of it. In the vast repertoire of his soul there were facets to meet every joy, every surprise, every emergency that life might produce. He was able to make large allowances, even for the less aggressive forms of stupidity, and the only aspect of life that had the power to really frighten him was unimaginativeness.

Another thing: Although Altenberg died a bachelor at sixty, I think he knew more about women than anyone else who ever lived on this earth—more than Stendahl, Flaubert, De Maupassant, Freud, Simone de Beauvoir and Dr. Kinsey. I'm going to translate, or, rather, I'm going to try to transmute, some excerpts from his thirteen books into English, not only because I want my friends to have the pleasure of getting to know him, at second hand at least, but because such a piece of loving labor on my part is sure to help *me* in realizing the problem of Eve when I finally get around to painting her. Yes, I'm going to make Altenberg available to the English-speaking reader as soon as I've finished this book. Meanwhile I'm going to offer you a sketch of his right now.

It is called "Theater, Evening."

She couldn't take her poodle along with her to the theater, so he stayed with me, and the two of us were going to await her return at my favorite coffeehouse.

From the moment of our arrival he kept his eyes frenziedly focused on the entrance door. Well, I thought, that's pretty premature. After all, it's only a quarter past eight, and we certainly have to wait until a quarter of twelve at the very least.

We sat and waited.

Every passing carriage woke trembling hopes in his heart, and a couple of times I said to him, "It's quite impossible, she can't be here yet. Just think about it! It's simply impossible!"

Sometimes I looked down at him and said, "Our adorable mistress!"

He turned his head away from me, and it was plain he was absolutely sick with longing.

"Is she coming, or isn't she?"

She's coming, she's coming . . ." I assured him.

Once he gave up his watching post, placed one paw on my knee and put his head in my lap.

As if he said to me, "Tell me the whole truth, I can stand anything!"

At ten o'clock he began to whimper. I kissed him and said, "Don't you think I miss her too? We are men! Please, remember, we have to control ourselves!"

But he didn't care anything about self-control, he just went on yammering.

"Is she coming or not? Yes or no?"

"She's coming . . . she's coming!"

He lay down flat on the ground, his head away from the entrance, like someone who has completely given up hope. Only an occasional shiver of anguish ran across his beautifully corrugated back.

He didn't whimper any more, and finally I stopped looking at him. I just sat there quietly, crushed in my chair, and waited.

It was a quarter of twelve.

And then she came. With soft, gentle steps she came toward us, and she smiled at us sweetly and sat down.

The poodle stood still in frozen unbelief, then gave an insane yodel of joy and wildly leaped up at her; leaped up at her again and again, as he continued singing—singing!

While I hung up her silken evening wrap, she said, "Did you both miss me?"

As if one had said, "What sort of day is it?" or "How do you feel?"

Then she said, "The play was simply enchanting!"

But *I* felt: Longing—Longing which pours endlessly from the hearts of all living creatures—what, oh, what becomes of you?!

Are you gathered up like vapor into clouds?! Is the world saturated to its very limits with dense mists of longing?!

Are there any answers to these questions?!?

Do these treasures of feeling go altogether to waste?! Or are they gathered up lovingly and compassionately by someone, to fill a deep need in those hearts for which they were intended?!?

Does it help *them?!?*

Does it give them strength to bear the great burdens of their own lives?!?

Does it have a meaningful, noble answer somewhere in the universe?!?

Oh, Longing—Longing that pours out of all living creatures—where do you go?

What, oh, what ever becomes of you?

And, just for the hell of it, here's another vignette by Altenberg:

Today on the Graben, in the late September sun, I saw an old bearded peddler selling some patented clothes hangers. They were extremely cheap, and practical too, and I'm sure many people would have stopped to buy them if they hadn't been afraid that the merchandise might be damaged, or shop-worn, or in some other way quite worthless.

Next to this peddler sat his enchanting, tawny, fifteen-year-old granddaughter. Because of this, I bought six clothes hangers for twenty-five cents apiece. The little one was absolutely radiant over this fantastic stroke of good business.

"Can my granddaughter take the package anywhere for you? Why should you drag it around with you all over town? She'll deliver it."

I hesitated for a moment. "No, thank you."

As I turned away I prayed, Oh, beautiful brown-skinned masterpiece, may you never be ashamed to sit beside your old grandfather in the public streets while he is trying to earn his humble living! May you always believe that the sale of six patented clothes hangers at twenty-five cents apiece is a whale of a business. And may you never deliver a package to the room of any man who loves you as much as I do!

These two fragments are all I can offer you at the moment, because I'm too busy with my own affairs.

My own affairs, curiously enough, are concerned with the reading of a lot of letters that people are sending me from all over the country, asking my advice on various strange and unanswerable matters, such as choices of careers, decisions on marriages and even whether they ought to commit suicide or not.

Kids, it's a big hassle for everybody. There are no graphs to study and no charts to follow on the road toward death. The best advice I can give you is: Try to please yourself. You'll go wrong, of course, but you'll have the satisfaction that *something*, no matter how small, paid off for a couple of minutes, for *you* at least.

I also think it's a good idea not to work at something you absolutely hate. You ought to have a little spare hate left over

for the bitcheries that life is going to dish up for you anyway.
Don't waste it all on your job. I consider that reckless and im-
provident.

Another thing: If you have a real vocation, or just even a
knack for something, you'll probably get around to doing it
sooner or later. Just see that it doesn't happen too later.

In 1916, when I was sixteen years old, I wrote some fables
and illustrated them with rather elaborate decorative borders.
To make the artwork more interesting for myself, I pretended
that they were fables from the Chinese.

When I had eight of them completed, I decided to take them
up to the offices of the old *Life*, a weekly joke magazine of
those days which was in many ways as influential as *The New
Yorker* is right now.

I was so green in the business that I picked some kind of
holiday to go up there with my stuff, and, sure enough, the
place was deserted. They were located on West Thirty-first
Street, and it was not until I got to their locked reception
room that it first occurred to me it was Decoration Day or
something.

Just as I was about to turn away, a plump, bespectacled
gent suddenly waddled out from a little cubicle and asked me
what I wanted.

"I'd like to submit some drawings," I said, "but I'm afraid
I picked a wrong day for it."

"You did," said Chubby. "I'm the only one in the office."

"Thank you," I said. "I'll call tomorrow."

"Just a minute," he said. "My name is Metcalfe, I'm one of
the editors, and if you'd like me to look at your stuff I might
just as well. Why don't we step into my office?"

I remembered his name being signed to all the *Life* play re-
views. As a matter of fact, he was their much-feared drama
critic, and his interest was certainly a big break for me.

So I quickly unwrapped the parcel and produced my work.
He liked it.

329

I mean, you can tell right away when somebody goes for your stuff. There's a kind of fluid in the air, a sort of magical vibration that says, "Yes!"

I got warm all over and my eyes turned definitely moist. Remember, this was my first try anywhere, and after all, I was only sixteen.

"They're very nice," he said. "The drawings are very deft, and the text is— Let me see: 'Yoshihito, the fox, lay on his deathbed . . .'"

His voice trailed off while he went on reading my little yarn, and as I studied his features I could see he dug the text too.

After about a minute he put down my first fable and looked carefully at all the rest of them. He liked them all.

"How much," he said, "are you planning to ask for these?"

"A hundred dollars apiece," I said. It was an absolutely insane sum, of course, but I figured I'd let him screw me down.

"That's a very good price," he said, still studying the stuff. "Yoshihito—is that what you call the hero of your first fable?"

"Yes," I said, "Yoshihito, the fox—"

"These are supposed to be fables from the Chinese, are they?" he asked.

"Yes," I said, "because it gives me a chance to put all the animals in Chinese costumes. It's more picturesque that way."

"Right!" he said. "I'm just wondering about Yoshihito."

Slowly he walked over to a bookcase, bent down and pulled out the volume marked "Y."

Eight fables at a hundred dollars a smack was enough to last me for God knows how long. I'd go on making about one fable a month and the rest of my life I'd just paint, and study at the academy. It was *the* answer. *I was in.*

"It says here," said Mr. Metcalfe, looking up from the book, "it says here that Yoshihito is the name of a *Japanese* prince."

"Yes?" I said. "Well, I can change that easily enough."

Mr. Metcalfe turned his back on me and replaced the book on the shelf. A sudden panic took possession of me, and I started to sweat—as I always do when I'm in a jam.

"I didn't bother looking it up," I said, "but I'll check all the names carefully before they're published."

Even I could tell that something almost hysterical had crept into my voice. When Metcalfe faced me again, I was conscious that a strange, cold wind was suddenly blowing through that office. Everything was wilting all around me, and a hoar frost was settling on the windowpanes and all over the petals of my bright, blossoming hopes.

"No," said Mr. Metcalfe, "we're not really interested. Maybe some other time . . ."

When I hit the street again, I started bawling, for real. I bawled all the way up to Grand Central Station, where I deposited my package in the public check room. I hated those pictures so, I didn't want to have them anywhere near me. When I got out of Grand Central I even tore my parcel check into tiny fragments, so that I could never redeem those disastrous miscarriages of mine.

I was through, once and for all.

I stood for a full minute on the corner of Forty-second Street and Vanderbilt Avenue, about as confused and revolting a corner as you're liable to find anywhere in the world, and as I stood there I vowed a holy oath: I shall never make another picture or write another line as long as I live. Never! Never! Never!

Well, there you have it. Luckily for Margie and me, I didn't quite manage to keep my word. You see, picture making and writing were still a lot easier for me than shoveling manure in a ninety-mile gale.

CHAPTER TWENTY-FOUR

Many people who were close to me at one time or another are now dying out all over the world, and it has finally come to such a pass that I hardly dare to open the morning papers, for fear that some other dear person has permanently gone from my life. It is true that most of these good and gay comrades disappeared from my immediate periphery long before they died, but somehow the knowledge that they were still available was always reassuring to me.

Geza Herczeg is dead too. He died in Italy, and no one seems to know exactly what happened to him there toward the end. I suppose time and breaded plum dumplings finally did him in. I collaborated with him on three or four scripts some years ago, and I shall always think of him with great affection. He taught me much about life, and particularly about show business, and I would have missed some wonderful good times if I had never known him as well as I did.

One of the plays Geza and I got mixed up in was a musical that he and I were supposed to translate from the Hungarian. That is to say, Geza had gotten himself permission from the authors to translate it and he'd even managed to find himself a potential backer. What's more, an early production had been promised, and so everything was in tip-top shape when I landed on the scene.

I think I'll just take a moment here to say a few words in praise of show business.

The silly Communists, who are dead wrong about so many things, are, of course, dead wrong when they say that capitalism has no more frontiers. A fat lot they know about it. They simply forget all about show business, which is just one long, endlessly unexplored frontier.

Man! I myself have made good money for quite a few years on the merest *notions* for plays that never even got into the rough-draft stage. I once sold the same unfinished script four times to the same producer, and I've known people around Broadway who've made handsome livings for themselves by just carrying around a lot of coffee-stained manuscripts that whole committees had written and that other whole committees had already rejected.

Actually, I'm mildly amused by the way certain well-known men in the theater eventually sit down and compose their memoirs. From the gutter to the sidewalk in one generation. So what? They actually did write, or collaborate on, or produce, or do *something* with at least one real hit play! That's for sure!

But how about the characters who never get involved in anything so tangibly solvent? Who just give or take endless options, hire press agents, announce titles to forthcoming productions, sign leases, pre-empt advertising space, and never,

never, never, under any circumstances, get connected with anything that has an actual curtain going up on any of their strange and elusive prospects.

Now, then, let me tell you once and for all that to me these boys represent the real romance of the theater. *They* are my great heroes, because they are the only ones still left who give show business any kind of really colorful flair. The smart cookies who write their cunningly contrived Broadway clap-trap, who adapt dreary comic strips into nauseating musicals, who, two years before they even start writing their emetic messes, manage to cut in an influential director (who also happens to be the son-in-law of some big theater owner)—these boys all make me sick, up to here!

But the others, the dreamers whose dreams never come true for anybody—the moist-eyed lads who are going to bring repertory to Broadway, the cats who have options on plays that aren't even copyrighted—believe me, these are the sole custodians of any iridescence and fantasy that the legitimate theater still has.

Let's face it—the legitimate theater is mostly in the hands of cold-blooded connivers who just make themselves tidy fortunes serving as stooges and errand boys for a lot of millionaire real-estate operators. They divvy the spoils among them, that's all these kids do, and there is about as much color and romance in the machinations of these adroit manipulators as you're likely to find in a cement factory.

I'm giving you all this stuff straight. I know a lot more about it, too, than just any old grudging and envious outsider. As I've just told you, I did very well for myself whenever I dipped my schnozzle, no matter how casually, into the show business trough for a while, and I've been bemused for many years by watching the boys at the main table—flanked by their tax experts, their psychiatrists and their alimony lawyers —pretend that they were all just a bunch of carefree heedless poets having a cheerful sup at the Mermaid Tavern together.

But back to Geza. As I mentioned before, he had this Hungarian play, and one day he called me up and asked me to help him turn it into English.

"Vee'll go helf and helf," he said. "Dere is no use heggling about percentages. Dere vill be enough money for everybody!"

So I came up to his place in the East Sixties and we started to write. That is to say, *I* started to write and he walked up and down the apartment and talked up a cyclone.

He was great!

The play we were doing was a typical Central European musical that had been a smash hit in Budapest about twenty years before—a kind of horror. The plot was simplicity itself really. It concerned a colonel of hussars who, during the summer Army maneuvers, is stationed on a vast estate in the Bukovina somewhere, and you will not be surprised to hear that in this lavish but nonetheless forlorn outpost an absolute skyrocket of a love affair ensues. *Three* love affairs ensue, as a matter of fact, and all of them with the same man. You see, there are present on the premises a very young-looking grandmother, a mother and, of course, a daughter, and, what's more, all of these seductive ladies are at once and to the same desperate degree smitten by our colonel of hussars. He's in a real jam, too, because he, in his turn, can't seem to make up his own mind which of these three delectable tootsies to go for. Remember that woman, at each stage of her development, has something peculiarly memorable to offer, and so the colonel sings some pretty meaningful songs about his attractive dilemma. He sings about spring, about summer, about autumn, and the various rich fruits that each of these seasons brings to man, he sings about the juices and even the pits of these fruits, and believe me, there wasn't a single lemon in the lot of them.

As I said in the beginning, a real horror!

Geza wasn't the least bit upset by this little plot. "Vee vill modernize it," he said. "Vee vill Brodvayize it, so dat dee original autors vill buy dee rights from us to trenslate it beck into Hungarian. It vill be an altogedder noo play."

Well, I was ready for a new play, because the old one certainly stank.

By the way, I'm not going to try to give you Geza's accent from now on, because I'm just making a botch of it. He had a Hungarian accent, of course, but also over the years he'd managed to add to it certain strange German and French inflections and involutions of speech that most other Hungarians of my acquaintance never even heard of. Let it suffice you that he talked with enormous conviction and fluency, and I realized, after working with him a couple of days, that he certainly had no intention of doing anything else. The writing part of it was going to be *my* job. But, to tell you the truth, I didn't do very much writing either. He wouldn't let me.

"We must be sparing with it," he said. "If we flood their offices with a lot of manuscript we will have a tough time getting any money out of them. It will be like a dam that will prevent any of their cash to flow in our direction."

I didn't understand his process of reasoning and I suppose I must have looked it, because he instantly sat down beside me and very patiently started to explain his technique of play salesmanship to me.

"These people aren't really interested in the theater," he said. "You see, dear boy, as a matter of fact, *nobody* is interested in the theater. They're just interested in being mixed up in a lot of theatrical activity and with a lot of theatrical girls. That's perfectly understandable, too, isn't it? Now, then, I don't for a minute mean that they are *opposed* to producing a hit play, or that in an emergency they don't want to *sell* a hit play for a lot of money to the movies. Not at all. They are

336

not antisocial. Oh, no! But, by and large, they really like most of all the *tummeling* that goes on in and around the theater. Lunches at the Algonquin, cocktails at Sardi's, dinners at the Plaza and so on—you understand?

"Very well! Now, then, we will give them, first of all, a synopsis—a kind of foretaste of the pleasures to come. That should take about six pages. Three is not enough, and ten is too much, but six is just about right. Okay! So let us go ahead and make out our little synopsis. We cannot have the locale in the Bukovina because that is too far away and too strange for America. We must bring it a little nearer to Broadway, so we will make it Algiers. You see, that gives us a lot of harem dancers, French Zouave uniforms, with caps, and diapers floating around their necks, and the whole thing is at once more friendly and familiar to people. All right!

"Next, for America we must make the husband, who is also a son-in-law and a father, a lot more interesting than in the original play. In the old script he is just a cipher waiting to be cuckolded by anybody who comes to upholster the furniture, but we will have to rescue him and make him a great *ingénieur*. He is building a bridge or a tunnel somewhere that keeps him away most of the time. Still, he must have a certain stature so that when he finally comes home in the last act for his daughter's wedding he too can wear some kind of uniform, like the rest of the cast, and maybe he can even be decorated by the government for his great accomplishments. Fine! Next we have to take care of the grandmother, who is still quite young-looking and attractive. Maybe the local French governor, who comes to give a medal to the *ingénieur* . . . or maybe . . . I tell you what, we'll just leave it all in suspense for the moment. We'll worry about the ending later on. Right?!?"

"Right!" I said.

But we never did worry about it really, we just *tummeled*

and after about a week we had some kind of synopsis going. We finished around seven one evening, but Geza waited up with me till about one-thirty in the morning, and then he finally rang up the prospective producer.

"Well," he said, "we have *just this minute* gotten finished with your job. *Just this minute* the pen fell out of our hands! We both feel it is *great!!!*"

The producer was, of course, dying to hear the story and Geza kept tantalizing him about it on that phone till nearly two-fifteen.

Result?

Luncheon at the Algonquin the next day.

The luncheon still stands out in my mind as one of the most bewildering charades that I have ever in all of my life participated in.

There were ten of us at the meal and I never really got to figure out who anybody was supposed to be in relation to the impending production. There were three good-looking women, and of course *their* relationship to some of the men at that table was perfectly plain to anybody. It was just the rest of them, the permanently balding, prematurely paunchy, chronic smilers at that gathering, that I never got to place properly.

Naturally there were only toasts and high spirits during the luncheon and nobody expected us to *read* anything in that dining room. That was coming later. In the meanwhile I had a chance to get acquainted with the one man at that shindig whose character, I'm happy to say, was clearly defined for me, and that was Mr. William Tecumseh Levy, the producer.

That was his real name, too, and he was very proud of it. He didn't look so much like a Levy either. He could easily have dropped that last monicker of his, and since he hadn't I concluded he *must* be something of a real sport.

He was, too. He was, first of all, quite a rich man. What's

338

more, he'd had the good sense never to have hustled for his dough at all. He had inherited it, quietly and in good taste, and now he was spending it.

"I like the European-type musical show," he told me. "The waltzes, the mazurkas, the pretty sets and costumes, and all the rest of it. I think 'Love Divided by Three' (that was the name of our little lulu) has everything."

"Everything and to spare," I said.

"I think Geza is a great man," he said. "I'm dying to hear your synopsis."

"Well, it's just a sketch," I said.

"That's all right. I've seen quite a lot of sketches in the last two years, and I've learned to fill out wherever it's needed."

"Great!"

The luncheon took till a quarter of four. After the last round of brandies had been dispatched we started to amble over to the producer's offices, which were in the Graybar Building.

Now, this was particularly unfortunate, because I had some deep-seated, long-standing prejudices against this building. I have prejudices against whole boroughs in New York City, and I'll try to explain why.

You see, there are certain buildings in which, the very moment you enter them, you have a sudden, deep conviction that you'll never manage to earn a goddamned cent in them. I don't quite know how to clarify this feeling, but you just must believe me that the minute I spot them I realize with cast-iron certainty that no check of any size worth mentioning is ever going to be handed to me inside those walls. I don't care how modern the elevators, or how slick the walls (as a matter of fact, most of their entranceways look as if they had been lined with slices of ossified salami)—something, somewhere, sends me a message announcing that a deep, arid failure is in the offing.

I'm quite certain that lots of other people must have had these or similar feelings in different buildings around the world and probably weren't aware of them at the time. Now that I've made you conscious of it, think back! Aren't there certain buildings in your own past, or perhaps even whole blocks in some towns, that seemed almost on sight to preclude any possible form of good fortune for you?

Well, we were in for it. We were heading straight for the Graybar Building, and I can tell you, I entered those unpromising portals with deep misgivings.

When we hit Tecumseh's office the assembled company draped itself over the overstuffed chairs and couches and, putting on appropriately eager and expectant faces, waited for Geza Herczeg to begin.

I myself was nervously fingering the six measly pages inside my coat pocket, but at the last minute, catching a stern, reproving glance from Geza's somber, meaningful eye, I decided to desist for a while.

Remember, we had already been talking for about three hours about a nonexistent play, and I couldn't for the life of me imagine what else there might be left for any of us to say. There *is* nothing, I decided. We've just got to start reading our script and get it over with.

Well, I was dead wrong!

Geza got up from his chair. He was a tremendously fat, short, bald-headed man with an enormous nose, bushy eyebrows and large, limpid walrus eyes, and I tell you, he looked at that crowd of stupefied art lovers with a glance of benign command, like a bringer of truth among the Waramungas. He quietly surveyed that mob of hard-breathing lushes crowded together in that silly office and, by some magic peculiarly his own, managed to convey by just that look of his alone that they were an unusually privileged group to be present there with him at that particularly important moment in theatrical history. I don't know why, but I suddenly expected him to lower his head and pronounce a Latin benediction of some kind. The drowsiest sap in that room removed his exploring hand from his girl friend's knee and made some effort to pull his rambling faculties together. Everyone had the sensation that something special was impending, and even I felt a certain sacred spasm run across my abdomen.

"We are here," said Geza, "to tell you the story of a musical play which is as heartwarming as the memories of yesterday and as slick and streamlined as the hopes of tomorrow."

And then he went on for the next hour and a half and told a story that had not the slightest connection with anything that we had written. Not one damned thing. I was as spellbound as the rest of those dunderheads in that room, and when he got through and finally sat down again there was a solid round of applause from all hands present, including my own.

"Great!!!" said Tecumseh. "Great!!! When can I have the outline?"

"We are working on it day and night," said Geza. "Mr. King and I are struggling to give you a synopsis that will present the true values of what I have just told you. As you must have noticed, the story line is really quite unimportant. It is the spirit of the play, combining the best features of three generations and five continents, that carries the audience along to its breathless conclusion.

"Of course," said Tecumseh. "I understand. But when do you think we can have some actual material that we might submit to some prospective backers? After all, we've got to have something for *them*, don't you see?"

I instinctively stuck my hand into my pocket to reach for those six pages, but I instantly desisted when I again caught Geza's strong, forbidding look hurled in my direction.

"We are working like beavers in an underground tunnel," he said. "Mr. King sleeps and eats in my house and he hasn't seen his family for the past ten days. We cannot go on like this without some tangible help from someone. Neither one of us has earned a single penny since we started on this project and we are not in a position to finance ourselves indefinitely. We will make any arrangements you like, but I think others besides Mr. King and myself should help carry this artistic burden. Even when you dig gold out of a gold mine you first have to sink shafts, lay pipelines, cart in a lot of gravel and make the ground ready for the excavation of treasure. Right? So I leave it up to you what the next move will be. I've just explained to you briefly, and in rough outline, what this gold mine contains. The next move, gentlemen, is yours!"

Well, to make the agony short, their next move was to hand us two checks for fifteen hundred dollars. Just like that!

When Geza and I finally left with the dough in our pockets, I took a long, apologetic look at the Graybar Building. I had been quite wrong about that grim, repulsive pile. Geza had certainly broken the spell of its unresponsiveness, and gold had actually sprung for me out of this totally unpromising quarry.

It was early spring when that first meeting took place at Tecumseh's office, and I can truthfully tell you that I wrote about half a dozen assorted outlines of musicals during the next six months. I don't remember exactly how much money we got in advances but it was certainly enough to keep us going comfortably for about a year.

In the end, of course, nothing came of it all. It took me quite a few weeks before I realized that nothing had been *expected* to come of it. I remember we were already well into the fall and I still had occasional feverish fits of sudden typing, but slowly I, too, caught on and let things drift just as everybody else did. I don't want you to think for a minute that Tecumseh or anybody else in his entourage ever felt cheated. Nothing of the sort. They got a hell of a lot of entertainment out of us, they and their girls. I still recall how some of their more impressionable females would get absolute shivers of delight at the mere thought of being allowed to be present at such creative theatrical séances.

No, they got their money's worth, the lot of them. Later on, when somehow or other they drifted out of our ken, we had just one problem left, how to find an entirely new set of producers for ourselves. And we did, too. That is, Geza during the next two years found us three completely new groups of angels, and we parted pretty good friends with most of them too.

In other words, if you're planning to write a play don't bother looking for an idea, just find yourself a Hungarian collaborator and your worries are over.

By the way, I think I ought to mention, for those of you who never heard of Geza Herczeg before, that by the time I met him he already had scads of successful movies to his credit. Once he had even won an Oscar for his collaboration on a screen play about Zola (with Paul Muni), and earlier still he had written a musical called *Die Wunderbar*, in which Al Jolson made an enormous hit on Broadway. But that was all years and years in the past, of course.

And now he's dead. In Italy, of all places. May the earth rest lightly on his whimsical and courageous heart.

I told a Hungarian friend, Sandor Hatvanyi, just yesterday that I'd written a sort of *in memoriam* for Geza Herczeg, and he immediately told me another amusing sidelight on his life in America.

"You know," said Hatvanyi, "there was a press agent some years ago who'd had a very active life and who had even managed to save quite a bit of money. His name was Danny Zilzer. One day he came to me and asked me if I knew anyone who might help him write his autobiography. Because Geza wasn't busy just at that time, I naturally suggested him. So the two of them met, and they instantly took a great liking to each other. When I asked the press agent a little while later how things were going along, he said, 'Just fine! We will meet twice a week in some restaurant and we will talk for a few hours, and then Geza will go home and digest this material and write it all up.' Fine! Meanwhile Zilzer had given Geza a drawing account of seventy-five dollars a week. I didn't see either of them for about six months, and then one day I ran into Zilzer again, and when I asked him what kind of progress they were making he seemed a little thoughtful before he answered me. 'To tell you the truth,' he said, 'this Geza likes to talk so much *himself*, that I haven't been able to tell him as much as I should like to. But I suppose we'll get around to it in time. We'll wait and see!'

"And then, the following winter, Zilzer came to call on me at my office. 'Mr. Hatvanyi,' he said, 'this friend of yours who's been getting seventy-five dollars a week from me for almost a year now is certainly a champion talker. Of course, I enjoy listening to him, because I must admit that the story of his life is certainly more interesting than mine. I'm just wondering whether in the long run it mightn't be a much better idea if *I* were to sit down and write *his* autobiography. What do *you* think?"

The life of the elderly intellectual immigrant is often founded on such a grotesque series of heartbreaks and misunderstandings that, if I had the time, I could easily fill out many purposeful years by just writing about their strange adventures and misadventures in the new millennium.

I'm thinking now of Karen Wollner, who has lived in New York City more than thirty years and who is actually as little acclimatized to America as if she'd just arrived last week.

Karen is a receptionist and adviser at some large altruistic enterprise that acts as a sort of clearing house for the problems of new immigrants. Actually it doesn't work out that way at all, because an immigrant is *always* new. *That* is his true and permanent status over the years, and unless he came here as a very young child indeed he never quite manages to get used to everything!

Karen Wollner is probably the one ideal woman in the whole world to fill the job that she has picked for herself, because despite the fact that she's been in the United States over a quarter of a century and has held her position for most of that time, she has never become blasé toward the problems of her multilingual, overly-anxious, poisonously persistent, boring clients. In fact, she carries most of their fears and misgivings right home with her every evening, and her private conversations are constantly loaded with references to their feverishly oafish attempts at acclimatization.

Because she is a woman of enormous imagination and of great human sympathy, she even established many years ago a secret private fund out of which she blindly and impulsively distributes small sums to the most despairing cases that happen to come to her attention. I mean that on a shelf right under the counter where she is seated she generally keeps a small stack of single-dollar bills, and if she happens to hear a particularly soul-shattering story she quickly puts one or two bills into an envelope and, in an absolute typhoon of embarrassment, manages to slip her gift of personal kindness into the pocket of the bewildered, stupefied and usually ungrateful applicant.

But I'm misleading you. There is no such thing as a "private fund." This money that she distributes comes straight out of her own not very lavish salary, and it is a matter of peculiar pride with her to go the bank every week and to select only the crispest and most newly minted bills for these special donations of hers. Also, it isn't always necessary for a potential recipient of her charity to tell her any kind of story at all. If the face or clothing of one of these unfortunates makes some special unaccountable impression of helplessness upon her, she doesn't even wait to hear any verbal elucidation of his personal disasters at all; she just shells out on sight.

So that's Karen Wollner for you. She has gone on quietly through the years, giving saintly aid and comfort to the truly bedeviled in our midst, and you will not be surprised to learn that none of the million-dollar charity and endowment foundations active in America at the moment carries her name on its letterhead.

Since I love her dearly, she sometimes confides in me, and, so, a little while back, she told me a rather interesting anecdote out of her life.

"There was a man," she said, "who came to visit our establishment about six years ago, and from the very beginning he made a terribly strong impression on me. You see, he had been some kind of writer and editor in the old country, for Ullstein, I think, and he'd arrived in the United States at the age of fifty-six full of hope and with a whole suitcaseful of his clippings. Of course it's the old familiar story—there wasn't really anything for him to do along the lines of his profession. Naturally not. He spoke very bad, halting English, and who would bother to translate the work of an elderly writer who was known only to a few rather special people in Europe? In the beginning he went every day to some of the newspaper or magazine offices, hoping to do feature articles about certain aspects of the German and French literary and cultural scene. Well, you can easily imagine that he got nowhere. He had a wife and a twenty-three-year-old daughter, too, and the three of them lived somewhere up in some wretched furnished room in the West Seventies.

"What was so heartbreaking about him was his clothes and his manners, which must have seemed rather old-fashioned even back in Europe. He wore a shiny, rather loose-fitting brown suit which I'm sure his poor wife ironed for him every day, because whenever he came here it was always meticulously pressed. Unfortunately, she also attempted to clean it for him, and even before he came through the door I could always smell the unhappy effluvium of that cleaning fluid floating in two minutes ahead of him.

"Well, as time went on he got more and more desperate. Around Christmas time he addressed envelopes for a while— in fact, his wife and daughter did too—and then on the twenty-third of December, when he came in to wish me a Merry Christmas, I gave him my first small donation. I put it in his pocket, and since he was carrying a lot of parcels from the five-and-dime he hardly noticed what I was doing. But about half an hour later he came back again and he walked toward me as if he were drunk. In his hand he held the envelope with the five dollars I had slipped him, and when he came closer I saw that his poor fat face was just streaming with tears.

" 'Madame Wollner,' he said, 'I really can't . . . I mean I absolutely can't . . . My name is Kurt Hartweil and everybody in Dresden will tell you that my family . . . that I myself . . .'

" 'Please,' I said, 'it's just a trifle for the family, for Christmas. It makes me very happy, Mr. Hartweil, and next year you'll buy me a twenty-pound stuffed turkey. Please, Mr. Hartweil, people are beginning to notice!'

"That made him pull himself together. He still was anxious to keep up appearances, and he finally tottered out into the street again.

"After Christmas his wife and daughter came to see me and brought me a present. They had knitted me a muffler and a kitten-eared cap out of brown wool trimmed with beige, and I must tell you those two poor women depressed me even more than the father. You see, they were still full of

347

Old World pretensions of gentility and they were absolutely heartbreaking in their faith and their devotion to the old man. He'd been so much looked up to, back in Dresden, don't you see, and here nobody knew him or cared about him at all. Editors to whom he applied for jobs would make him wait endlessly in their antechambers and would finally dismiss him like an importunate mendicant. They were getting about twenty-five dollars a week from our organization, which the women eked out by baby sitting and selling some preserved fruits to other immigrants who were better off than themselves. Mrs. Hartweil, who had been something of a cook back in Dresden, had even begun to compile a cookbook of some kind, and she asked my advice about a possible collaborator, with whom she would be happy to share the profits. Well, all I can tell you is that, between them, they certainly managed to ruin my holidays for me.

"But later on our relationship fell into a regular routine. I used to give him two or three dollars every time he came to see me, and he never protested any more. He would just stand there and look at me every time I slipped the envelope into his pocket, blink his eyes like a sick bird and then slowly turn around and walk out again. His walk, by the way, had changed a great deal in the course of that year. From the back he now looked like a man who had suffered a stroke and was just learning how to toddle along all by himself again.

"And there was, of course, that suit of his. He obviously had only that one brown one, and by the following Christmas it had become so stiff from all that cleaning fluid, and all that ironing, that it looked more like some sort of metal sheeting than any kind of cloth at all.

"And then, suddenly, around Easter he took to his bed, and his daughter dropped in to tell me about it. Luckily they had some friend, a refugee doctor, who took care of him and even supplied him with medications. He never got up out of that sickbed. He died one Sunday afternoon, and the following morning the two women came to inform me of their loss.

"I think I ought to tell you at this point, if you don't know already, I have an absolutely insane dread of funerals. I had never attended one in my life and I had never yet seen a dead person. I'm sure *you* can understand my feeling in this matter, but I was absolutely certain that those two bereaved women would never understand such an attitude, and, what's more, conventionally brought up as they both were, they would have considered my staying away as a deliberate insult to the dead man.

"I was nearly beside myself with worry and anxiety. I had such dreadful migraine headaches that for the next three days I could hardly drag myself down to work.

"Another thing made me heartsick, too. I couldn't get it out of my mind that that poor man was surely going to be buried in that dreadful brown suit of his. I just couldn't stand the thought of it. I know it's silly, of course—what difference does it make what you get buried in?—but somehow I was just shattered by the thought that this sad, innocent failure of a man was destined to march through all eternity in that hideous brown suit smelling of cleaning fluid. He had acquired, shortly before his death, a particularly nasty stain on one of his lapels, and I saw him tramping along toward the heavenly host with that ghastly grease spot, like a coquettish, post-culinary nosegay, in his cast-iron buttonhole. I know it's all silly, but the thought of it just destroyed me.

"Finally the day of the funeral came around and, after a sleepless night, I decided to attend after all. I did, however, make one reservation to myself: Under no circumstances would I approach the catafalque and look at the dead man's face.

"When I got up to the funeral parlor there must have been at least two hundred people there. I have never been so frustrated and bewildered in my life. I didn't see the mother or the daughter around anywhere, and I had brought along ten dollars for them in an envelope. I was clutching it so desperately in my hand that, in my anxiety, I tore the envelope in half.

"Finally I landed with a dense mob of people who were all seemingly headed toward the head of the chapel. And then a terrible thought came to me: These people were obviously going to the front of the room to take a last look at the deceased. Well, I would have none of *that!* I tried to fight my way out of that line but I simply couldn't budge anybody. I was carried along relentlessly by their chests and elbows, and every step I took just brought me nearer to the exposed coffin. So, in absolute despair, I decided to close my eyes and to let these morbid fools guide me blindly past the exposed corpse. And that's what I did. But from time to time I just *had* to open my eyes to see whether we had already passed the danger point. And now I'll tell you something really crazy: When I actually stood beside the coffin I had my head turned aside, but I suddenly opened my eyes and looked, just for the fraction of a second, at that corpse.

"I nearly fainted. He was wearing *that brown suit*.

"Luckily I was wedged so securely among all those people that I couldn't have dropped to the floor, even if I had wanted to. That was my one great piece of luck, too, because, by the time we reached an exit I had recovered sufficiently to make a wild dash out into the street.

"But, I still hadn't gotten rid of my ten dollars, so I went back to the main entrance, asked somebody for a new envelope, addressed it to the wife and left it in care of one of the assistant undertakers. Then I went home and went to bed.

"Now the strangest thing happened. You know how meticulous those Germans are about all their social obligations and official courtesies and all that stuff. Well, to my great surprise

350

a whole week had gone by and those two women had never even bothered to acknowledge receipt of the money, nor of the note of condolence that I had enclosed. I was a little miffed with them, anyway, for not realizing what a terrible sacrifice I had made to all my instincts and feelings by just going to that funeral parlor in the first place.

"And then, on the very afternoon when I'd decided to go up to the undertaker's to see whether anybody had perhaps misplaced or stolen my little contribution, the daughter dropped in to see me. She looked terrible, of course, but I noticed that her manner toward me was just a little reserved, almost reproachful. I couldn't have been more annoyed. What in heaven's name did they expect of me, anyway?

" 'Did you get my note?' I finally asked her.

" 'Yes,' she said. 'We got it just at noon today. The man brought it from Campbell's funeral parlor. It was very kind of you.'

" 'Not at all,' I said. 'I just wonder why they didn't give it to you on the day of the funeral. I left it there *then*.'

" 'My poor father was not buried from Campbell's,' she said. 'I think it was very nice of them to send it up to us at all . . .'

??? !!! ???

"I clutched the desk in front of me with both my hands, as I realized with ultimate horror that—*I had attended the wrong funeral!*"

CHAPTER TWENTY-FIVE

When I got to be seventeen years old, in New York, I became familiar for the first time with the ritualistic intricacies of the life of the Jewish ghetto. It happened just then because I'd gotten a job as a cartoonist on a Jewish weekly joke paper called *The Big Stick*. Jack Marinoff, the editor of that wild sheet, is still alive, and his sister, Mrs. Carl Van Vechten, told me only recently that he is still around, and still full of ginger and catnip juice.

There was just one minor drawback to that job of mine: I used to get very peculiar pay checks at the end of each week. That is to say, instead of the twenty dollars that were due me, I used to receive eighteen dollars and seventy-five cents, or nineteen dollars and a quarter, and other such equally strange sums. I really couldn't figure it out at all, and for quite a long

352

while I was too timid to ask anyone about it. Remember, this was a hell of a long time ago, and there weren't any withholding taxes, old-age pension funds or any other such nonsense around just yet.

Wild!?!

Finally, one fine payday, I just stepped right up to Old Man Marinoff himself and demanded to know what shook with my crazy salary checks.

"It's perfectly simple," he said. "You don't write any Yiddish, so I have to pay somebody to print the necessary captions into your cartoons. That's why there are deductions."

"But why is it never the same sum twice?" I asked.

"Because sometimes the captions are longer, and I have to pay more. It's obvious!"

It was obvious, all right, but I just didn't like it one damn bit.

Well, if I didn't like something back in those high-spirited years, I generally did something about it, and so I instantly looked around that East Side neighborhood for a suitable school where I could learn how to write my own Yiddish captions.

I think it was somewhere on Forsythe Street that I finally found a *cheder*, that is to say a Hebrew School, where they generally taught only children, of course.

I must say, the classroom made a rather weird impression on me. I had never before conceived it possible that anybody could learn anything under such thoroughly disorganized circumstances. The teacher, a Mr. Fachmann, a wispy little man with an enormous nose and a huge, fan-shaped gray beard, seemed to be less in charge and more like an active competitor against his noisy, individualistic pupils. In fact, it seemed to me, on first contact with that academy of learning, that they were all just loudly sassing each other back and forth; certainly there was no rhyme, no reason, no system or harmony of any kind evident in their apparently extemporaneous gibberish. Later on I understood better. I was dead wrong about the whole thing. It was just Mr. Fachmann's own peculiar little system of pedagogy, that's all. If any of the youngsters ever really got out of line, that fine teacher would at once lean forward and, without missing even a syllable in the droned Biblical liturgy, and without the slightest show of anger, whack the delinquent smartly across the ears with a tightly folded Jewish newspaper.

At any rate, when I dropped in, the novelty of a grownup unexpectedly appearing in their classroom managed to silence the kids long enough to give me a chance to explain my purpose to their teacher.

"I want to learn how to read and print Yiddish," I said, "because I'm a cartoonist on *The Big Stick* and I have to do my own captions, you understand?"

"That will be four dollars," said Mr. Fachmann, "and that includes Hebrew."

"I don't need Hebrew," I said. "Yiddish is all I have use for at the moment."

"Nonsense!" said Mr. Fachmann. "Hebrew is even more important. No man is complete without Hebrew."

"Please," I said, "I've gotten along fine without even Yiddish all these years, so what in God's name do I need Hebrew for? Our paper is printed only in Yiddish, don't you see?"

Mr. Fachman got up from behind his table, came up to me and put a long, bony, wonderfully translucent scholarly hand on my shoulder.

"What is your name?" he asked.

"Koenig," I said.

"Mr. Koenig, you're making a terrible mistake. Don't you see, the Gentiles are murdering each other off on all the battlefields of the world. [The First World War was still on.] Nobody will finally be left except us. I'm telling you, Mr.

354

Koenig, that Hebrew is definitely the language of the future! Take Hebrew!"

"Just a minute!" I said. "Aren't the *Jews* dying in all the battlefields of the world too?"

"Certainly," said Fachmann, turning away from me wearily. "They are killing off the youth and the flower of our race. And who will finally remain? Nobody but *old* Jews like myself, and *our* language is definitely Hebrew. That's what I've been telling you from the beginning. There is no extra charge—four dollars covers the complete course. Sit down, you can start right now!"

So I started, but I finally won out over Fachmann, and although he cunningly tried to sneak in a little Hebrew on me from time to time, Yiddish is all I ever came up with.

Another thing that annoyed me about my job was the grub I was compelled to eat. I mean, we editorial workers on *The Big Stick* all ate our meals in a restaurant called the Kibitz-arnyeh!

That'll give you an idea.

I wasn't used to the rich Jewish food they used to dish out there and I was never able to finish one single portion of anything they served me. The portions were absolutely enormous, and, worst of all, the waiters took it as a personal affront if you left anything on your plate.

There was a particularly annoying waiter called Simcheh (which means "joy") who had a face like a steamed turnip and who just used to irritate the ass off me. Every time I left anything on my plate, a little soup or something, this guy would instantly become the lawyer for the rejected residue. He'd spin the goddamned stuff in front of me on the table, sloshing a little of it into my lap likely as not, raise his silly colorless eyebrows up to the top of his head and say, "What's wrong wid dis plate zoop???"

He was an absolute horror, but since everybody in the office went to the Kibitzarnyeh I naturally didn't like to go off to eat by myself somewhere else. Another misfortune of mine was the fact that this monster, Simcheh, had for some reason or another—probably because I was the youngest in the lot— decided to extend his particular concern and patronage to me. Whatever the hell the reason, he always brought me the biggest helpings, the richest pastries and the largest marrow bones. He was impossible.

So one day, when my stomach felt already a little queasy, I went out a little earlier for lunch than the rest of my confreres, and without even looking at the Kibitzarnyeh I hurried to a restaurant three blocks away where they sold only dairy dishes. It was great! I ate what I wanted, as little as I wished, and nobody dictated to me or put up any arguments. And that's what I did every day from then on. I mean I did it for about five days, and then a very strange thing happened to me.

I was sitting in this dairy restaurant having my modest little luncheon, when suddenly I spied a big fat face topped by a ridiculously small derby staring through the front window of this dairy dump—and the face that stared was, unmistakably, Simcheh's. I got deathly pale, of course, and my first thought was instant flight!

You have to try and visualize the circumstances of my dilemma. You see, a real Jewish dairy restaurant is a special and very peculiar institution. First of all, the moment you sit down, and even before you order anything, the waiter brings along a platter of bread. But I'm describing this very inadequately. There is not just bread on this platter, there are at least *three* kinds of bread, a dozen assorted rolls, sweet rolls, crackers, matzoth and God knows what else, and there is also served for your immediate comfort a side dish of cold chick-peas. By the way, years ago there used to be no charge whatever for this service, and the breadstuffs were piled up so high in front of you, you couldn't possibly see the man sitting across the way from you. The windows, always sweating with steam, had huge pyramids of flyspecked grapefruit piled up to their very tops, and the topmost grapefruit invariably carried a small American flag. So you see that anyone who tried to spy anybody through the window of that restaurant had to get past not only all that citrus window trimming, he had to be able to see successfully behind that towering ambuscade of bread too.

I knew I just had to take a chance, so I quickly got up, paid my check and walked into the toilet. Unfortunately the toilets in such joints were always just casual afterthoughts on the part of the management. They were not designed for casual loitering. In fact, they sufficed only for the bitterest necessities, and nobody in his right mind ever remained there but for the most urgent exigencies alone. Also, the windows of these toilets were always heavily barred and there was certainly no question of getting out the back way.

I stayed in that dreadful stinkatorium for as long as five minutes and then I had to call *Kamerad*. I tottered out of there and finally fell into the street, straight into the arms of Simcheh. The son of a bitch had outwaited me. Besides his crazy derby hat, he was wearing an enormous black overcoat, and, since it was a particularly slushy day, I could see his big, flat waiter's shoes squidging water all around us at every step. Although he had hardly any features at all, it was obvious that this steaming troglodyte was deeply disturbed. At any rate, when I stepped out of that dairy place he just grabbed me by one arm and without uttering a single word led me purposefully toward the Kibitzarnyeh. He pushed me ahead of him through the door of the restaurant, led me to a chair, gave me a long reproachful look and started to take off his hat and overcoat as he waddled somberly off toward the kitchen. A minute later he was back with a steaming plate of chicken soup, studded with *kreplach*.

"Dis is de kind of food dat a growing boy should eat!" he said. "Dairy food is for goils. It tins de blood and gives you pimples. Eat!!!!" he commanded.

I was as if in a trance, so I started to shovel the stuff into me, while he stood stonily in back of my chair to see that I did proper justice to his prescription. Luckily for me, at that point another customer demanded some of his attention and he grudgingly shuffled across the room to wait on a less irritating client.

The minute his back was turned, I jumped up from my chair, grabbed my hat and coat and ran breathlessly out into the street. I was so furious I nearly wept with rage and frustration. The dirty, flat-footed bastard! How dare he? What did he think I was, anyway—some snot-nosed kid that he could lead around by his apron strings?!?

I ran along the street toward the office simply spluttering with rage. Well, I'd show him! I'd show everybody! Goddammit, I was planning to get married in a couple of weeks, and here I was being treated like a puling infant. It was enough to drive one stark, raving mad!!!

I landed at *The Big Stick* in a fierce mood of truculence and banged the door so hard it nearly came off its hinges.

Unfortunately there was nobody in the front room (the offices were in an old-fashioned East Side railroad flat) and I had to dash all the way to the back before I finally found Marinoff, quietly reading the afternoon paper.

I exploded right on top of him. I let him have it from 'way 'way back.

"What the hell is the meaning of all this crap?!?" I shouted. "How does this goddamned waiter dare to run my life?!? What does he mean by dictating to me where and what I should eat! I want you to tell this insane character that if he ever butts into my life again I'm gonna blacken both his goddamned eyes for him!!! You hear, Marinoff? I've had enough of it!!! This is a showdown, and you'd better tell him so!!!"

Marinoff had lowered his paper when my little harangue began and he looked at me speculatively over his bifocals as I proceeded to the final ultimatum. As I stood there and looked at him in furious expectancy, he put down the paper altogether and raised his glasses high up on his forehead.

"You're talking about Simcheh?" he said softly.

"Yes, I'm talking about Simcheh, God damn his gall!!!"

"Well," said Marinoff, "if you're talking about Simcheh, I want you to know you're talking about a man who still has six unmarried daughters in his home, and all I can tell you is that you ought to be ashamed of yourself for bringing a lot of additional worries into the life of a man who already has so much to think about!"

Well, there, for all it was worth, was a peculiarly Jewish reaction to a given situation. I found it equally strange, or at least unique, on quite a few other occasions. For instance, once I discussed with a Jewish playwright whose name was Nochem Petstein the condition of the Yiddish theater.

Somewhere during the course of our talk he said. "Shakespeare never managed to become popular in the Yiddish theater."

"Why not?" I said. "The Jews are surely most appreciative of every form of cultural expression, so how do you account for it?"

"It is very simple," said Petstein. "His heroes just bore them."

"Bore them?!? Why, that's impossible."

"Not at all. Just think about it for a moment. Take Hamlet, for instance. He rants on for five acts about some wrong that was done to his father by a wicked uncle. *Five acts!* It is really too boring—his indecisiveness, I mean. Either his suspicions are right, in which case he should seek justice, or they're

359

wrong, in which case he should shut up. It just wearies a Jewish audience to the point of utter exhaustion. The man is obviously a schlemiel and it is silly to waste precious time on him, that's their reaction."

"And is this true about all of Shakespeare's plays?" I said.

"There was one exception," said Petstein. "It was a play called *The Jewish King Lear*."

"*The Jewish King Lear?* Was that just a translation, or what?"

"No. It was the King Lear theme under small-town Jewish circumstances. Ungrateful children, an embittered father—you understand? All the rest of it. As a matter of fact, when Old Man Kessler, the great Yiddish actor, used to play the role of King Lear, the private bank across the way, Mandel's bank, used to keep open till two o'clock every morning, because people would come weeping out of that theater and in the middle of the night send money home to their old parents in Europe."

"For mine," saith the Lord, "is a peculiar people!"

CHAPTER TWENTY-SIX

Y EARS AGO, when any of my friends were planning to get married or to set up a household of some kind with some toothsome tootsie, the groom would generally take his prospective bride to the nearest cafeteria, where they would both proceed to help themselves to some basic table silverware. The more ambitious ones among them sometimes swiped jars of mustard and ketchup too, not to mention salt and pepper shakers, and I know of one particularly provident bride who even managed to get away with a largish ice pitcher, which she successfully concealed under her maternity mantle.

These creature comforts can, of course, be lifted easily enough in any of the thousands of cafeterias that flourish around the country, but the steadier ones among my shoplifting acquaintance were always particularly partial to the sturdy cutlery put on view at the Horn and Hardart self-service restaurants. The presence of these substantial tools in any new domestic situation were like an augury of permanence and gave tangible promise that the contracting parties had pledged themselves pretty definitely to an enduring commitment. It was the sort of arrangement where progeny was likely to be anticipated rather than dreaded.

My friends Valerie and Stewart Petchell bivouacked in just such a cozy warren for many years in Greenwich Village, until destiny, in the shape of an unexpected, substantial inheritance, lifted them forever out of our midst and transplanted them to the arid joys of Southern California. And there, after quite a long time had passed, I finally saw them again. This removal to the Coast, by the way, was the pivotal point of the critical stipulation that made them eligible to become incumbents of the estate in the first place.

At any rate, I found them, after many years, marooned on some hideous cliff on the outskirts of Hollywood, and, with their wonderful talent for reducing everything they touched to instant antiquity, they weren't really so badly settled at all. The house they infested had originally been a combination of Swiss chalet with Alhambra overtones, and the garden that descended from their doorstep at a forty-five-degree angle was completely overrun by poison ivy.

They had managed to qualify for this inheritance of theirs chiefly because they had unconditionally agreed to look after some fifteen cats which had been the cherished pets of the deceased testator, who had happened to be Valerie's spinster aunt. It stands to reason that by the time I landed in their midst they had worked out a whole meaningful philosophy about cats, and even about Southern California. Life is just too unbearable on any other terms.

"It isn't only that cats were considered sacred among the ancient religions," said Stewart, "but even in Christian demonology they have always played a significant role."

"So did owls," said Valerie.

"We can't accommodate owls," said Stewart. "Besides, the cats mightn't like it."

We were sitting in their back patio, a perilous perch over-hanging a rocky gulch and festooned with mildewed ferns and withered stinkweed.

"It's really not so bad out here," said Valerie, "once you get to see the beauty of the uneven landscape. I mean, nature is more like a willful housekeeper in this place, showering all the moisture in one spot and then putting a lot of aridness right across the way from it."

"It has its own compelling beauty," said Stewart.

To my surprise, they'd gotten rather thin out there. They were both pretty tall and bony people, and a little weight wouldn't have done either one of them any harm. They were both rather hairy too, and I noticed with some alarm that in the intervening years they had gotten to look rather more like animals than like people.

"What do you do with yourselves all day?" I asked.

"Oh, there's lots to do around the house," said Valerie.

"The cats, I suppose," I said.

"Oh, no!" said Stewart. "They're no bother at all. They're all toilet-trained. Aunt Martha had them using the bathroom from the time they were kittens. That's why there isn't any smell around here. Didn't you notice?"

"Yes," I said. "Where are they, anyway? When they aren't on the toilet, I mean. I haven't seen a one of them around yet."

"They're upstairs in the dormitory. You want to look at them?"

"Why not?" I said. "I might as well take a gander at your kind benefactors."

The dormitory had six beds in it and looked like any child's nursery. The cats were all just ordinary alley cats.

"There are only eight of them," I said. "Weren't there fifteen to begin with?"

363

"Yes," said Stewart, "but the others all passed on. The last one, Micky, died just two weeks ago. I'll show you his grave in the cemetery later on."

"Were they all too old to have kittens, or what?" I asked.

"Well, it isn't really like that, at all," said Stewart, somewhat embarrassed. "You see, they *could* have had kittens when we first arrived here . . ."

"Yes?"

"We had them all fixed," said Valerie.

"I see!"

"The will provides," said Stewart, "that we have to live here and take care of them until the last one passes on, see? Somehow, Aunt Martha forgot to make any stipulation about having them fixed. I suppose she just couldn't imagine that anyone would so such a thing. Well, we *did*."

"You were quite right!" I said.

"But *some* cats get to be as much as twenty years old," said Valerie plaintively.

"Why didn't you just poison the lot of them right at the start?" I asked.

"Couldn't," said Stewart. "A vet comes out here every month to examine them, and when they die he makes an autopsy."

"When they found out we had them fixed," said Valerie, "the lawyer for the estate took us to court, but luckily the judge hated cats, and, besides, there was nothing in the will to prevent us from doing it."

"Well, you've got it licked now," I said. "At least there won't be any *more* cats."

"Yeah," said Stewart. "We've got it licked all right if we're only lucky enough and they all manage to catch rabies! They sometimes get it if they're bitten by a rabid fox. I read about it in *Time* magazine recently."

"Don't you fool with any rabid foxes," I said. "They're lia-

364

ble to bite *you*, and then Valerie will be alone here, marooned on this goddamned cliff with eight toilet-trained cats for company. Why in hell don't you chuck the whole thing and come on back east?"

"We can't," said Valerie. "Don't you see, we've invested too much in this thing already. We've been here almost ten years now. After all, they can't last forever, can they?"

My final glimpse of them, when I left them late that night, was to see them gauntly silhouetted against the dark-gray sky. They were leaning far over the rickety banister of their crazy eyrie, trying to catch a last, hungry look at my departing taillight.

They all burned to death two years later, all of them, including the cats, and the only reason I bothered to recount this dreary tale at all is because I feel that my book, at this far-gone stage, seems to be lacking a parable that carries a certain strong moral flavor.

Of course the moral of this little story is, don't ever get involved with *money!*

And yet it's damned hard *not* to, as I perfectly well know. Not that money really makes very much difference to me, at this stage of the game. I've reduced my needs to the barest essentials, and I can truthfully say I was never particularly greedy in the past, either. Luckily the human body has altogether only nine small apertures. Don't bother counting them, I once wrote a lyric about this for a musical that was never produced.

> *Nine little holes in the body of man*
> *To take in the world and its wonder . . .*

I've forgotten how the rest of it went, but I think it concluded that man should really have been built like a great big sieve, to accommodate all his ruinous, multiform varieties of gluttony.

I'm not going to pretend that I don't *like* having a lot of money. All things being equal, it is certainly better to be rich even if you happen to be afflicted with cancer. You can afford a pleasanter sickroom, softer pillows, prettier nurses, and you can at least manage to march off in some kind of style.

It is perfectly true, though, that money alone isn't enough to grease the activities of life into any true sort of locomotive splendor. The joyless boneheads, embedded in their slickest Rolls-Royces, certainly give satisfaction to nobody, not even to themselves.

I knew all about this when I was just a youngster. I used to sit on top of a bus with my pretty girl friend (there were open-top buses in those days) and we would look commiseratively down on the deadpan dyspeptics who were grimly belching their discontent into the fragrant spring air. It wasn't a case of sour grapes with me, either; I just realized, when I was sixteen years old, that I didn't need a couple of million dollars to have myself a ball. I had love, and joy, and passion, and such a thrilling awareness of the staggering beauty of the world that I needed only a few cents in my pocket to fill my most extravagant needs at the richest fountains of life's offering.

A friend of mine, Toldi Zoltan, talked to me about an interesting case in point the other evening. I'd had him over to the house for dinner, and I had just apologized to him for various lacks in our social accommodations, due to the fact that I was still living in a rather small apartment, since my illness had prevented us from finding better and more spacious quarters.

"Please, don't even give it a thought!" said Zoltan. "You could entertain successfully in a grotto or in the belly of a whale, because you and your wife *love* people, and so there is never any worry about having a good time in your house, wherever it might happen to be. By the way, did you ever know a chap called Bertrand Brassard, a French publisher?"

"No," I said. "I've heard a good deal *about* him, though, and once I was even supposed to illustrate a book for him, but for some reason or another nothing ever came of it. Why? Am I *supposed* to know him?"

"No," said Zoltan, "but he just came to my mind as a good example of what we've been talking about. You see, this Brassard person used to throw just about the most lavish parties in Paris some years ago, and a lot of my friends used to know him. He was a very rich man to start with, and he had married some kind of perfume heiress on top of it, and so naturally they ran the most splendid establishment that you can imagine. At any rate, in no time at all their parties became notorious for their deadly dullness. Nobody would ever have gone to them at all but for the fact that he was the head of a powerful publishing house and his wife was part owner of a distinguished art gallery. It stands to reason that a lot of unfortunate artists and writers, and their various wives and mistresses, simply had to attend these dreary festivals. Each time, all these poor people nearly yawned themselves into lockjaw before the evening was over. Well, then, once a few years ago my friend Miklos was invited to one of these official embalming sessions, and he told me later that by the time it got to be ten o'clock he noticed that moss had started to form on the crystal chandeliers and that creeping fungi were beginning to settle on the rims of the champagne glasses. Miklos suddenly decided to do something radical about this tottering evening that was about to come tumbling down about everyone's ears, and so he discreetly approached the host, with the kind intention of administering some sort of quick first aid.

" 'Monsieur Brassard,' he said, 'I think this party of yours is showing strong signs of stagnation, and I really believe we ought to do something pretty drastic about it right away.'

"Brassard, a short, potbellied, amiable man, was not at all shocked by my friend's outspoken diagnosis, but smiled at him in a perfectly benign way and said, 'Perhaps you are right, Miklos. Why don't you suggest something that we can do about it?'

" 'I think,' said Miklos, 'that we all ought to get completely undressed. I'm quite sure that that ought to liven things up quite a little!'

"Brassard looked at him in some surprise, of course, but, since it was his great ambition to be considered a real *boulevardier*, a thoroughly worldly man, he didn't expostulate or grow indignant at this wild idea, he just looked at Miklos rather searchingly for a moment to make sure that his suggestion had been made in earnest.

" 'You actually think that would help any?' he asked.

" 'I'm absolutely convinced of it,' said Miklos. 'I believe it will give the whole party a completely new dimension! It's certainly worth trying. What can you lose?'

" 'All right,' said Brassard. 'Let's get undressed, then, and get it over with!'

"And, what's more, he was as good as his word and started at once, slowly but systematically, to remove his clothes.

"In less than a minute the idea had caught on, and in less than three minutes every person in that room was completely naked.

"So naturally the fairies teamed up with the fairies, the Lesbians with the Lesbians, and even a few normal people started to cluster together in the far-distant corners.

"Miklos, who told me about it, said, 'You know, the funny thing about it all was that when I looked around that room later on, I saw our host going from table to table, emptying out the dirty ash trays.'

"So you see, Alex," said my friend Zoltan, "this poor Bras-

368

sard, dressed or undressed, just didn't ever seem to have the proper party spirit. And you, obviously, always had!"

Well, not quite always. No! There were good long spells in my life when I had damned little to celebrate.

Yesterday afternoon I pulled down from the shelf a book that Margie had brought along with us from the city, and as I opened it a letter fell out of it. It was a letter I wrote her five years ago, when I was confined in the Public Health Service Hospital in Lexington, Kentucky. This correspondence of ours had certain heartbreaking overtones, since we were newly married when I landed down there for the fourth time.

It occurs to me that on the three previous occasions I had hardly sent, or received, any mail at all, because very few of my friends had the vaguest idea of what in hell had become of me. During my third visit my dear friend David Lober did send me some kind, hopeful words that were uncontaminated by even the faintest trace of commiseration or good advice. The rest was self-imposed silence.

But in 1955, when I was suddenly separated from my beautiful young bride, I just practically lived to await the afternoon mail delivery each day. During the six and a half months we were separated, Margie wrote to me at least once every twenty-four hours, and, occasionally, after a weekend, I had as many as two and even three letters from her at one time. I was allowed to answer her only twice a week, each time on a single sheet of paper, and so when this five-year-old letter fell out of that book yesterday it certainly woke some pretty grim memories in my heart. Here is what I had written her:

MEIN SCHATZERL,

Not all of my days are valiant. There are indeed moments when I fall into deep despair and I can't conceive how I can go on enduring it all. I tell you this, lest you imagine *yourself* deficient in fortitude. Don't you believe it. Once, the whole wide world was too small for my roamings and now I am obliged to function within a few circumscribed, square yards. So it happens that from time to time I become quite stunned by my helplessness and the end of my bitter dilemma seems nowhere in sight. You know, I can sometimes barely imagine the next five hours, much less the next five months, that still separate me from you.

Oh, my darling, these are the breaches that love has made in my armor, since tenderness is surely the most potent means of undermining a man's self-sufficiency. Happily, it has its glorious compensations, and it is these in the largest measure which sustain me through the worst of times.

It is Sunday, and I am writing this letter while you are singing in church. I am sitting in the dayroom and it is drizzling miserably outside; standing up against the wall are three of my paintings, ready to be varnished, and I have purposely dawdled these last two days, so that some absorbing chores would come to occupy me today, when there isn't any mail delivery.

As I sit here and stare at my pictures I try to conjure up the meaning of my legend. I look at my work, which has never been so good, and I realize that with God's help my tale may still have many facets to unfold. I will varnish one of my paintings and return to this letter in a little while. I don't have to return to you, because your image is constantly before me, and guides me, like a peripatetic lighthouse.

The varnishing is done, and now I must tell you what else happens to me here. Mostly I just do my painting and give opinions and advice to some of the people who drop into my room. Just this morning a young man came to see me, while I was deeply absorbed in some drafting problems, and, I'm afraid, I answered his questions rather injudiciously. He had asked me what qualities I considered absolutely essential and basic in a lovable woman. Before I knew what was happening I heard myself saying:

"A good mind, of course; high cheekbones, clear eyes, a long neck, slender wrists, beautiful hands, impeccable ankles, and, deep down somewhere, only known to me, an unmistakable streak of whorishness. May heaven preserve me from ever going to bed with a righteous female. Take my word for it, when a doll thinks she's got the holy grail under her skirts, she'll finish you off faster than heart failure in a typhoon."

So, you see, my love, I'm not altogether harmless even here, in the strictest confinement.

I don't know whether I mentioned to you that I've reread half a dozen biographies of some really great people, during the past month, or so, and as I read about these noble lives, I was absolutely choked with gratitude for the many sensitive and precious hearts that have lived and loved and suffered here before us. (I don't mean Gladstone or Billy Sunday or Bruce Barton, I mean the poets and the artists and the sages who all had true intimations of mankind's possibly great potentials.) I hear them singing and rhyming and whispering to us, out of the past, and giving us encouragement and good cheer on our road through the wonderful human adventure. If we only pause to listen to them, for a moment, what fateful and significant things may we not overhear for our heart's comfort, consolation, and delight. Some of these people were actually stupendous failures, as the world measures success, but, the significance of their lives and their work remains to contradict and to reproach their blind and deaf contemporaries.

Oh, my love, why do I go on ranting like this about all these trifles—when all I really want to say over and over again, is, that I miss you so desperately, my dearest—that I don't know how I'm going to face tonight without you, and

371

tomorrow—and the day after—and the day after that—and all the other one hundred and fifty-four bleak days, for the next five months to come. It is quite inconceivable to me how I'm ever going to live so long without even once kissing your lovely smile, my darling.

But, I am resolved to work hard and to bear my bitter lot patiently, until the will of destiny will bring us happily together again.

My love, my dearest one, you live so constantly in

ALEX

P.S. Because, as you know, I'm only allowed two letters a week, which I can certainly share with no one else, will you please write to Clare and Earl, in my name, and send them my thanks and my affection.

XANDEL

P.P.S. In the second chapter of the Canticle of Canticles, Solomon says:

> Stay me with flagons, comfort me with apples:
> For I am sick of love.

Because they are having some kind of a successful apple harvest in the world, we are getting endless apples with all our meals. So many, in fact, that I've thought of paraphrasing those dear sentiments to say:

> Stay me with kisses, comfort me with love:
> For I am sick of apples.

X

I have given you this letter exactly as I originally wrote it, in all its terrible syntax and its emotional confusion, simply because I want to belie a friend of mine who said to me only the

372

other day, "I notice that you are not going to ruin your autobiography by putting your life into it."

Well, he's quite wrong! I put all of it in, just as it occurs to me, and heaven is my witness, I have prettified very little.

By the way, the Clare and Earl referred to in my letter are Margie's parents, who live 'way out in Chadron, Nebraska. All through our period of grief and separation, these two dear people displayed the greatest possible amount of kindness toward us. Remember, I'm not exactly the sort of son-in-law that good, average American parents are quite likely to be prepared for. After all, a short while after their precious only child had gotten involved with me I landed smack in Lexington for six months, and they had no immediate reason to believe that I was ever going to reform, either. But they were strong and steadfast through that whole ghastly period and they went right on taking care of my darling just as if I had never appeared in her life at all. They wrote me encouraging letters to the hospital, too, and on very slender evidence indeed they remained consistently cheerful and optimistic about our future together. And what had trained them for this particular role in minor sainthood? Nothing, of course, but the natural goodness and loyalty which had always been the basic and integral part of their characters. I'm sure that they were deeply concerned and uneasy about the safety of their child— I think it is inconceivable that they should *not* have been—but they trusted her sound and decent instincts, and, guided exclusively by their deep affection of her *and by nothing else*, they left all the rest of it trustingly in the hands of God.

And now, since this book is really *me*, what is my greatest hope and my wildest and most ambitious dream for it?

Only this: that when all the dissertations on abstract art shall have been reduced to finicky footnotes in neglected tomes full of pretentious scholarship, *I* shall be patiently waiting under a willow tree while the burning adolescent who brought me along in his sweaty hands will be neglecting me for the sweeter glory of tumbling his gigglish but complaisant girl friend in the tall, fragrant summer grass, somewhere!